ISBN: 9781313426442

Published by:
HardPress Publishing
8345 NW 66TH ST #2561
MIAMI FL 33166-2626

Email: info@hardpress.net
Web: http://www.hardpress.net

CORNELL UNIVERSITY
LIBRARIES
ITHACA, N. Y. 14853

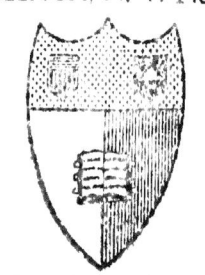

Fine Arts Library
Sibley Hall

Cornell University Library
ND 623.L91B41 1901

Lorenzo Lotto; an essay in constructive a

3 1924 016 782 140

LORENZO LOTTO

BERNHARD BERENSON

By the same Author

The Study and Criticism of Italian Art

With 41 Illustrations. 10*s*. 6*d*. *net*.

CONTENTS: 'Vasari in the Light of Recent Publications'—'Dante's Visnal Images and his Early Illustrators'—'Venetian Painting'—'Correggio'—'Giorgione's Lost Originals'—'Amico di Sandro.'

A Second Volume containing the following Essays will shortly be ready:

A Word for Renaissance Churches—Alessio Baldovinetti—The Caen Sposalizio—An unpublished Masterpiece by Filippino Lippi—The 'Raphael' cartoon for a Madonna at the British Museum—An Altar-piece by Girolamo da Cremona—The Drawings of Andrea Mantegna, &c.

LONDON: GEORGE BELL & SONS

Brogi photo.] [Brera Gallery, Milan

PORTRAIT OF LAURA DI POLA

LORENZO LOTTO

AN ESSAY IN CONSTRUCTIVE ART CRITICISM

BY

BERNHARD BERENSON

REVISED EDITION WITH ADDITIONAL ILLUSTRATIONS

LONDON
GEORGE BELL & SONS
1901

OXFORD: HORACE HART
PRINTER TO THE UNIVERSITY

TO

W. P. E.

PREFACE

THIS book has another object in view than the bringing together of mere information regarding Lotto. It is an attempt to reconstruct Lotto's character, both as a man and as an artist. Consequently only such data as served this purpose have been considered. No document that can throw light on the painter's career, no authenticated work, at all accessible, has been neglected. Such documents, however, as would bring more increase to the pages of a book than to the intimacy with an artist have been left to the delectation of lovers of old paper, in and for itself. As to pictures known only by hearsay, they cannot and must not be considered in forming an estimate or in defining the quality of an artist, vicarious experience of the work of art being less than useless in criticism. Nor has it been thought needful to encumber the following pages with refutations of all the catalogue-makers whom it has pleased to attach Lotto's name to pictures. Such refutation might be made amusing, if not edifying reading, but could not add to our knowledge of the master. Happily criticism is so much of one accord regarding the bulk of paintings attributed to Lotto, that the study of him can afford to become something more than 'Bilderbestimmung'—the discussion of what was and what was not painted by a given artist. The author is confident that the student who has devoted as much time as himself to the study of Lotto, and has as many of the painter's works fresh in his mind, will agree with him in the exclusions he has made,—even when he has against him Messrs. Crowe and Cavalcaselle, as when they attribute the Pitti *Three Ages*[1] to Lotto, or Morelli when ascribing to him *The Concert* at Hampton Court, or the *Lot and his Daughters* of the Milanese Museo Civico.

Considering at what length Alvise and his school have been treated in the present work, it has been a sore temptation to make the study of them more exhaustive, but the writer has constantly had to remind himself that his book deals with Lotto, and that Alvise and his following may come in only when they can throw light on the subject in hand.

In this second edition, besides the rectification of mortifying misprints and some few obvious errors, there will be found a considerable increase in the number of works by both Lotto and Alvise, which are here discussed. Otherwise, the book remains unchanged, and I doubt whether, from the point of view taken by the writer, the part concerning Lotto himself will ever require much more change. Further documents may be discovered, and further pictures, but scarcely in either case of a kind to add to our knowledge of Lotto's artistic personality.

[1] For the happy suggestion that this and the following, both obviously from the same hand, are by Morto da Feltre, see Mary Logan, *Guide to Hampton Court*, the Kyrle Society, London.

But the point of view taken by the writer eight or nine years ago, when he first composed this book, was determined by interests that then seemed much more important than they do now. Yet as he has no means of arriving at the certainty that his present interests are essentially more real than the earlier ones, as these earlier interests also are at all events permanent ones, and as, moreover, if the author's present point of view, and this point of view only, were regarded, the new edition would have perhaps no greater likeness to the old one than if the subject were handled by a different writer, the author has thought best to stick to his old position. But he feels bound to confess that he now concerns himself little with the work of art as a document in the history of civilization, and laments the confusion that such an interest is apt to create between historical and aesthetical standards. He feels even more greatly bound to warn his readers against the assumption that in art there is such a thing as progress. Technical advance there has been and may be, but it is by no means identical, nor even coincident with advance in art; and a counsel of perfection would be to avoid confounding an interest in the history of technique with love of art, and most of all to beware of finding beauty where there is only curiosity.

If further documents can be of no great service in the study of Lotto himself, there is much they still may do to clear up the question touched upon at considerable length in this book—the question of his antecedents. That Alvise formed him there can be no legitimate doubt; nor can it be reasonably argued that the position here given to Alvise, his father, and his uncle in the history of Venetian Painting is exaggerated. Further documents, read by the competent, will, it may be hoped, but help to establish the author's theory. The precise relations, however, between the various painters in this group may be considerably changed by further researches in archives. Thus far, to give an instance, we know the date of birth of relatively few Venetian artists.

Thanks are due to Dr. Georg Gronau and to Dr. Max Friedländer for several hints helpful in preparing this new edition.

CONTENTS

	PAGE
PREFACE	vii
LIST OF ILLUSTRATIONS	xiii
INTRODUCTION	xvii

CHAPTER I

LOTTO'S EARLY YEARS: 1480–1512 1

CHAPTER II

LOTTO'S ANTECEDENTS: THE SCHOOL OF ALVISE VIVARINI	17
I. Lotto, Giovanni Bellini, and Giorgione	17
II. Jacopo di Barbari	26
III. Francesco Bonsignori	39
IV. Bartolommeo Montagna	47
V. Cima da Conegliano	53
VI. Testimony of Lotto's entire career to his descent from Alvise	62
VII. Alvise Vivarini	65
VIII. The purpose of knowing the artist's antecedents	95

CHAPTER III

THE TRANSITION: 1508–1517 100

CHAPTER IV

THE BERGAMASK PERIOD: 1518–1528 . . . 137

CONTENTS

CHAPTER V

MATURITY: 1529–1540 181

CHAPTER VI

OLD AGE: 1540–1550 211

CHAPTER VII

LAST YEARS: 1550–1556 232
    Appendix to Chapter VII 239

CHAPTER VIII

LOTTO'S FOLLOWING AND INFLUENCE . . . 243

CHAPTER IX

RESULTING IMPRESSION 249

INDEX TO PHOTOGRAPHS OF PICTURES AND DRAWINGS NOT BY LOTTO 279

INDEX TO NAMES MENTIONED INCIDENTALLY . 283

INDEX TO PLACES 285

LIST OF ILLUSTRATIONS[1]

	TO FACE PAGE
1. PORTRAIT OF LAURA DI POLA . . . *Frontispiece*	
2. DANAË	1
3. LOUVRE, ST. JEROME	2
4. SANTA CRISTINA ALTAR-PIECE	6
5. CENTRAL PANEL OF RECANATI ALTAR-PIECE . . .	11
6. S. VITO, AND BARBARI'S HERALD. (On same page.) . .	12
7. CRACOW, MADONNA AND SAINTS	15
8. BONSIGNORI, MADONNA AND SAINTS. (In S. Paolo at Verona.)	40
9. BONSIGNORI. (Details of Polyptych in S. Giovanni e Paolo at Venice.)	44
10. BONSIGNORI. (Portrait of a Gonzaga.)	46
11. MONTAGNA. (Vicenza Altar-piece.)	48
12. MONTAGNA. (Brera Altar-piece.)	52
13. CIMA, MADONNA WITH SIX SAINTS	58
14. ALVISE. (Polyptych at Montefiorentino.)	66
15. ALVISE, MADONNA AND SAINTS. (Venice Academy.) . .	68
16. ALVISE. (Berlin Altar-piece.)	72

[1] When no painter's name is given the illustrations are after originals by Lotto.

LIST OF ILLUSTRATIONS

                                                                               TO FACE PAGE

17. ALVISE, MADONNA. (National Gallery.) 74
18. ALVISE. (St. Clare, Venice Academy.) *To follow preceding*
19. ALVISE, REDENTORE MADONNA 76
20. ALVISE, SANTA GIUSTINA 78
21. ALVISE. (Frari Altar-piece.) 82
22. ALVISE. (Portrait of Man, Mr. Salting's) 84
23. ALVISE. (Portrait, Padua.) . . *To follow preceding*
24. ALVISE. (Layard Portrait.) 86
25. ALVISE. (Mr. Salting's Bust of Boy.) *To follow preceding*
26. ALVISE. (Louvre Bust of Salla.) 88
27. ALVISE. (Bust of Man, Comtesse de Béarn's.) . . . 90
28. ALVISE. (Windsor drawing.) 92
29. ALVISE. (M. Mathey's drawing.) 94
30. JESI, ENTOMBMENT 106
31. PORTRAIT OF PIERO SODERINI 108
32. ASSASSINATION OF PETER MARTYR 112
33. NAPLES. (Bust of Man.) 116
34. PORTRAITS OF AGOSTINO AND NICCOLÒ DELLA TORRE. (National Gallery.) 118
35. KAUFMANN. (Portrait.) 120
36. S. BARTOLOMMEO ALTAR-PIECE 122
37. DRESDEN, MADONNA 140
38. S. BERNARDINO ALTAR-PIECE 142
39. S. SPIRITO ALTAR-PIECE 144

LIST OF ILLUSTRATIONS

TO FACE PAGE

40. CHRIST TAKING LEAVE OF HIS MOTHER	146
41. CARRARA. (Portrait of Lady.)	148
42. PROTHONOTARY GIULIANO. (National Gallery)	150
43. CARRARA, MARRIAGE OF ST. CATHERINE	152
44. MADRID, BRIDAL COUPLE	154
45. FAMILY GROUP. (National Gallery.)	156
46. BERLIN. (Portrait of Young Man.)	168
47. MILAN. (Portrait of Youth.)	170
48. VIENNA. (Portrait of Man.)	174
49. HAMPTON COURT. (Portrait of Andrea Odoni.)	174
50. VIENNA, SANTA CONVERSAZIONE	176
51. RECANATI, ANNUNCIATION	178
52. VENUS AND CHASTITY	180
53. CARMINE ALTAR-PIECE	186
54. HOLFORD, 'LUCRETIA'	190
55. JESI, VISITATION	192
56. MONTE S. GIUSTO, CRUCIFIXION	194
57. LOCHIS, HOLY FAMILY	198
58. DORIA PORTRAIT OF INVALID	204
59. CINGOLI ALTAR-PIECE	206
60. BRERA PORTRAIT OF OLD MAN	220
61. LORETO, PRESENTATION IN TEMPLE	236
62. MR. WAGNER'S DRAWING	242

INTRODUCTION

BEFORE approaching the first chapter, with its dry analysis of data, a bare word of explanation is necessary.

Given a few documentary notices, and a number of pictures, to reconstruct the history of an artist's education, and of the early years of his career—such, at the beginning of our task, is the problem before us. How shall we solve it? In one way only, and that is by discovering what habits have become so rooted in the artist as to be unconscious, and under what influences he formed them, the training of the painter being altogether a training in habits of attention, visualization, and execution.

Of all perceptible phenomena the painter is taught to observe only a few—a certain type of face, let us say, a certain type of figure, a certain type of movement are singled out for observation from among the multiple types existing. Of all possible ways of picturing this type in his memory he is taught but one way, and of all possible ways of transferring his visual image to wall, panel, or canvas he again is taught but one way. He may get more ways later, and even get over his first way, but while fresh from school the young painter's way is sure to be his master's way.

Conclusions, therefore, regarding a painter's origin, drawn from the existence of general resemblances between his works and the works of other masters, do not surprise us. We are, however, likely to be troubled by the constant reference to certain details singled out from the many, details apt to be neglected in our general impression of a picture, but pounced upon by recent connoisseurship as likely to yield the best clue to a master's antecedents.

These details are the ears, the hands, the ringlets of hair, certain constantly recurring bits of landscape, certain awkwardnesses of attitude, and other such unimportant and even trivial things.

It is his most inrooted habits, we bear in mind, that the painter acquires from his teacher. What, then, is more likely to reveal habit, the general look of a picture depending so much as it does on the subject, or on the sitter's whim, or the details just enumerated, which the subject scarcely affects, and the sitter never notices? Let us see in which habits are most likely to take root.

Habits tend to become fixed in measure as they meet with the least resistance. The child [1] is taught to draw in a stereotyped way, but the habits of execution that he thus tends to form encounter the resistance of the teaching in observation that he is having at the

---

[1] Whatever I say here about the education and the habits of the artist I mean to apply to the Italian artist of the fifteenth and sixteenth centuries only. For all I know it may not be true of the artist of to-day.

INTRODUCTION

same time. The resistance, however, is not the same all along the line, because attention itself tends to crystallize into habits of regarding certain features and details, and disregarding others. Habits of execution will, therefore, tend to become strongest where habits of attention are weakest.

Now, where are the habits of attention weakest? Surely not in that which is of greatest general human interest, the expression of the human face. Its pleasantness or unpleasantness makes or mars a picture. A habit of execution which resulted in eyes invariably wild, in a mouth invariably sour, in a nose invariably mean, would be fatal to any painter's career; while the artist who has the wisdom to please in these points, may give the less expressive features any shape, not grotesque, that he chooses. It is in the less expressive features, then, that habits of attention are weakest, and habits of execution, consequently, strongest.

It remains to be seen which features are the less expressive, and therefore the less noticed. They must be those which are less capable of a sudden change of look.

Of all the exposed parts of the human figure, the ears are least capable of sudden change of character. After the ears come the hands. The ears therefore get the least attention, so little that not one person probably in a thousand knows the shapes either of his own, or of his dearest friend's. Nowadays the hands are noticed, but in the fifteenth century they were scarcely ever observed, and it is only in the sixteenth, that their shape began to glimmer with a suggestion of individuality. The painter's public never noticing them, and consequently never criticizing them, there was no reason for doing them otherwise than in the way first learned, and consequently the ears and the hands, more than any other exposed parts, permitted of the formation of habits in their execution. And all that holds true of the ears and hands holds true of even less expressive and less noticed details, as, for instance, hair and dress, regarded not as a whole where they are entirely at the mercy of fashion, but in such details as a particular ringlet, or a particular fold. As long as a painter gives our hair and clothing a certain cut, we do not demand the exact reproduction of every hair and fold. Even if the artist had the patience to reproduce them, we should lack the patience to audit his account. The hair and clothing, then, also permit of the formation of habits in their execution. And we might thus examine every detail of every conceivable picture with figures, to see what chance it gave for the formation of habits of execution; and at the end of our task we should come back to the ears, the hands, the hair, the folds, certain idiosyncrasies of pose, and certain settings and backgrounds, as pronest to being executed in a stereotyped fashion.

In other words, the details just mentioned are least liable to change from the way they were done, when first learned. Now, as a master cannot but teach his own ways, those habits of the pupil which, once formed, have undergone the least change can scarcely help being, as much as the pupil's personality will permit,

INTRODUCTION

like the master's habits. It follows, therefore, that the ears, the hands, the hair, the drapery, and whatever other details most permit of the formation of habits of execution are the best clue to a painter's origin, and to the history of his novitiate.

I cannot here pursue this subject further. Its full development would take a volume. I must add, however, that although habits of execution are the most obvious, they are not necessarily the most tyrannical. Habits of attention, and of visualization; habits of feeling and of thinking do, no less than habits of execution, intervene between the artist and the object, and all of them the spectator must be able to deduct before he is approximately sure of having before him the idea of the master, and not a projection of his own fancy or fantasy.

With this, and with the further word of warning that the artist is not a botanical but a psychological problem, the reader is invited to examine the data upon which rests my theory of Lotto's origin and development [1].

[1] To follow me in my arguments, the reader should have before him the photographs of the various pictures discussed. Photographs of Lotto's works are indicated in the text; of others in an index following after the last chapter.

[Sir W. Martin Conway

DANAE

LORENZO LOTTO

CHAPTER I

LOTTO'S EARLY YEARS

FROM 1480-1512

LORENZO DI TOMMASO LOTTO must have been born in 1480; for, in a will made by him on March 24, 1546, he speaks of himself as being 'about 66 years old' (Gust. Bampo, *Il Testamento di Lorenzo Lotto, Archivio Veneto*, vol. xxxiv). Other documents published by Dr. Bampo (*Archivio Veneto*, vol. xxxii, p. 169) prove conclusively that Lotto was born in Venice. 1480.

LONDON COLLECTION OF SIR W. MARTIN CONWAY.
  DANAË.

Danaë, completely clothed, reclines in a wooded landscape. To the L. a female satyr peers from behind a tree, and a faun lies in the foreground to R., while Cupid pours a shower of gold from the clouds. 1498 ?).

On wood, 16 × 13 in.

This is clearly the least mature of Lotto's existing works. It resembles Alvise Vivarini in type, draperies, landscape, greyish tone, and cool effects of light. The face of the Danaë, with its full oval and round chin, recalls one of Alvise's later pictures, the *Madonna* of the Redentore at Venice. Her loose construction and

1498 (?). awkward pose suggest Jacopo di Barbari's engravings. The Cupid, with his turned-up nose, fat cheeks, and chubby limbs, is identical in general build with the *putti* in Alvise's Redentore picture. The hand of the female satyr, with its long, clumsy fingers, recalls the hands in Alvise's Berlin altar-piece (No. 38), while the clinging drapery of the Danaë, composed of soft stuff that tends to arrange itself in close lineal folds converging at a point (vividly recalling the draperies of the *putti* in the Redentore Madonna, and of Alvise's *Sta. Giustina de' Borromei* in the Casa Bagati at Milan, and certain details in his last picture, the altar-piece of 1503 in the Frari at Venice), is even more strikingly like the drapery of Jacopo di Barbari. The landscape, containing full-foliaged trees of small leaves, painted with great minuteness, has closer affinities with German or Lombard than Venetian painting. The greyish tone and cool lights recall such of Alvise's pictures as the Berlin altar-piece and the altar-piece of 1480 in the Venice Academy (Sala IX, No. 11). In spirit, the picture is closely akin to the *Endymion* and the *Apollo and Marsyas* in the Parma Gallery, which were painted by Cima da Conegliano, and no less akin to the mythological and allegorical engravings of Jacopo di Barbari.

LOUVRE, No. 1350. ST. JEROME.

1500. The saint crouches against a rock in the foreground of a mountainous landscape, while his lion and St. Antony appear around the edge of a boulder to the L. In the middle distance a horseman is seen riding through a forest clearing.

Inscribed: LOTVS. 1500. On wood, 58 cm. h., 40 cm. w.

Photographed by Braun.

The style is much more mature than in the first

Braun, Clement & Co., photo. Louvre, Paris

ST. JEROME

work. The trees are similar, but the tone is warmer, 1500. coming nearer to Alvise's *Resurrection* in San Giovanni in Bragora at Venice. The movement of the figure is far more articulated and expressive than the *Danaë*. The drapery is not so pronouncedly Alvisesque as before, for its large papery folds recall Giovanni Bellini. The rocks in the foreground suggest the same master. But the movement of the figure is neither Alvisesque nor Bellinesque. It already betrays an artist who is able to use the human form as an instrument of expression in a way and to a degree the older Venetian masters rarely attained.

Lotto was living at Treviso, as appears by a document of this date, published by Dr. Bampo in the *Archivio Veneto* (vol. xxxii, *Spigolature dall' Archivio Notarile di Treviso*). Sept. 6, 1503.

NAPLES, SCUOLA VENETA, NO. 56. MADONNA AND SAINTS.

The Madonna, seated against a curtain to R. with St. Peter Martyr standing to L., places her hand on the infant St. John at her knee. Behind the saints is seen a landscape deepening to a watered valley, with low hills beyond on the sky-line. 1503-1505.

Signed: L. LOTVS. About 85 cm. h., 1 m. w. Figures three-quarters. Much repainted, the knife in the head of St. Peter Martyr looking like a much later addition, and the little St. John completely painted out of shape. Indeed, Messrs. Crowe and Cavalcaselle go so far as to say that he was put in much later, replacing the head of a donor [1].

[1] This composition occurs, with slight changes, a number of times in the Venetian Painting of about 1500, e. g. Berlin Gallery, No. 287, attributed to Previtali; the *Madonna and Saints* signed 'Marcus Venetus,' and supposed to be by Pensabene, in the Lochis Collection in Bergamo;

1503–1505.

Photographed by Brogi, Florence.

In this picture we again find traces of the influence both of Bellini and of Alvise Vivarini. The Virgin is not only draped as in Bellini's early Madonnas in the Contarini Collection of the Venice Academy (Nos. 17 and 24), the one in the Lochis Collection at Bergamo (No. 210), the one with the Greek inscription in the Brera (No. 261), and the one in Turin (No. 779), but resembles the last two even in type. Her L. hand, however, is Alvisesque, close to such a hand as that of St. Antony of Padua in Alvise's altar-piece of 1480 already mentioned. The structure of the Child is identical with Alvise's in the Berlin altar-piece, although its movement has a greater resemblance to that of the Child in a picture belonging to Miss Hertz, of London, painted by Bartolommeo Montagna, or to the Child by the same master in the Vicenza Gallery, representing the Madonna between SS. John and Onofrio. In type the St. Peter Martyr, severe and ascetic, recalls Cima. His ear is Alvisesque, much narrower than in Giovanni Bellini, and having a marked indentation where it meets the cheek, a peculiarity scarcely ever wanting in Alvise and never in Lotto, except possibly in one or two portraits. The thumb of St. Peter's L. hand, with the second phalanx broader than the first, we shall find frequently in Lotto, and as frequently in the works of Jacopo di Barbari, Bonsignori, and Savoldo.

LONDON, BRIDGEWATER HOUSE. MADONNA AND SAINTS.

The Madonna is seated, with, to R., SS. Clare and Francis, whose wound she is touching, and, to L.,

a Madonna by Basaiti in the Stuttgart Gallery; and a Madonna, probably by Catena, formerly in the Pourtalès Collection (woodcut in Lafenestre, *Peinture Italienne*, p. 317).

SS. Jerome and Joseph, Jerome offering a scroll to the Child who turns eagerly toward him. Two woodmen are seen in a hilly forest in the background. *1503-1505.*

Inscribed: L. LOTVS F. On wood, about 85 cm. h., 1 m. w. Figures three-quarters.

The Madonna and all the saints, except the Francis, are practically the busts of the figures in the altar-piece at Santa Cristina near Treviso, although the drier and more timid treatment, and the ash-coloured flesh-tints, make it certain that this picture was painted first. The St. Francis resembles the St. Peter Martyr in the picture at Naples.

One copy of this is exhibited in the Dresden Gallery (No. 195). Another is said to be in the Grosvenor Gallery in London.

Next in date comes a small allegorical picture, which belonged to the late painter Gritti, of Bergamo. Just before his death, he sent it to London, and it has not been heard of since. Several authorities quote the following inscription on the back: *July, 1505.*

BERNARDVS. RVBEVS.[1]
BERCETI. COMES. PONTIF. TARVIS.
AETAT. ANN. XXXVI. MENSE. X. D. V.
LAVRENTIVS. LOTTVS. P.
CAL. IUL. MDV.

The picture represented a tree with trophies, a shield with the arms of the Rossi di San Secondo, a *putto* playing with instruments on the ground, a satyr among urns and vases, and a genius making a path up a high mountain.

---

[1] Bernardo Rubeo, Legate of Bologna, is well known to students of Italian art through his medal struck by Francesco Francia.

NEAR TREVISO, SANTA CRISTINA. HIGH ALTAR.

1505-1506. The Madonna is enthroned in an apse, with SS. Liberale and Jerome standing below her to R., and SS. Cristina and Peter to L. Above, in a lunette, the Dead Christ upheld by Angels.

Signed: LAVRENTIVS LOTVS. On wood, 2·46 m. h., 1·42½ m. w.

Considerably damaged by recent attempts at restoration and by bad varnishing.

Photographed by Alinari, Florence.

The pose of the Madonna's head, bending to the L. with a kerchief rising in a peak over the crown, is commonly found in Alvise's works (e.g. the Venice altar-piece of 1480, and the National Gallery Madonna), but almost never in Bellini's. The finger-tips resting on an object (a book in this instance) are also found in Alvise (e. g. the Berlin altar-piece) and his school alone among the elder painters. The position of the Child, standing with both his feet on his mother's L. knee, with her L. hand only around his body, is never found in Bellini, but is precisely paralleled in Alvise's altar-piece of 1480, where, indeed, the proportions and action of the Child closely resemble Lotto's. The Virgin's L. hand is almost identical with the hand of St. Antony of Padua in the altar-piece of 1480, and her drapery, distinctly outlining the knees with folds in the shape of half diamonds, resembles Alvise's draperies in the Berlin altar-piece. The long-drawn, parallel folds over the arm and shoulder of the angel to R. in the *Pietà* recall the figure stretched out at full length in Basaiti's *Agony in the Garden* of the Venice Academy (No. 69), a picture in which, as Messrs. Crowe and Cavalcaselle have already noted, Basaiti is still purely Alvisesque. The hand of the St.

[Treviso, Santa Cristina

ALTAR PIECE

Jerome, with its bony fingers wide apart, and with 1505-knotty joints, recalls the hands of Alvise, as for example the hand of the St. Jerome in the Frari altarpiece. St. Peter's hand, with its scattered fingers, is even more Vivarinesque. The St. Cristina is of the same type as Lotto's early *Danaë*. The only ear visible, that of St. Peter, much rounder than Alvise's, but retaining the characteristic indentation into the cheek, remains in this form practically throughout Lotto's entire career. It is, by the way, strikingly like Montagna's ear in such a typical instance as the St. Margaret in the Sacristy of San Nazzaro e Celso at Verona, or like Bonsignori's ear in the portrait in the Sciarra-Colonna collection at Rome. St. Liberale, with his feet almost parallel although not alongside of each other, and St. Peter, with his feet at right angles, stand in a way characteristic of Alvise, as, for instance, the saints in the Venice Academy altarpiece. The capitals of the architecture are close to those in Alvise's Berlin altar-piece. Alvise's influence is traceable not alone in all these details, but in the more general characteristics of an exaggerated contrast of light and shadow and a zinc-washed grey tone.

But there are traces of Bellini's influence as well—not only of his general influence (as in the composition of the *Pietà*, which recalls such a composition of Bellini's as the *Pietà* in the Correr Museum at Venice, Sala IX, No. 54), but, I think, of one particular work, his altar-piece of 1505 in San Zaccaria at Venice. The arrangement of Lotto's work, although more crowded, recalls Bellini's—the Jerome and Peter closing in both compositions at the sides—and his Jerome may be reminiscent of the Jerome of Bellini. Furthermore, the decorative Mosaic pattern in the apse appears to have been suggested to Lotto by a similar feature in the San Zaccaria picture, although

1505-1506. Lotto's design already betrays that marked originality in decoration which becomes later so distinct a characteristic of his work. The fig-tree, a feature seldom found elsewhere in Lotto's pictures, may be a further indication of his having studied Bellini's work. If this hypothesis be correct, we can assume that the altar-piece could not have been begun before the end of 1505, that being the date, it will be remembered, of Bellini's picture. The maturity and ambitious character of the painting, moreover, help to confirm this later date rather than the somewhat earlier one which has sometimes been assigned to it.

ASOLO. ALTAR-PIECE. ASSUMPTION OF THE VIRGIN.

1506. The Virgin rises, surrounded by a glory of cherubs, while SS. Antony Abbot and Basil stand below to R. and L., looking up at her.

Inscribed: LAVRENT LOTVS IVNIOR MD. VI. According to Messrs. Crowe and Cavalcaselle, the present inscription is not the original one, which, they say, was LAVRENT LOTVS IVNII 1506.

On wood, 1·69 m. h., 1·54 m. w.

The Madonna is of the same type as the Cristina of Treviso and the Catherine of Munich, but even more Alvisesque than either. The landscape recalls the Naples picture, but is larger in treatment and much more elaborate, with fine effects of light on the horizon. The flesh colour is blonder than in most of Lotto's early works, and is almost of the tone found in Alvise's latest pictures. For a Venetian work of this date, this Assumption is singularly expressive. The feeling is distinctly devotional, and Lotto's power of psychological analysis appears here for the first time in the attitude of sentimental ecstasy he has given the

MUNICH: MARRIAGE OF ST. CATHERINE

young St. Basil, as contrasted with the calm reverie of the old St. Antony. 1506.

Lotto quits Treviso, leaving his furniture and most of his clothing behind him to pay for the rent of his house. (G. Bampo, *Spigolature*, &c.) The same collection of documents proves Lotto's presence at Treviso on February 24 and November 25, 1504, and on April 7, 1505. On the last occasion he is mentioned as *pictor celeberrimus*. We can assume, therefore, that from September, 1503, to June, 1506, Lotto was constantly in or near Treviso, becoming more and more well known as an artist. Oct., 1506.

In June, 1506, Lotto was instructed by the commune of Recanati to paint, for the price of six hundred florins and the keep of himself and of his assistant, an altar-piece which should be 'much better even than the works of his adolescence and first manhood with which they were already acquainted[1].' This proves that Lotto must either have visited Recanati himself or have sent his pictures there years before. The altar-piece mentioned in the last entry is the one finished for San Domenico in 1508. It may therefore be safely assumed that from November, 1506, to some time in 1508 Lotto made his head quarters at Recanati, and that he there painted the following works: Nov., 1506.

MUNICH, No. 1083. MARRIAGE OF ST. CATHERINE.

The Madonna, seated against a green curtain, bends over St. Catherine, who kneels to the L., placing the tips of her fingers on her neck. She holds on her R. knee the Child, who, with a lively gesture, leans forward to place the ring upon the saint's finger. These three 1507 (?).

---

[1] *Nuova Rivista Misena.* March–April, 1894. P. Giannuizzi. *Lorenzo Lotto nelle Marche.*

1507 (?). figures form a pyramidal group. To the R. an elderly saint looks over the Virgin's shoulder, holding a green book under his arm. To the L. is seen a forest landscape, with a mule-train in the foreground.

Signed: LAVREN. LOTVS. F. On wood, 70 cm. h., 90 cm. w. Figures three-quarters.

Photographed by Hanfstängl, Munich.

Again distinctly like Alvise, except the old saint, who is a trifle Bellinesque. The hair of the Child and of the old saint is painted with great minuteness, as in Jacopo di Barbari. The treatment of light and shadow is subtler and more harmonized than in the Santa Cristina altar-piece. The landscape resembles that of the Louvre *St. Jerome*. Over the Madonna's knee is a very Alvisesque fold, two long, almost straight and almost parallel lines (cf. fold on Madonna's knee, over her arm, or on curtain, in Alvise's Redentore picture). The hand of the kneeling saint is very close to the L. hand of Jacopo di Barbari's *Galatea* at Dresden. Lotto's fondness for the decorative use of bows of ribbon appears here for the first time, in the shoulder knot of the St. Catherine.

ROME, VILLA BORGHESE. MADONNA AND SAINTS.

1508. The Madonna is seated, turning toward St. Onofrio (R.), while the Child in her arms tries to grasp the Sacred Heart held out to him by a Bishop (L.).

Inscribed: LAVRENT. LOTVS. M.D. VIII. On wood, 53 cm. h., 67 cm. w. Figures three-quarters.

Photographed by Anderson, Rome, and Alinari, Florence.

The composition as a whole, with the Child turning toward the figures on one side and the Madonna toward those on the other, is, to my knowledge, never found in the Bellini, but occurs in such cases as Cima's

Recanati

THE MADONNA AND CHILD, WITH SAINTS
CENTRAL PANEL OF ALTAR PIECE

works at Munich (No. 1033), at Vienna (No. 156), and 1508. at Parma (No. 360), and in Jacopo di Barbari's engraving of a *Santa Conversazione* (Bartsch, vol. vii, p. 518, No. 5). In pose of head, type, and expression, the Madonna stands close to Jacopo di Barbari's *St. Catherine* of Dresden (No. 58). Her hood has the Alvisesque peak, and the sealing-wax red of her dress recalls the National Gallery *Madonna* by Alvise. The damask of the Bishop's mitre resembles the curtain in Barbari's *Portrait of a Youth* at Vienna (No. 203). The almost parallel, close fold on his R. arm and on his skirt recall Barbari again, as well as Basaiti and Alvise. The accentuated and mobile nostrils, which are peculiarly noticeable in the Bishop, are more or less characteristic of Alvise and his whole school, appearing most pronouncedly in Jacopo di Barbari and Lotto. The heavy protruding eyelids of the Madonna are also characteristic of Alvise and his following. A likeness between the St. Onofrio and the old man on the R. in Dürer's *Christ among the Doctors*, in the Barberini Gallery, has been noted by Thausing (*Dürer*, p. 265), but instead of the Onofrio being, as he says, an 'out and out transcript from Dürer,' the resemblance is scarcely more than the likeness between any two white-haired old men. If anything, the St. Onofrio is of the type of such of Cima's old men as the one in the Vienna altar-piece. The sweeping tufts of his hair recall the treatment of hair in Alvise and, more particularly, in Jacopo di Barbari.

RECANATI, MUNICIPIO.

ALTAR-PIECE in six parts from San Domenico.

Central Panel: Madonna enthroned between SS. Urban and Gregory, who stand on the pedestal to R.

1508. and L., giving a robe to an angel, who presents it to the kneeling St. Dominic. On the steps of the throne, two *putti*, one playing a mandolin, the other tapping him on the shoulder with the bow of his lute, to call his attention to what is going on.

Inscribed: LAVRENT. LOTVS. MDV IIJ. The entire work is on wood. *Central Panel*, 2·25 m. h., 1·04 m. w.

Photographed by Alinari and Anderson.

Side Wings: R., St. Vito and St. Peter Martyr; L., St. Flavian and St. Thomas Aquinas. Each 1·68 m. h., 69 cm. w.

Photographed by Alinari and Anderson.

Above these, smaller *square panels:* R., SS. Catherine of Siena and Sigismund; L., St. Vincent and the Magdalen. Each 65 cm. square, half-length figures.

Photographed by Alinari.

Top Panel: The Dead Christ, with Joseph of Arimathea, the Magdalen, and an angel. 76 cm. h., 1·09 m. w.

Mentioned by Vasari, but carelessly described. He speaks of three predelle, 'una cosa rara . . . con le più graziose figurine del mondo,' which have disappeared.

The composition of the central panel, with the saints on different levels and the architectural setting—a coffered vaulting—is on Alvise's scheme (cf. the Berlin and Frari altar-pieces), but is knit together more closely than any of Alvise's altar-pieces or Lotto's own earlier ones. It is as yet, however, entirely free from exaggeration of movement. The Madonna, of the same type as in the Santa Cristina and Borghese pictures, but with less expression than either, is draped in the Alvisesque hood, in this point, and in bend of head, recalling Alvise's National Gallery Madonna; but her mantle falls down over the steps of the throne in ample folds, as in Bellini. A fold on her R. arm is as nearly as may be like a fold on the R. arm of Alvise's Santa

LORENZO LOTTO

[Recanati

S. VITO (DETAIL)

JACOPO DI BARBARI

Alinari photo]   [*Treviso*

A HERALD
DETAIL OF A FRESCO

Giustina in the Bagati collection at Milan. The Child, 1508. in structure and movement, comes close to the Child in the Naples picture. The smaller of the two *putti* bears a striking resemblance in type, build, and movement to the *putto* on the R. in Alvise's Redentore *Madonna*, while the long oval of the angel's face recalls Alvise's Santa Giustina. The hand of the Madonna around the Child is almost identical with the R. hand of the Madonna in Montagna's *Nativity* in the Vicenza Gallery (Sala V, No. 3); the R. hand of the angel, with its enormously thick fingers, is distinctively Alvisesque (cf. Berlin and Frari altar-pieces).

Dramatically, this is perhaps better rendered than any previous Venetian altar-piece. The interest is concentrated upon the relation between the Child and the kneeling St. Dominic, the other figures looking on reverently and attentively. It marks a happy moment in the artist's career; he was sufficiently master of his craft to construct and interpret as he wished, but his hand was not as yet so obedient as to tempt him to push movement to an extreme, or to sacrifice the figures to the mere interpretation of feeling.

The St. Vito in the R. panel has not only Alvise's characteristic heavy chin, but a mouth cut nearly as in Alvise's signed *Portrait*, formerly in the Bonomi-Cereda collection at Milan, but now belonging to Mr. Salting, and in the Louvre *Portrait* ascribed to Savoldo (No. 1519), but also by Alvise—a mouth, by the way, almost always found in Alvise, particularly in his later works, and frequently in Lotto's earlier works. But close as this figure stands to Alvise, it stands even closer to Jacopo di Barbari. There is scarcely a characteristic of that master which is not to be found in the St. Vito. In mere general resemblance the head recalls that of the warrior on the L. in Barbari's frescoes around the tomb of Onigo in S. Niccolò

1508. at Treviso, and the full-face bust of a youth in the Lochis Gallery at Bergamo (No. 147), having with the latter even stronger affinities in such characteristics as the toss of the head, the proportions of the features, the long nose with accentuated nostrils, and the curly hair in close corkscrew ringlets, with high lights on separate hairs. The awkward position of the legs is Alvisesque, and particularly close to the figure of St. Liberale in the Berlin altar-piece. Vito is clad in the romantic costume of the time, with long, rich sleeves, ribbons, and jewels over his armour.

The thick fingers in some of the figures have a tendency to spread, as in Alvise and his followers. The R. hand of St. Thomas, with two fingers drawn in and two stretched out on the edge of a book, is identical with the hand of St. Nicholas of Bari in Bartolommeo Vivarini's altar-piece of 1465 at Naples, and with the hand of St. Augustine in the *ancona* at Bologna dating from 1450, and painted by Antonio and Bartolommeo Vivarini, the masters and predecessors of Alvise. The capitals and mosaic decoration are almost identical with those in the Santa Cristina altar-piece. The Magdalen in the L. upper panel closely resembles the St. Catherine in the Munich picture, and the St. Catherine in the R. upper panel comes very near to the early Madonnas of Basaiti. The composition of the *Pietà* is almost the same as in the polyptych in San Giovanni e Paolo at Venice, attributed to Alvise and Bartolommeo Vivarini, but really by Francesco Buonsignori, their follower.

The whole altar-piece has something of that dryness of expression and sobriety of colouring which is characteristic of Alvise, and also the low tones and the tendency toward bituminous flesh-tints which is found in Alvise and his school.

[*Count Sigismond Pusłowski, Cracow*

THE MADONNA AND SAINTS

CRACOW, COUNT SIGISMOND PUSLOWSKI.

The Madonna seated with her head in profile to L. adores the Child who lies fast asleep sunk between her knees on her lap. St. Catherine looks at the Child over His mother's shoulder; St. Francis joins in worship; between him and the Virgin appears the head of St. Jerome, while the infant John looks up to the Madonna. All against a dark green curtain.

Signed: L. LOTVS. On wood, 40 m. h., 29 cm. w.

I owe what knowledge I have of this picture to the photograph and information furnished me by Prof. Count Georges Mycielski of Cracow.

We scarcely can go wrong in assigning this little panel to 1508 or a little later. The action of the children recalls the Munich and Recanati works of that year. The Francis is the Peter Martyr in the latter polyptych, but reversed. The Catherine is own sister to the Vito in the same panel. Like him also, she is bedizened with finery and ribbons. Her hand anticipates Lotto's later forms. As this original little painting seems to have been acquired about 1803 in Rome, it is not at all unlikely that it was painted in Central Italy.

There is no lack here of Alvisesque traits. Thus Catherine recalls Barbari's heralds, and her mouth is quite like Alvise's. The R. hand of Francis is almost, without a change, the hand of St. Anna in the latter's Venice Academy picture of 1480.

1508.

HAMPTON COURT, NO. 114. BUST OF A YOUNG MAN.

Full face, with head tossed back somewhat as in the Recanati St. Vito, but more energetically; hair parted in the middle, flowing down to shoulders, and beard

1508-1509.

1508-1509. carefully combed out to the sides. Black silk doublet over white shirt; grey background.

On canvas, 53 cm. h., 39 cm. w.

Photographed by Simpson.

Engraved by Van Dalen for the series made from the Van Reynst pictures before they were sent by the Dutch States to Charles II.

In all morphological characteristics and technical qualities, this picture agrees with Lotto's works of 1508 already discussed, but, being a portrait, and not a sacred picture, it is a trifle freer in pose and more personal in interpretation.

CHAPTER II

LOTTO'S ANTECEDENTS: THE SCHOOL OF ALVISE VIVARINI

I.—LOTTO, GIOVANNI BELLINI, AND GIORGIONE

With the Recanati altar-piece, the Cracow panel, and the Hampton Court portrait, closes the first part of Lotto's career, there being a sharper division between the works considered so far and those next in date, than exists between any two consecutive works by Giorgione, Titian, or Palma, Lotto's contemporaries. We can thus speak with a literalness rarely possible in such cases, of all of Lotto's paintings up to 1509 as works of his first manner.

If we could see arranged in a row all these early pictures, and in rows above them the pictures Giorgione, Titian, and Palma painted at the same time, the first glance would reveal a striking likeness in general tone, types, and artistic aspiration between the three artists last mentioned (none of them younger than Lotto, it will be remembered), and a striking difference between them and Lotto. Beside them, Lotto is timid in colouring and antiquated in types, and, while it would seem that to them the *Quattrocento* had become a mere reminiscence, he appears to be still almost completely embogged in it. Their colouring is rich, deep, and mellow, while his swings from dark bituminous to highly transparent, cool, but hard tints. Their medium has a more even flow than his; their lights and shadows are so well distributed that our attention is scarcely drawn to them, while his are still as sharply contrasted as in those Quattrocentists, who first systematically devoted themselves to the study of *chiaroscuro*. Giorgione, Titian, and Palma either glaze thickly or else paint entirely in oils, while Lotto's glazes are so thin that his pictures look more like tempera than oil paintings. The people in their pictures are well formed, comfortable, happy as mere animals, while his are ascetic, severe, even melancholy, as if still overburdened with the *ennui* of the cloister, or the *accidia* Petrarch complained of. In the building up of his compositions, Lotto is even more of a Quattrocentist than in other features. The Virgin, flanked to right and left by brooding saints, is still enshrined like an idol in the apse of a sanctuary in those altar-pieces that he painted at a time when Giorgione was already enthroning her over a radiant landscape as queen of the earth and of the dazzling sky, with saints standing below her as a guard of honour. We have no such thing as an *ancona*—the old form of altar-piece in many parts, with the Virgin or chief saint in the principal panel—by Giorgione or Titian, but Lotto has left us one (at Recanati) at least as elaborate as any of the fifteenth century; and it is an interesting fact, in this connexion, that we have no indication that Giorgione, Titian, or Palma ever painted a *predella*—that last remnant of the *ancona* to disappear—while we know of a number painted by Lotto. In short, Lotto, as he reveals himself to the cursory spectator of his early works, seems not so much the contemporary of Giorgione, Titian, and Palma, as of an artistically older generation, of Bissolo, Basaiti, and Catena. As he is, however, somewhat younger than Giorgione and Titian, and no older than Palma, we might infer that Lotto was either one of those unhappy painters destined never to outstep the circle of their first master's influence, or that he was an artist of exceedingly slow development.

But we shall see before long that, whatever Lotto's limitations may have been, his capacity for growth was not limited, for in certain points, as will appear, he actually went beyond any of his closer contemporaries; and we have already seen that in certain features indicative of early maturity, such as giving the figures expressive movement and analysing situations and characters, Lotto was for his age rather advanced than backward. Incapacity for growth and sluggishness of temperament can consequently have no place in explaining the belated character of his first manner. We are therefore obliged to seek for another explanation, and we shall be the better prepared to find it when we have noted and discussed another consideration peculiarly interesting in this connexion. It is this. As we examined Lotto's early works, we observed his affinities with other painters, but among these artists the name of Giorgione did not once occur. As an artist Lotto, as we shall see later, was very susceptible, and indeed Messrs. Crowe and Cavalcaselle find in him little more than 'a mush of concessions' to outside influences. How then shall we explain the fact that this easily swayed, easily influenced young painter gives in his early works no indication of having known the fascinating, irresistible Giorgione? The explanation is all the more difficult because we must bear in mind that there is no such thing as a pre-Giorgionesque Titian, and scarcely such a thing as a pre-Giorgionesque Palma. If Lotto, as is generally supposed, had been the fellow pupil of these three artists, working in the same studio with them, how did he contrive to escape the spell of Giorgione, when the sturdy Titian, destined to outmatch them all, was for the time absorbed by him, and when even the slow-trotting Palma followed after as best he could? So great confessedly was the charm of this boy-magician, Giorgione, that even his own master, the more than seventy-year-old Giovanni Bellini, is said to have fallen under his influence to the extent of trying to remodel his own style on that of his pupil. It need scarcely be added that the influence which the master presumably could not resist, the influence which such pupils as Titian and Palma fell under almost to the extinction for a time of their own personalities, could not have been resisted by so sensitive a person as Lotto, if he had been constantly at work with them. We are driven, therefore, to the inference that Lotto could not have been in the same studio with Giorgione, Titian, and Palma, that he could not have been their fellow pupil under Giovanni Bellini.

Now, if we could clear our minds of the old tradition that Lotto was Bellini's pupil, we should at once be put on the track to an explanation of the archaic character of his early works. But Vasari and Ridolfi state that Lotto's master was Giovanni Bellini; Messrs. Crowe and Cavalcaselle repeat the statement, and Morelli accepts it as a matter of course. When we look into it, however, we find that we have here nothing but a case of successive copying. Vasari's personal acquaintance with the Venetian school was exceedingly small, as becomes evident when it is noted, for instance, that he divides Lazzaro Sebastiani into two persons, sees Basaiti double, and names a host of tenth-rate artists in one paragraph pell-mell, dashing an epithet of appreciation at one or the other for purposes of mere rhetoric. The truth is that Vasari's contemporaries were living fast, felt as if they were already ages away from the fifteenth century, and consequently took little pleasure in artists of two or three generations ago, scarcely caring to burden memory with their names. Hence the habit, so easily explained psychologically, but so fatal to criticism, of making one great name stand for a whole art-epoch or style. When Vasari was preparing the second edition of his *Lives* (published in 1565), Giovanni Bellini had already become a generic term for 'superior fifteenth-century Venetian Master,' and what could be more natural than to speak of Lotto as his pupil? It must also be remembered that Vasari and his contemporaries felt none of that keen interest which we, inspired by our general evolutionary philosophy, take in artistic genealogies. The question was not of such absorbing interest to Vasari that he would have taken trouble to ascertain the precise facts, and even if he had wished to do so, it would not have been so easy as might be thought. Lotto was dead. He had lived a wandering life, and Vasari might have had the greatest difficulty in finding a single person who had known him intimately. Titian himself might have forgotten whether Lotto had been or had not been his fellow pupil. Even in our own day it is by no means easy to ascertain who were the masters of still living painters. In fine, we need give no weight to Vasari's statement, except in so far as it is borne out by facts.

Ridolfi, who after Vasari is considered the best source of information on Venetian painting, is not worth refuting. He merely repeats Vasari in Marinistic Italian, adding at times to Vasari's lists, but scarcely ever to Vasari's statements. Coming down to modern critics we know that Messrs. Crow and Cavalcaselle are noted for their skill in reconciling the observation of their own eyes with an almost blind acceptance of the printed word, by means of a theory of influence which wholly ignores psychological probability, and scarcely takes cognizance of time and space. They observed, for instance, an affinity between Lotto and Cima da Conegliano, and between Lotto and Basaiti, but it did not occur to them to inquire into its cause, the vague word 'influence' seeming to them a sufficient explanation. Morelli, in this particular instance, saw even less clearly than his rivals. He never speaks of Lotto without calling him the pupil of Giovanni Bellini.

I am aware, however, that certain facts had not escaped the notice of this acutest of all critics of Italian art. He had an hypothesis, in his own mind probably too vague to permit his venturing to print it, that both Cima and Alvise Vivarini were foremen of Giovanni Bellini's *atelier*. Such a theory would explain why so many of the supposed pupils of Bellini seem to have been far more under the influence of Cima or of Alvise than of their nominal master himself. But on looking into it closely, we find that this hypothesis is unfounded. Alvise could not possibly have been the foreman of Bellini's workshop. The struggle between the Muranese and the Bellineschi, of which we have a plain statement in Alvise's letter of 1488 to the Signoria of Venice, must have been far keener than has yet been supposed, although the mere traces of it still remaining should lead us to suspect one of those rivalries which it would be poor psychology to think of as continuing on a high level of generous emulation and not sinking to bitter hatred. Alvise, morever, was at work in the Doge's palace on his own account from 1489 on, and seems to have had so much other work on hand that at the end of fourteen years he had not quite finished the second of the subjects entrusted to him [1]. We can, therefore, dismiss the idea that Bellini had for foreman of his shop a rival who was absorbingly busy on his own account, and probably an enemy to boot. Cima's

[1] It would seem that he was ailing—for our argument the same.

foremanship in Bellini's studio has more mere probability in its favour, Cima being at least thirty years younger than Giovanni Bellini and presumably a stranger without a footing in Venice. A curious fact seems to confirm this hypothesis. It is this. Sebastiano del Piombo's earliest known work, a *Pietà*, belonging to Lady Layard in Venice, is so distinctly Cimaesque in drawing, types, and composition, as to leave no doubt that the painter was a close imitator of Cima; yet, odd as it sounds, Sebastiano on this particular work proudly inscribes himself the pupil of Giovanni Bellini. Messrs. Crowe and Cavalcaselle, staggered by this flagrant contradiction, deny the genuineness of the inscription, but without the least reason. The fact remains. To Morelli it seems to have proved that Cima was the foreman of Bellini's workshop, Sebastiano naturally preferring to be known as the pupil of the already famous master rather than of the assistant to whom he actually owed his training. But if this were the case, why is it so solitary? Why do we not find traces of it in other painters—in Previtali, for instance, who in 1502, in his first known work, also recommends himself to future patronage by declaring himself the pupil of Giovanni Bellini? In his *Madonna and Donor*, now in the gallery at Padua, Previtali shows no trace of Cima's influence, although he probably painted it in the very year in which Sebastiano, born scarcely earlier than 1485, painted his *Pietà*. An even greater objection to the hypothesis that Cima held such a position in Bellini's shop arises from our personal knowledge of Cima's career. Don Vicenzo Botteon's monograph on that artist (to which I must refer my readers) enables us to trace his career with much greater precision than was possible in Morelli's lifetime. Cima, like Alvise, seems to have been a busy artist on his own account, as the mere number of his remaining works and the comparative brevity of his life indicate. That he had an *atelier* of his own can be assumed from the distinctness and unswerving tension of his own style, and from the way he and *his* assistants are spoken of in the documents concerning his own pictures in S. Giovanni in Bragora at Venice. Morelli's hypothesis concerning Cima's foremanship is therefore as untenable as the one about Alvise. As to Sebastiano's *Pietà*, the explanation is probably this. Sebastiano must have begun his studies under Cima, in Cima's *atelier*, and then, for a reason we are not deeply concerned with, changed over to Bellini. Just about 1500 the triumph of the Bellini over all rivals was so definite, their fame had got so noised abroad, that the younger pupils, as we have seen in the case of Previtali (and other instances are not rare), found it expedient to let their pictures declare not merely their own names, but their artistic origin as well. Sebastiano followed the fashion and adopted it the more gladly, perhaps, as he may have had some personal reason for letting his picture announce his break with Cima and adherence to Giovanni Bellini.

Morelli's idea concerning the relation of Alvise and Cima to Bellini being thus proved untenable, no explanation remains of the archaic style of Lotto's early works, if their author were actually the pupil of Giovanni Bellini. We are therefore obliged to seek elsewhere his artistic origin, and, as we have seen, the weight of extraneous evidence concerning Lotto's connexion with Bellini is not great enough to make us hesitate in declaring the tradition unfounded.

We have already observed that in the sixteenth century, from which time we still draw most of our information about the century preceding, ' Giovanni Bellini ' had become a generic name for superior Venetian Quattrocentist, and it followed as a matter of course that all superior painters a generation or two younger were his pupils. But we have just had occasion to note that Alvise Vivarini and Cima da Conegliano had each his own *atelier*, and nobody disputes the fact that Gentile had also his own *bottega*, and Carpaccio as well. All these artists must have had their own assistants, their own apprentices, and their own pupils, and before we can have a clear idea of the Venetian school as a whole we must divide it up into its various branches during the fifteenth century, and see what each contributed towards the art of the Cinquecento. Only by this kind of articulation can the term 'School' get more than a mystical meaning, and art-history become a proper subject for the student of humanity's autobiography.

But such is not our task. We are concerned with Lorenzo Lotto, and with the fifteenth-century Venetians only in so far as they help us to understand him. We have seen that Giovanni Bellini could not have been his master. We are now ready to discard all tradition, and, benefiting by the analysis we have made of Lotto's first pictures, we are free to decide that the artist with whom the young Lotto had the closest affinities must have been his first teacher.

Alvise Vivarini, Jacopo di Barbari, Cima, Montagna, Giovanni Bellini, Basaiti, Bonsignori, Bartolommeo, and even Antonio Vivarini are, in order of frequency, the painters we have been reminded of in those of Lotto's pictures that we have thus far examined. Giovanni Bellini we have already excluded, so that we can leave him out of consideration. Alvise's influence we have found always predominant not only in Lotto's types, forms, draperies, setting, and grouping, but also in his colour, tone, and technique. It is with the few works by Alvise still remaining that Lotto's early pictures have in common by far the greatest number of characteristics, and we are therefore strongly inclined to assume that Alvise and no other was Lotto's master; but before yielding to this inclination, we must account for the apparent jumble of other painters with whom Lotto has affinities. I say 'apparent jumble' because the name we encounter with greatest frequency after Alvise's is that of Jacopo di Barbari, a painter supposed to have been a pupil of Giovanni Bellini, and rarely in Venice; because Montagna, inhabiting Vicenza, with slight interruptions, from 1480 upwards, has thus far scarcely been connected at all with the Venetian school, except by Morelli, who makes him the follower of Carpaccio; because Bonsignori also has never, except in a cursory note by Morelli, been connected with Venice, having, according to Messrs. Crowe and Cavalcaselle, before he fell under the influence of Mantegna, been the pure product of the Veronese school; because, finally, Antonio Vivarini died some time before Lotto was born, and if Bartolommeo Vivarini lived on till Lotto's adolescence, the point of striking likeness we found between them (the hand of St. Thomas in the Recanati picture of 1508) is not in the works of the old Bartolommeo, which Lotto might well have known, but in a picture now at Naples, painted for Bari in 1465, which it may safely be assumed Lotto had not seen up to this point of his career.

II.—JACOPO DI BARBARI

In the first place, let us try to account for the affinities between Lotto and Jacopo di Barbari. Fortunately, Morelli has reconstructed this matter so admirably (*Die Galerien zu München und Dresden*, pp. 255–266) that comparatively little remains to be done to perfect our idea of his artistic personality.

BARBARI AND THE VIVARINI

Morelli was, however, not so happy in reconstructing Barbari's artistic genealogy, which he traces back to Giovanni Bellini. For this I see no grounds whatever. Although born between 1440 and 1450, the earliest works of Barbari of ascertainable date that have come down to us are the decorative frescoes around the Onigo monument in San Niccolò at Treviso, executed in the last five years of the fifteenth century. Barbari was more than forty at this time, and had, as Morelli has observed, already passed under the influence of Antonello da Messina and the Lombardi. We should therefore expect to find but faint traces of his first schooling, yet we find them in fact strong enough to clearly betray his origin. The face of the herald on the R. is too far gone to repay examination, but the one on the L., better preserved, has the projecting eyelids, the prominent nostrils, the full-flexed lips, the oval of face, and the heavy, almost double chin of Alvise. The emphatic, even vehement, pose of the two figures is a characteristic never found in Giovanni Bellini, but is not rare in Alvise [1], and is even less rare in Bartolommeo Vivarini. Each of the heralds has an arm akimbo with the back of the hand against the hip—a peculiarity never found in Bellini, but in Alvise (in his Frari altar-piece), in Bonsignori (whom we shall presently discover to have been a pupil of Alvise), and in an altar-piece in Vienna (No. 6) formerly ascribed to Catena, but obviously by Lazzaro Sebastiani, a painter who was in his earlier years an indisputable follower of the Vivarini. Finally, the unbalanced position of the herald on the R. with his legs almost parallel and slanting from R. to L., is one of those gross awkwardnesses frequently found in the Vivarini,

---

[1] Cf. St. Antony Abbot, St. Matthew, and similar figures in the Venice Academy, and the St. Liberale in the Berlin altar-piece.

and perfectly matched by the St. Sebastian in Bartolommeo's polyptych at Vienna (No. 10).

The two portraits in the Bergamo Gallery (Lochis, Nos. 147, 148), earlier probably than the foregoing, share the same character. The oval of the full face, the heavy chin, the long nose with inflated nostrils, the hair almost silken and in ringlets[1] in the one, betray its many affinities with Alvise; while the marked indentation in the upper lip of the other, with the black shadows outlining the inflation of the nostril, again bear witness to the painter's connexion with Alvise, although here the wide-open eyes, with the pupil perfectly distinct from the iris, as well as something in the whole conception, betray Antonello's influence also.

At this point I must allow myself a parenthesis to meet an objection likely to arise in the minds of my readers. They may say that certain points I have noted as distinctly Vivarinesque are found in Antonello also, and that Antonello might therefore account for all that I have explained by the Vivarini in the case of Barbari, as well as in the cases of Bonsignori and Montagna which I am going to take up in due course. I take this first opportunity, therefore, of declaring my adherence to Morelli's opinion regarding Antonello, to wit, that as an artist he owes nearly everything to the Venetians, although in the mere technique of oil-painting he, in turn, exerted upon them an overwhelming influence. I venture to disagree with Morelli, however, in so far as he sees in Antonello's Antwerp *Crucifixion* of 1475 the influence of Carpaccio, and in other pictures, as, for instance, the *Portrait of a Youth*, at Berlin (No. 18), and the *St. Sebastian*, at Dresden, the strong influence of Giovanni Bellini. In the

[1] Cf. Alvise's St. John, the one nearly in profile, in the Venice Academy (No. 621).

ANTONELLO AND THE VENETIANS 29

Antwerp picture I can find no trace of Carpaccio. (What, by the way, do we know of Carpaccio's activity as early as 1475, his earliest known work, the *Madonna with two Saints*, in the Berlin Gallery, being at least as late as 1485?) The influence of Bartolommeo Vivarini, on the contrary, is faintly discernible in the Madonna's oval, and more clearly in the small angular folds of her mantle spreading on the ground. In the *Youth* at Berlin it is the general Venetian character that strikes me, rather than distinct signs of Giovanni Bellini's influence. As to the *St. Sebastian* of Dresden, his oval is Alvisesque, the close parallel folds of his loin-cloth are characteristic of the Vivarini, and even the pose, with the legs slanting and almost parallel, comes close to Alvise. That Antonello came under the influence of the Bellini I would not deny; my point is that their influence, far from being the only, does not seem to have been even the dominant one, that having been exerted upon him by the Vivarini. Nor would I deny the probability that Antonello himself had an influence upon the youngest of the Vivarini, on Alvise; if however it existed, it is not easy to ascertain, all the peculiarities that Alvise has in common with Antonello, the exaggerated perspective of the eye [1], the prominent nostrils, the full-flexed lips, being characteristic of the Vivarini before Antonello came to Venice at all, so that he must have taken it from them, and not they, Alvise in particular, from him. Moreover, excepting possibly the exaggerated perspective of the eye, the above-mentioned peculiarities are not at all so marked in Antonello as in Alvise.

Returning now to Barbari,—we have already noted

[1] This peculiarity is found already in the St. Peter in Alvise's earliest remaining work, the polyptych at Montefiorentino, dated 1475—that is to say, possibly only one year after Antonello's arrival at Venice. In Antonello himself it occurs for the first time in the *Condottiere* of the Louvre, also dated 1475.

that besides sharing with the Vivarini characteristics which they, in turn, share with Antonello, he has others which are not found in Antonello at all, but in the Vivarini frequently, so that, in any case, he owes very much more to them than to Antonello. Let us now continue the examination of Barbari's works. Turning next to the Berlin *Madonna with SS. Barbara, John, and a Female Donor*, which dates from the earliest years of the sixteenth century, we are struck by the roundness of the Child's head, by the Madonna's R. hand with its longish palm narrowing down to fingers pressed close together, both features characteristic of Alvise, by the close parallel folds on the Virgin's waist, and the close crumpled folds on her sleeve, and the large angular folds of her skirt spread out on the ground, drapery found frequently in Bartolommeo or Alvise Vivarini, less frequently (with these precise characteristics) in Gentile Bellini, and never in Giovanni. In the landscape, in the middle distance to L., and in the knoll to R., we have striking reminders not of Giovanni Bellini, but of Cima da Conegliano [1], whom we shall also find to have been a pupil of Alvise. In the Dresden pictures, the Saviour in type and movement is but a variation on Alvise's of 1493 in San Giovanni in Bragora at Venice. The slightly open mouths in all these figures, and elsewhere in Barbari, are probably a mannerism derived by exaggeration from the Vivarini, although in them, frequently as the open mouth occurs, it is always to be accounted for [2]. Morelli would derive this mannerism, and the close parallel folds as well, from the Lombardi, with whom

[1] Cf. Berlin, No. 7, *Madonna and Donor*, and Venice Academy *Madonna with Six Saints* (No. 36). For reproductions of Alvise's principal works, see section VII of this chapter.

[2] Antonello, however, gives his Dresden St. Sebastian an open mouth without making him look as if he were crying out or speaking; so does Cima in the head of the *Female Saint* in the Museo Poldi at Milan.

Barbari doubtless had business connexions. But Barbari was forty years old at least when—so far as we know—he first worked in company with Lombardi, and at that age a man's mannerisms change only through their own momentum, not through communicated impulse. It seems patent moreover that the Lombardi were themselves very much influenced by the Venetian painters. Surely their works, particularly such as the Giustiniani chapel at San Francesco della Vigna, and the *Coronation* at San Giovanni Crisostomo at Venice, would not have borne such striking resemblance to the paintings of Bissolo, Girolamo Santa Croce, and other minor Venetian painters if Tullio and Antonio Lombardi had been as uninfluenced by Venetian masters as their father Pietro on his arrival at Venice. Most interesting in this connexion is the sculptured altar, probably an early work by Tullio, in the Duomo of Cesena. Here the Resurrected Christ is so Vivarinesque that He reminds us at once of the Christ in the *Resurrection* in the Verona Gallery by Jacopo da Valenza, Alvise's slavish imitator. The St. John and St. Catherine are equally Vivarinesque. The mannerisms which Barbari and the Lombardi have in common are thus probably due to a common source, the Vivarini.

Returning to the Dresden pictures, we note that the silken ringlets and twisted locks, here and elsewhere so characteristic of Barbari's work, are also to be found in Alvise, and with comparative frequency in his pupil Cima. As to the top of the thumb in these figures, particularly that of the Saviour, which Morelli notes as being one of the most peculiar of Barbari's mannerisms, that also is derived from Alvise[1], in whom (and in

---

[1] For a striking likeness between Barbari's thumb, as in this Saviour, and Alvise's, cf. the R. hand of St. Lawrence in the Venice Academy (No. 621).

whose school as well) the second phalanx of the thumb is, as a rule, much larger than the first.

In the Dresden *Galatea* (No. 59 A), we have still further indications of Barbari's connexion with Alvise. The feet are at right angles to each other, as we find them frequently in Alvise. The big toe is shorter than the others, a peculiarity not uncommon in Alvise, very frequent in Bartolommeo, and universal in the latter's probable fellow pupil, Carlo Crivelli. That this is no mere accident in Barbari will be seen in his engravings and in another picture, hitherto unnoticed, which I venture to ascribe to Barbari, the *St. Sebastian* in the Pitti (No. 384), attributed to Pollajuolo [1].

We have finally to consider the two splendid heads in the Habich collection at Cassel, both of them drawings, the one in charcoal, representing a youth who wears a small cap over his bushy *zazzera*, and the other in red crayon, also representing a youth. Not only do these drawings proclaim even more loudly than the paintings their affinity in morphological details with Alvise, but the mere technique tells its own story. Unfortunately, drawings by Alvise are so very rare that the terms of comparison between his and Barbari's are almost lacking, although all the heads known to me (see later under Alvise) have innumerable points of likeness in technique. But much more striking is the resemblance between these heads of Barbari and the heads by Bonsignori in the Albertina, Chantilly, and in the Uffizi. That this resemblance should have escaped Morelli is, by the way, a singular instance of the truth that no individual

---

[1] Cf. ear in this with ear of Female Donor in Barbari's Berlin picture; hair and eyes with Bergamo portraits, and drawings in the Habich collection. Note the prominent nostrils, the mouth slightly open, the feet identical with those in the Dresden *Galatea*, curving out at the joint of the little toe. The outlines are sharp and almost engraved, as is the portrait at Bergamo (Lochis, No. 148). Probable date, 1480–1490.

can do more than so much to advance a science, science being pre-eminently the result of intellectual co-operation. Now Morelli had already observed that 'judging from his drawings, Bonsignori owed all that was best in him to Alvise' (*Die Galerie zu Berlin*, p. 75). We shall see later how correct Morelli was in this hypothesis, which, unfortunately, he did not even attempt to prove. Meanwhile, we can take it for granted that the likeness between Barbari and Bonsignori is due to their common origin, the Vivarini, and thus my thesis, that Barbari was an offshoot of the Vivarini, is confirmed from this quarter also. A drawing in the Uffizi, hitherto unnoticed, will be the last to be examined in this connexion [1]. It is in red crayon, the head of a smooth-faced youth, slightly turned to the L., with straggling hair, pensive, wide-open eyes, and firm mouth. The characteristics of technique and form are unmistakably Barbari's, but the conception, the feeling, are so Alvisesque that I never look at it afresh without being reminded of Alvise. In such a drawing as this, we have one of those precious links that connect master and master all the better for the difficulty of deciding precisely to which it belongs.

Now that we have made Barbari's works yield up all the information they can give us regarding his origin, we are free to turn to evidence from without. In 1511 Barbari was pensioned off by the Grand Duchess Margaret, Regent of the Netherlands, because of his 'great age and debility.' This means that he could scarcely have been under seventy in 1511, and

---

[1] Uffizi: attributed to Garofalo, whose name is printed on the top. Cf. mouth with mouth in Bergamo portrait (Lochis, No. 148). The hair is more as in No. 147 in the same collection, and also recalls many of his engravings, particularly the *Resurrected Christ* (Bartsch, vii. 519, 7). The lids are as in nearly all of Barbari's works, and the nostrils also. Most characteristic of all is the small pupil, perfectly marked off from the iris. The technique is identical with the Habich red crayon drawing.

consequently that he was born about 1440, and would thus have begun his apprenticeship as a painter no later than 1455. Now as late as April, 1470, the Bellini had made so little headway in Venice that Giovanni is glad to receive a commission from the Scuola di San Marco on the same terms accorded a few months earlier to Lazzaro Sebastiani[1], a parasitical painter, who in his first fifty years was a follower of the Vivarini, and towards 1500 fell under the influence of Gentile—a painter than whom no one ever habitually kept a lower level of attainment. Mere historical grounds, therefore, do not compel us to assume that the Bellini were Barbari's teachers. The Vivarini, on the other hand, were firmly established, receiving commissions from near and from far, and, unless we have positive documentary or morphological proof to the contrary—such as we have not found at all in the case of Barbari—we are justified in assuming that a Venetian born about 1440, as Barbari was, would naturally have frequented their *atelier* and been their pupil. We have seen already how this historical view is borne out by the examination of Barbari's works.

We have still another source of evidence bearing upon Barbari's origin. Dürer writes on February 7, 1506, from Venice, that 'Giovanni Bellini is still the best painter; and *the sort of thing that pleased me so much eleven years ago* pleases me now not at all, and if I did not see it with my own eyes, I could not believe it[2].' We have here the distinct confession that on his first visit to Venice, Dürer was captivated not by the Bellini, but by others so different, that on his second visit, when Giovanni Bellini was revealed

---

[1] P. Molmenti, *Carpaccio, son Temps et son Œuvre*, p. 33.
[2] Thausing, *Dürer*, p. 79.

BARBARI AND THE VIVARINI

to him, he could scarcely believe that the others had so taken his fancy. Now the contrast between Giovanni and Gentile Bellini, on the one hand, and between Gentile and Carpaccio, on the other, is not at all of the kind to make it possible that 'the others' were either Gentile or Carpaccio. These others could have been none but the Vivarini and their followers. Two explanations suggest themselves for Dürer's frequenting the Vivarini on his first visit to Venice, both of which are interesting to us. Although by 1494 the great superiority of the Bellini over the Vivarini must have been as clear to the cultivated Venetian as the superiority of the 'impressionist' over the old landscape painters, of MM. Degas, Puvis de Chavannes, Carrière, and Besnard over Bouguereau, Laurent, and Constant, is to us, yet to the mass of the Venetians the Vivarini were still *the* painters, and outsiders, always provincial in such matters, might scarcely have heard of the Bellini, any more than the American or Scandinavian youth of ten years ago, who was leaving home for Paris, had heard of MM. Pissaro or Degas. It requires no stretch of the imagination to realize how lost the provincial, and how much more lost the foreign new-comer, must have felt in the Venice of 1500, and how much he must have been the victim of the traditional view of this city, brought from home, and of the guidance of his townsmen established in Venice. As to the competence in matters of taste on the part of Dürer's intimates during his visits to Venice, we have his own statement that Anthony Kolb, a leading member of the Fondaco dei Tedeschi, thought Jacopo di Barbari the greatest painter in the world. We are free to infer, then, that the Vivarini in 1494 were still the most popularly known painters, and that Dürer frequented them as a countryman frequents the inn with the old and well-known sign.

But granting my hypothesis about the relations between them and Jacopo di Barbari, Dürer may at the same time have had special recommendations to the Vivarini. Morelli has established satisfactorily that Barbari must have visited Nürnberg as early as 1490, and that at this time he must have had an overwhelming influence upon Dürer. As it was not until many years later that Dürer discovered his own great superiority to Barbari, on his first visit to Venice he was still Barbari's warm admirer. Now, Barbari might himself have been there during Dürer's first visit, or if not, he might have introduced him to the Vivarini. If these reciprocally supplementing hypotheses are correct, we have brought still further evidence in favour of the close connexion between Jacopo di Barbari and the Vivarini.

Having, I trust, established the relation of Barbari to the Vivarini, his relations to the young Lotto become at once easy of explanation. A great deal that they have in common is due to common origin, Barbari having probably been the fellow pupil, under Bartolommeo, of Alvise, and very much influenced by the latter. But there are, besides, certain affinities between Barbari and Lotto which are explicable only on the supposition of a personal acquaintance between them. I am aware, of course, that all the resemblances we have found between Lotto's early pictures and Barbari's frescoes at Treviso, executed towards 1500, might be explained by the fact that Lotto was living at Treviso from 1503 to 1506. But there are likenesses with others of Barbari's works, and, considering how very improbable it is that Lotto had actually seen these also, we must conclude that he was personally acquainted with the man, familiar with his gamut of mannerisms, and influenced by his character. No objection can be made to this hypothesis. That Barbari was in or near

Venice from about 1493 to 1502 we know from his works at Treviso, in the Frari, and from his map of Venice, executed in 1500. He may have had no *atelier* of his own, but worked in that of Alvise, whose personal friend he must have been. There the boy Lotto might have made his acquaintance, watched him at work, and perhaps had his direct instruction. Between the ageing man and the mere boy there may have been a sympathy arising from kindred temperaments. In both there was a streak of extravagance; in both, a great sensitiveness; in both, unevenness of attainment; in both, a restless roving disposition. When one reflects on the determining and indelible impression made upon a sensitive personality by the influences it falls under when it first wakes to the consciousness of self and of distinct interests, who shall make sure that Barbari, besides influencing Lotto the artist, may not have given a bias to Lotto's entire personality[1]?

Personal contact with Barbari would moreover explain a certain likeness existing between Lotto's early works and Dürer's pictures. Often, although a general impression of such a likeness is correct, it is yet too vague to permit of analysis, or even of precise localization. This was doubtless the case with Thausing's impression regarding Lotto's affinities with Dürer. He felt it strongly, but when he came to define it, he discovered no other ground than what we have decided to be a fanciful resemblance between an old man in Dürer's *Christ among the Doctors* and Lotto's St. Onofrio in the Borghese *Madonna*. His analysis is better

[1] A further confirmation, from the outside, of Lotto's intimacy with Barbari may possibly be found in the fact of Lotto's residence at Treviso. I am aware that this confirmation is neither necessary, nor in its nature convincing, but it is possible that Lotto got his first commission at Treviso upon Barbari's recommendation, and possibly even as Barbari's own successor.

where he notes the Child's hair in the same picture as being fine and silken, like Dürer's. But this kind of hair is found as well in Lotto's Munich picture, and in most of his early works, being a peculiarity derived from Alvise and Barbari. Now Barbari, it will be remembered, had a distinct influence on Dürer also: hence the trait the latter shares with Lotto. From the same common source, Barbari, the follower of the Vivarini, we may derive all the other likeness between Lotto and Dürer, viz. the movement of the children in the Munich and Borghese Lottos and in Dürer's *Adoration* of 1504 in the Uffizi; the small, dense foliage, painted almost as in miniature in most of Lotto's early pictures, particularly in the very earliest, Prof. Conway's *Danaë* and the Louvre *St. Jerome*; and certain peculiarities of movement and drapery of a Vivarinesque nature found in both [1]. What adds all the more to the impression of likeness between Dürer and Lotto is that their common source, Barbari, acquired a slightly Northern tinge in his first visit to Nürnberg which leaves its trace, through him, in Lotto, as in the miniature painting of the trees.

I trust my dwelling so long on Barbari has been justified, not only by the need of explaining how it is that he and Lotto come to have so much in common, but by the conclusion we have been enabled to reach that Lotto, the pupil of Alvise, was in all probability also strongly influenced and even determined by his master's friend and companion, Jacopo di Barbari. We have by this means not only greatly strengthened our hypothesis that Lotto was Alvise's pupil, but we have also distinguished another element in his composition, an element the due consideration of which we

[1] How much of a Vivarinesque residuum Dürer carried along with him even into his maturity may be seen by any one who carefully examines his *Rosenkranz Madonna*, his *Trinity*, or the copy of the *Hellersche Altar*.

shall find most helpful when we come to define and reconstruct Lotto's quality and personality. We must now turn to Bonsignori, and account for the fact that in certain points Lotto reminds us of him also.

III.—FRANCESCO BONSIGNORI

While examining Barbari's drawings, we noted the great likeness between them and the drawings of Bonsignori, and noted, in turn, how the likeness between the drawings of the latter and those of Alvise had led Morelli to infer that Bonsignori was the follower of Alvise. Establishing this hypothesis, therefore, would lead to the inference that the points of resemblance between Lotto and Bonsignori were derived from a common source, Alvise, and would thus confirm still further the evidence already assembled to prove that Lotto was the pupil of Alvise. Let us therefore devote our attention, for a while, to the early works of Bonsignori.

Although a Veronese by birth, Bonsignori is not a member of the school of Verona. His earliest painting noted by Messrs. Crowe and Cavalcaselle is in San Paolo at Verona. It represents the Madonna enthroned on a low platform of rock, with a giant Magdalen to R. and St. Antony Abbot to L. In the middle distance are quiet, mysterious pools, and beyond them low, jagged rocks, with a suggestion of an unfathomable sky stretching above them. *Naïf* and awkward as this picture is in many respects, it is yet overwhelmingly impressive, the figures towering majestically over the sky-line, and thus producing one of the most cosmic effects in art. Turning to morphological considerations, we note that the Madonna's oval and features are distinctly Alvisesque[1], while the build and movement of the Child, with his R. arm stretched out, recall the Child in Bartolommeo Vivarini's Frari triptych of 1487. The Magdalen's rather vehement look, loose flowing hair[2], and arm akimbo with the back of the hand against the hip, all remind us of Alvise and Barbari. Her enormous length from the waist down is also Alvisesque. The St. Antony Abbot at once suggests Alvise's in the Venice Academy (No. 621), a figure which Bonsignori may actually have had in mind while painting this picture. His thumb has the larger second phalanx of Alvise and Barbari, and his feet are at right angles, as in the Vivarini. The colouring is quiet, with a tendency to very pale greenish greys and unobtrusive bituminous tints such as we have in Alvise's earlier pictures. The landscape has the low sky-line found later in Alvise, and probably is precisely of the kind that Alvise had in his middle years.

In Bonsignori's first dated work, *The Madonna with the Sleeping Child*, of 1483 (Verona Gallery, No. 148), the Vivarinesque character is no less outspoken. Here, to note a feature not already dwelt upon: the Madonna's mantle forms almost a rectangle about her head, as in Bartolommeo and Alvise[3]—a feature which never occurs in the Bellini. In the altar-piece of 1484, also in the Verona Gallery (No. 271), the Vivarinesque character is so marked, and, it must be added, so exaggerated, that, barring the colour, it tempts one to place it beside the performances of Andrea da Murano[4]. The complicated, facet-like folds over

---

[1] Cf. Alvise's St. Sebastian and St. Lawrence in the Venice Academy (No. 621).
[2] Cf. the Magdalen in Alvise's Berlin altar-piece.
[3] A startling instance is the National Gallery *Madonna*.
[4] Cf. in particular Andrea's *Crucifixion* at Vienna (No. 9).

BONSIGNORI [Verona, San Paolo

THE MADONNA AND CHILD, WITH SAINTS

the St. Christopher are an exaggeration of Alvise's in the St. Paul in the Montefiorentino polyptych, and in the skirt of the Madonna of 1480, in the Venice Academy, and is very close to the drapery of the St. Lawrence in the same collection (No. 621). St. Christopher's feet are posed as in Alvise; the drapery over St. Jerome's chest is in close parallel folds; the almost naked St. Onofrio is thick-set, and in build and action vividly recalls the St. Sebastian in Alvise's Berlin altar-piece. Finally, the curtain behind the throne, across the entire breadth of the picture, is a striking feature, paralleled only in Alvise's Venice Academy picture of 1480.

In Bonsignori's *Madonna* of 1488, in San Bernardino at Verona, the Alvisesque character is even more predominant. The Madonna is enthroned between two windows as in Alvise's Academy and San Giovanni in Bragora pictures. The two music-making *putti* on the arms of the throne are of the build of Alvise's in his Berlin altar-piece, and draped almost identically[1]. Both the Jerome and the George stand with their feet at right angles to each other, as in Alvise, and George has his arm akimbo with the back of the hand against the hip, as in Alvise, Barbari, and Lazzaro Sebastiani. Furthermore, in all of Bonsignori's pictures that we have examined thus far, the fingers are thick and clumsy, as in Alvise.

Soon after 1488, Bonsignori settled at Mantua, and there gradually modified his style under the influence of Mantegna, but with that part of his career we are not concerned except in so far as we must establish his authorship of a portrait recently in the Sciarra

[1] In each the *putto* to the R. is tied around the diaphragm twice with a string, and the *putto* to the L. is tied under the navel with a narrow sash hanging in a long pendent knot.

collection [1], attributed to Mantegna, which I have had occasion to mention because of the striking likeness between the ear it shows and Lotto's typical ear. This bust of an oldish, smooth-faced warrior, in flat-topped cap and armour, bears the inscription 'AN. MANTINIA PINX. ANNO M. CCCCLV.' That this inscription is a mere forgery is amply proved by the slovenly lettering which Mantegna, the passionate classicist who played so prominent a part in the restoration and formation of the printed characters that we now use, would never have allowed himself, and least of all in 1455, when he was engaged on those eager restorations of Roman antiquity with which he filled his frescoes in the Eremitani. But, if this argument be not sufficiently convincing, the date alone is quite enough to prove the inscription a forgery. In 1455 Mantegna had just painted the *St. Luke polyptych*, now in the Brera, so timid and rigid as compared with this Sciarra bust. In 1455 he had not yet painted the Scarampo of Berlin, which in every probability was executed in 1459[2], and is nevertheless so much severer, so much more searching, so much more sculptural in conception and characterization. In style this Sciarra warrior is more advanced, in conception more pictorial, than even the portraits in the Camera degli Sposi at Mantua, which are dated 1474. The date on the Sciarra portrait being thus untenable, the entire inscription goes with it, and we are left free to assign the picture to the artist whose works it most closely resembles. For Mantegna the outlines are too vague, the drawing too feeble, the conception too pictorial. Mantegna's ear is rounder, with a wider cavity, and

---

[1] Now, I understand, in the collection of Mr. Johnson of Philadelphia.
[2] The style of the workmanship leaves no ground for doubting that Scarampo sat for this portrait while on a visit to Padua in the summer of 1459. (For this visit, see G. Voigt, *Enea Silvio*, iii. p. 46.)

BONSIGNORI AND THE VIVARINI 43

a lobe that curls back from the cheek. But the ear in the Sciarra busts corresponds perfectly with Bonsignori's[1]. The pose also is distinctly his, as in the National Gallery portrait, while the mouth and the look as well resemble the same picture. The accentuation of the double chin with the deep furrow under the lower lip is most characteristic of Bonsignori, and the prominent nostrils with the inflation outlined in shadow that we have here, we also find in his National Gallery portrait. The armour is painted in broad surfaces, as St. George's in Bonsignori's *Madonna* in San Bernardino at Verona. In short, one need only place this Sciarra warrior beside the National Gallery portrait head, or beside the bust of a Gonzaga at Bergamo (Lochis, No. 154), to feel convinced that they are all by the same author.

As I have said before, it is not my intention to pursue Bonsignori's career to the end. My purpose has been to prove his connexion with Alvise, and to establish his claim to certain works not hitherto ascribed to him on which I have based one or two statements. I trust that the reader who follows me patiently will find no difficulty in agreeing to the attribution to him of the Sciarra portrait. It remains for me to justify my ascribing to him the polyptych in San Giovanni e Paolo at Venice—an altar-piece containing a *Pietà* of which Lotto's at Recanati strikingly reminded us. Connoisseurship since Sansovino has boxed the compass of Quattrocento Venetian painting with this altar-piece, the majority agreeing, however, in connecting it, directly or indirectly, with the Vivarini. Boschini ascribed it to Bartolommeo; Messrs. Crowe and Cavalcaselle opined that it was painted by Carpaccio and Lazzaro Sebastiani in Barto-

---

[1] Cf. portrait signed and dated 1487, in National Gallery (No. 736).

lommeo's *atelier*; Dr. Bode in the sixth edition of the *Cicerone* claims the whole for Alvise; in Baedeker it is put down as a joint work of Alvise and Bartolommeo. The general Vivarinesque character of the altar-piece is, in fact, beyond question, so that its author, whoever he was, must have been, if not either one of the Vivarini themselves, at any rate of their school. If we can establish that the author is no other than Bonsignori, it will clinch the argument we have already made in favour of his connexion with Bartolommeo and Alvise Vivarini.

This polyptych consists of nine parts. The principal panels contain St. Vincent in the middle, with St. Sebastian to R. and St. Christopher to L. Above, on shorter panels, is the Annunciation, with a *Pietà* between. Below are three predelle with episodes from the life of St. Vincent. We note throughout the very sharp, strong outlines (as, for instance, in Botticelli's *Venus and Mars* in the National Gallery) with which we are familiar in Bonsignori's National Gallery portrait. We note also the shade of pale purple, so very rare in the Old Masters, except in Bonsignori, who seems to have taken special pleasure in it[1]. The hair of all the figures in the *Pietà*, and even more markedly the hair of the Gabriel, is curled like shavings, as we find it frequently in Bonsignori[2]. The folds of the drapery have throughout the complicated catches of Bonsignori; the fingers are thick and clumsy, and the back of Christopher's hand is furrowed as St. Anthony's in the San Paolo *Madonna* at Verona. The hands of the St. Vincent, with fingers like sharp pointed nails, are matched by the Mag-

---

[1] Cf. particularly Brera, No. 170, *SS. Bernardino and Louis holding the Initials of Christ*.
[2] Cf. especially the *Christ on the Way to Golgotha* in the Accademia Virgiliana at Mantua.

DETAILS OF A POLYPTYCH

dalen's R. hand in the same picture. The thumbs are beautifully drawn, and have, as always in Bonsignori, the larger second phalanx. The Child's head is almost the same as the Child's on the St. Christopher in the Verona *Madonna* of 1484, and in arm, leg, and general movement the two are identical. St. Sebastian's head, with aquiline nose, mobile, prominent nostrils, and self-possessed, proud look, is precisely in the character of all of Bonsignori's portraits, but especially of the *Gonzaga* at Bergamo. Sebastian's L. foot, with the toes awkwardly jointed, is identical with Christopher's in the Verona altar-piece of 1484. The landscapes have the subduing cosmic effect produced by gigantic figures towering over the sky-line, such as we found in Bonsignori's first work, the *Madonna* in San Paolo at Verona. Finally, the St. Vincent[1], although unmistakably by the same author, seems to betray a maturer hand, the colouring being more harmonized and soft, the draperies simpler and more functional—in fact, matching in nearly every point Bonsignori's *Vision of St. Osanna* in the Accademia Virgiliana at Mantua[2].

The final test of authorship comes only, however, when we can do more than merely say that a picture is by such and such a painter,—when we can place it chronologically among the other works of the artist to whom we ascribe it. I think we shall find no difficulty in ascertaining to what part of Bonsignori's career this polyptych belongs. Although it is on the whole more

---

[1] Cf. his hands with the Magdalen's R. in the San Paolo picture at Verona.

[2] The Christ in the *Pietà* and the folds of the curtain behind the Madonna are strikingly Montagnesque, and betray the close connexion that there was between this master and Bonsignori.

The predelle clearly are by no pure Venetian, but by one who betrays Veronese influence, such as we should expect to find in Bonsignori.

strikingly Vivarinesque than any other of Bonsignori's pictures up to 1485, this altar-piece is distinctly more mature. Here the artist is freer from crudities, less awkward, more sure of his line, far more capable of conveying his idea to a successful issue. The *Pietà* has rarely been treated with greater pathos and solemnity. St. Sebastian's head, taken by itself, is, as we have seen, a portrait in the character of the one in the National Gallery, or of the *Gonzaga* at Bergamo. The National Gallery head, it will be remembered, is of a Venetian Senator, and was painted in 1487, as we learn from the inscription. Now I can see no reason for assuming that this portrait was not executed on the spot, which would mean, of course, that Bonsignori was at Venice in 1487. On this occasion he might have come in close contact once more with the Vivarini, and perhaps worked in the *atelier* of one of them. Such an hypothesis would account for the San Bernardino *Madonna* of 1488 at Verona being, as we found, even more Vivarinesque than the earlier works, and would of course all the more account for the great *rapprochement* of Bonsignori to the Vivarini in the San Giovanni e Paolo polyptych. Soon after 1488, it can be assumed, Bonsignori settled down in the employ of the Gonzagas at Mantua. But between 1484, the date of an altar-piece in the Gallery at Verona, and 1488, the date of the *Madonna* in San Bernardino in the same town, Bonsignori's career is a blank, except for the head of a Venetian Senator that I have mentioned. I infer, therefore, that Bonsignori spent part, at least, of this interval in Venice, and that the San Giovanni e Paolo polyptych was executed at this time—all of it except the St. Vincent. This figure, evidently of later date, he may have sent down from Mantua, having in all probability been called away from Venice before he could finish it. Interesting as

BONSIGNORI

Alinari photo.] [Carrara Gallery, Bergamo

PORTRAIT OF A GONZAGA

it is to settle—I trust once for all—the authorship of an important and well-known work; interesting as it is also to help reconstruct the career of an artist like Bonsignori, in every way so fascinating, I should not have ventured upon this large parenthesis concerning him and his work, if it were not necessary to explain why Lotto should have reminded us of him. Now as any hypothesis of a personal connexion between Lotto and Bonsignori, at any rate in Lotto's most impressionable years, is untenable on account of Bonsignori's residence in Mantua from 1488 on, whatever they have in common must be due to a common source; and as we have established that in the case of Bonsignori this source was the Vivarini, it follows that Lotto must have drawn from the same spring, and we thus have further proof of Lotto's derivation not from the Bellini, but from the Vivarini.

IV.—BARTOLOMMEO MONTAGNA

We found in examining Lotto's early works more than one point which recalled Montagna, and it is now time to inquire into the cause of this resemblance. In 1480 Bartolommeo Montagna was already established at Vicenza, and, although he may have visited Venice not infrequently after this date, it is not possible to assume that these visits could have been of long duration. Especially in those years from 1496 to 1502, when Lotto was at the age to be most subject to the influence of artists other than his own immediate master, we know that Montagna was very busy at Vicenza. Here also, then, we are probably dealing not with a question of direct contact, but with one of common origin. But, as we have noted, Messrs. Crowe and Cavalcaselle make Montagna the offspring of the local school of Vicenza, which, in turn, they derive from—Signorelli! Morelli saw in Montagna the follower and pupil of Carpaccio. Let us now turn to his earliest works and see what in fact they reveal of their painter's origin.

Montagna's earliest important work [1] is the grand altar-piece originally in San Bartolommeo at Vicenza, and now in the gallery of that town. It shows us the Madonna enthroned on a high pedestal, under a portico open to the sky on every side. On a step against the pedestal three *putti* are making music. To the R. stand SS. Sebastian and Fabian, to the L. SS. John the Baptist and Bartholomew. Solemn, hieratic, mysterious, few pictures can rival it for quiet grandeur, and fewer still can compare with it for depth of twilight sky. It is more than usually difficult to tear oneself loose from its spell and turn to a scientific analysis. But its very quality already contains a strong reminder of Bonsignori's earliest works. Here also the grandeur of the effect is largely produced by making the Madonna's throne tower gigantically over the low sky-line. Here, too, we have in the landscape a quiet, mysterious pool. Coming now to more mechanical considerations, the open portico suggests another pupil of Alvise Vivarini, Cima da Conegliano, in whose paintings this feature is frequently to be found. The Madonna's oval is Alvisesque, and her drapery, in long-drawn, angular folds, is most characteristic of Alvise [2]. St. John's R. hand, with the long pointed forefinger, is identical with the one in Alvise's *St. John* in the Venice Academy (No. 621). The colouring is

[1] I am aware that Messrs. Crowe and Cavalcaselle are of a different opinion regarding the date as well as the importance of this work.

[2] Note in particular the knees wide apart, and the long, close, almost parallel folds connected at one end by a straight line, as in Alvise's Venice Academy and Berlin altar-pieces, or in Jacopo da Valenza, Alvise's slavish imitator.

pale, and the lights and shadows strongly contrasted, as in Alvise. The predella containing episodes from the life of St. Bartholomew has great affinities with Bonsignori's predelle in his San Giovanni e Paolo polyptych. In fine, this earliest important work by Montagna betrays at every point its author's affinities with Alvise, and the connexion with his school— although it reveals at the same time a genius superior to that master's. As to Carpaccio, I confess to finding absolutely no trace of his influence in this altar-piece, the nearest approach to it, the draperies of St. John, being, on close analysis, Alvisesque [1], and the colouring, far from being as in Carpaccio, even at his earliest, rich, deep, and warm, is pale and cool [2]. But Morelli based his theory of Montagna's derivation from Carpaccio chiefly on a picture at Bergamo (Lochis, No. 128), and on the Montagna drawings. As to the *Madonna with SS. Paul and Sebastian* at Bergamo, I fail to see its affinities with Carpaccio. The oval of the Madonna does not in the least remind me of Carpaccio's National Gallery or Berlin Madonnas, Carpaccio's earliest works, but decidedly of Alvise. The draperies, and the landscape even more, suggest Bonsignori's San Paolo picture at Verona [3]. With regard to the drawings, it is true that several of them resemble Carpaccio's in superficial technique, but I must protest against the sufficiency of such proof. In the drawings in the

[1] I say 'close analysis,' for such as are not acquainted with Alvise's polyptych at Montefiorentino (dated 1475), in which the drapery of the Baptist falls down in long-drawn folds directly from the shoulder, as in Montagna's *St. John* in this altar-piece. But cf. also Alvise's *Baptist*, a later work, in the Venice Academy (No. 618).

[2] As in Alvise's earliest known work, the polyptych at Montefiorentino, and in the same master's *Madonna* in the Venice Academy.

[3] I am not perfectly persuaded of the reliability of the date—1487—on the back of this Bergamo picture. It must be approximately correct, however, and in that case the St. Bartholomew altar-piece can be safely assigned to 1485.

Uffizi alone Carpaccio uses three distinctly different techniques: the pen alone, with short, straight lines; india ink, highly finished; and tinted paper with india ink and high finish of white. It is only this last technique that he has in common with Montagna, and it is by no means his most frequent. On the other hand, Montagna's superb charcoal head in the Habich collection at Cassel has, in common with the drawings of Barbari and Bonsignori, not only the superficial technique but the most striking morphological traits [1].

To return again to Montagna's early works, and in the first place to Miss Hertz's *Madonna*, we note an affinity in draperies and landscape with Bonsignori, in colouring with Alvise. After this, Montagna's colouring undergoes a change, becoming rich, deep, and warm— at times far too warm; but his forms for some time remain Alvisesque, and indeed never cease to betray his relation to that master. In the *Nativity* in the Vicenza Gallery, the Madonna's oval is Alvisesque; the Magdalen holds her ointment-box almost as she holds it in Alvise's Berlin altar-piece; the *St. Clare*, with her large eyes, reminds us distinctly of Alvise's in the Venice Academy (No. 593); while the landscape, the draperies, and the Magdalen's purplish-pink mantle suggest Bonsignori. In the *Madonna with SS. John and Onofrio*, also in the Vicenza Gallery, we encounter a recrudescence of Alvisesque traits [2]. The Madonna's

---

[1] Cf. proportions of face, prominent nostrils, with strong marking of inflation, and channel of upper lip.

[2] Contemporary with this work must be the portrait bust of a smooth-shaved man recently exposed at the Museo Correr, where it is tentatively ascribed to Carpaccio—if as I suspect, it really is by Montagna. The colouring, the technique, the few folds, the high lights on the hair and on the small trees are his. But the conception and the features are seen and executed in a way so singularly Alvisesque that one could almost take up with the foolish idea that it was drawn by Alvise and coloured by Montagna. At all events, this striking portrait (photo. Naya, No. 1751) is a connecting-link between the two artists.

oval, her long nose, her hood, the parallel close folds over her R. arm, the infrequent, angular folds of the drapery between her knees, the thumbs, the pointed index of St. John's R. hand, the build of St. Onofrio, and his feet posed at right angles are all decidedly Alvisesque. The Alvisesque characteristics by no means disappear when Montagna came, as seems apparent in his maturer works, under the influence of Gentile Bellini and of the sculptor Bellano. In the Brera altar-piece of 1499, for instance, the elaborate architectural setting, the St. Clare, and the feet at right angles, are all distinctly Alvisesque. In the Monte Berico *Pietà*, dated 1500, the Madonna's R. hand has the angular joints and pointed fingers that we find in the Bishop in Alvise's Frari altar-piece, while the curled hair of John and the flowing loose hair of the Magdalen remind us of Bonsignori. Even in such a comparatively late work as the *Magdalen with Saints* in Santa Corona at Vicenza, the St. Jerome is markedly like Cima's, and the St. Augustine is almost a transcript of the Bishop in Alvise's Frari altar-piece. Indeed, in general, throughout Montagna's works we note such Alvisesque or Vivarinesque features as these,—his Madonnas, as a rule, wear a pointed hood, and preferably (in the proportion of four to one) hold the Child, when He is represented standing, on the L. knee; when possible, the figures stand with their feet at right angles; the thumbs have the larger second phalanx, and the fingers are often thick and clumsy; the draperies have complicated catches, or are long-drawn and angular, and have, in early works, a tendency to parallel lines. Considering all this evidence drawn from a detailed study of his pictures, we need not a moment hesitate to declare Montagna the companion, if not the pupil of Alvise Vivarini; and seeing the number of resemblances we have found between Montagna and Bonsignori, we are tempted to conclude that, even before falling under the influence of Alvise, both had been fellow pupils under some provincial master. Just who I cannot tell; but I suspect it may have been Domenico Morone of Verona. Certainty on this point is at present unattainable; for we know Morone too little to be able to identify as his the slight un-Alvisesque residuum visible in Bonsignori's and Montagna's earliest existing works [1]. But, be this as it may, my object has been gained if I have established Montagna's derivation from the Vivarini, for this explains why Lotto, whom we already have many reasons to consider the pupil of the same master, should have points in common with an elder fellow pupil, and at the same time the existence of these points in common between Lotto and another pupil of the Vivarini confirms our hypothesis of Lotto's origin [2].

[1] I wish in final confirmation of my theory to call attention to the *Madonna* in the Berlin Gallery (No. 40), which Morelli correctly identified as an early Basaiti. The last Berlin catalogue hesitates to give full assent to this attribution, and is satisfied with labelling the picture 'School of Alvise Vivarini'—which for my purpose is even better. Now it is the non-Bellinesque character of such a picture which, at a time when 'Bellinesque' and 'Venetian' were still synonymous terms, determined its former attribution to the Veronese painter Carotto. In reality, it has considerable superficial resemblance to the works of Montagna and his school—in particular to such a *Madonna* by Fogolino as is owned by Mr. Robert Benson of London. The angels have the curls of Bonsignori and Montagna, and the landscape also suggests them. The point, however, in Basaiti's Berlin picture to which I wish to call particular attention is the Madonna's L. hand, in which the two middle fingers are closely pressed together, separated on one side from the index and on the other from the little finger. *Precisely* this peculiarity—derived, doubtless, from a common source—is found in the following of Montagna's most accessible works: in Miss Hertz's *Madonna*; the *Madonna* at Bergamo; the Madonna's hand in the *Presentation in the Temple* of the Vicenza Gallery; the Madonna's hand in the Brera altar-piece; the Madonna's hand in the Certosa altar-piece; the hands of the Madonna and of the alms-giving saint in the Berlin altar-piece (No. 44); and the hand of the Madonna in the Venice Academy (No. 80).

[2] Whether the Alvisesque traits in Buonconsiglio were derived in-

BART. MONTAGNA

[Anderson photo.] [Brera Gallery, Milan.

THE MADONNA AND CHILD ENTHRONED

V.—CIMA DA CONEGLIANO

We have now disposed of all those likenesses which have been most difficult to account for [1] between Lotto's early works and the works of other painters, and we have found every reason to believe that these resemblances are due to the fact that all the artists concerned are branches of the same tree—pupils of the Vivarini, and particularly of Alvise. But the artists we have discussed thus far have neither by the closeness of their likeness to Lotto, nor by the anterior probability arising from their constant residence in Venice, tempted us to believe that any one of them was, rather than Alvise himself, Lotto's first teacher. Jacopo di Barbari's great influence on Lotto we have explained as coming necessarily when Lotto was already more than half formed. We now have to discuss Lotto's connexion with an artist of whom, after Alvise and Barbari, he has thus far most frequently reminded us, with an artist in every way so superior to the meagre and mangled Alvise who has come down to us, that we are tempted to ask why he—Cima da Conegliano—rather than Alvise, was not the master who first taught Lotto.

In the first place, we must bear in mind that it is not the artist who now seems to us the greatest, who in his lifetime was considered the best teacher. Cosimo Rosselli, for instance, is a painter for whom we nowadays have a great contempt, yet it was out of his school, and not Botticelli's, nor even Ghirlandajo's, that Pier di Cosimo, Fra Bartolommeo, Mariotto, and Andrea del Sarto—in short, the bulk of Florentine

directly through his master Montagna, or straight from Alvise, is not to be determined. But they abound.

[1] Antonio and Bartolommeo Vivarini will be discussed later.

painting in the first quarter of the sixteenth century—sprang. Cima, moreover, did not settle in Venice before 1490[1], and it does not seem at all probable that a Venetian boy would have been sent to school to a new-comer from the provinces, when there was no lack of masters, such as the Vivarini and the Bellini, at home. We have noted, furthermore, that Lotto's early works did not remind us at all so often of Cima as of Alvise, and scarcely even so often as of Barbari, and we shall see later that reminiscences of Alvise and habits acquired under him may be traced even in Lotto's latest pictures, while reminders of Cima seldom occur after Lotto has attained maturity. We are therefore led to suspect that between Cima and Lotto some such relation existed as between the latter and Jacopo di Barbari. This relation, as we have seen, was of the kind that might exist between a grown-up brother and a much younger one, or at least between a visiting uncle and his boy nephew. Let us now see whether the common points between Lotto and Cima may not also be accounted for in the first place by common origin, and secondly by personal acquaintance; in other words, whether Cima also was not a pupil of Alvise Vivarini whom Lotto might have known through the relation continuing between the 'graduated' pupil, Cima, and his own master, Alvise.

Although born in 1460, Cima's earliest dated work is from 1489. It is the *Madonna with SS. Jerome and James*, which he executed for San Bartolommeo at Vincenza, and which now hangs in the gallery of that town (Sala IV, No. 18). The Madonna is enthroned under the frame of a coffered arch serving as a grape trellis, with St. Jerome to R. and St. James to

---

[1] Don V. Botteon e Dr. A. Aliprandi, *Ricerche intorno alla Vita e alle Opere di Giambattista Cima*. Conegliano, 1893, p. 32.

L.—a picture of severe, subdued feeling, great beauty of colour, and simplicity of line. But we note at once that sharp contrast of light and shade familiar in Alvise, the Alvisesque oval and pointed hood of the Madonna, the hands (particularly the R. hand of St. James) with thick fingers separating from the joints of the palm, the nose with marked inflation of nostrils, and the feet of St. James at right angles—peculiarities which we have already met with frequently in Alvise and his school. Nearly all of these Alvisesque characteristics reappear in another obviously early work, the *Pietà* in the Venice Academy (No. 604), wherein we note others as well, such as the thumb with the distinctly larger second phalanx, the angular joints of the fingers (as in Alvise, Bonsignori, and Montagna), and the sharp elbows of the Christ, almost exactly as in Alvise's *St. Sebastian* in the Venice Academy (No. 621)[1].

In the great altar-piece of about the same date in Santa Maria dell' Orto at Venice, wherein we see the Baptist standing under the ruin of a noble portico, with SS. Paul and Jerome to R. and Peter and Augustine to L., we note that the figures stand either with their feet almost parallel or at right angles to each other, as in Alvise, that the big toes are shorter than the others, that the perspective of the eyes is somewhat exaggerated, and—most Alvisesque of all—that the legs of the St. John are thin and badly modelled, curving in from hip to knee, with the knee-pan awkwardly placed, and curving out again from knee to foot[2].

[1] All the figures in this *Pietà*, except Christ's, have their mouths open, as in Barbari, but here they are wailing. The magnificent ' Deposition ' at Modena is no less Alvisesque: most strikingly so are the fluted folds of the Francis.
[2] Cf. Alvise's *St. John* and *St. Sebastian* in the Venice Academy (No. 612).

In Cima's early *Madonna*[1] at Bologna, the oval and hood are Alvisesque, the lights and shadows and colouring of the flesh are as in porcelain, the fingers are bent at sharp angles, the Child has a short, stubby nose, as in Alvise's *putti* in the Redentore *Madonna*, and curls, as in Bonsignori. Cima's somewhat less severe but still very early *Madonna with Donor* at Berlin (No. 7) has a Child almost identical with the last, except that His movement is precisely as in Miss Hertz's Montagna, or in that master's *Madonna with SS. John and Onofrio* in the Vicenza Gallery. The Child's ear in this Berlin picture is almost identical with the ear of the *putto* on the R. in Alvise's Redentore *Madonna*, and, as almost always in Cima, has that slight dent in the cheek which we find in Alvise without exception, and with great frequency in Bonsignori and Montagna. The Madonna's prominent nostrils (not to mention her oval), her stiff neck, the hand of the Donor[2], and his mouth[3], are all distinctly Alvisesque. Even the landscape here is not yet Cima's stereotyped one, but a variation of the river valley with hills on the horizon that we have in Alvise's San Giovanni in Bragora *Madonna*.

It would be tedious to follow Cima's paintings to the end, pointing out the Alvisesque traits in each separate one. I must content myself with only a few more examples, and then stop, hoping that my reader will by that time be sufficiently convinced of the connexion between Cima and Alvise. In the Munich *Madonna* (No. 1033), then, another early work, the Magdalen's R. hand is almost exactly that of the Magdalen in Alvise's Berlin altar-piece; in the *Madonna with*

---

[1] Mouths open without cause, as in Barbari.
[2] Cf. St. Sebastian's in Alvise's Berlin altar-piece.
[3] Cf. Alvise's portrait of 1497 in the Bonomi-Cereda collection at Milan.

SS. Paul and John the Baptist in the Venice Academy (No. 603), the Baptist is pointing, as we have found him in Alvise and Montagna, his mouth is open and his hair wild, as in Barbari; in the *Tobias and Angel*, also in the Venice Academy (No. 592), the almost impossible position of the St. James, with his R. foot in front of and at right angles to his L., we have found often in Alvise and Montagna[1]; in the Parma *Madonna with Six Saints* (gallery, No. 360), the Virgin's hood, the play of the hands, and the position of the feet are all Alvisesque; in the *Head of a Female Saint* in the Poldi Museum at Milan, the snaky hair, the pupil distinct from the iris, the prominent nostrils[2], and open mouth are all reminiscent of Barbari or Alvise; finally, in Cima's last picture, the *St. Peter enthroned*[3], of the Brera (No. 300), Peter's pose, with the white drapery over the knees, is singularly like the pose and drapery of the St. Ambrose in Alvise's Frari altar-piece.

Now to sum up: Cima's oval is usually Alvisesque; his nostrils are apt to be prominent, with the inflation clearly outlined; his mouths have a tendency to be open; his ears are narrow, with a dent in the line where they join the cheek; his hands tend to spread, and have clumsy fingers which separate off directly from the joints of the palm; his feet are awkwardly placed, at right angles or parallel; his limbs are thin and ascetic; the proportions of his figures, particularly in his earlier works, are too long, with the knees very low down, as in Alvise; his draperies tend to fall in long parallel or angular folds; his colouring is cool

---

[1] Cf. the Baptist in Alvise's Frari altar-piece, and the St. Sebastian in Montagna's *Madonna* in the Venice Academy (No. 80).
[2] Cf. with nose and nostrils here, Barbari's portrait at Bergamo (Lochis, No. 148), and his charcoal head in the Habich Collection at Cassel.
[3] Executed in 1516; cf. Don V. Botteon, op. cit., p. 101.

and porcelain-like [1]; his lights and shadows are strongly contrasted. All these characteristics are, I claim, distinctly Alvisesque and decidedly not Bellinesque. Nor am I by any means the first to notice this great divergence between Cima and Giovanni Bellini. I need only refer to the recent commentators on Vasari, to Selvatico, and to Messrs. Crowe and Cavalcaselle, who all have more or less strongly protested against the presumptive derivation of Cima from Giambellino. Messrs. Crowe and Cavalcaselle go so far as to say that 'his sharp contrasts of light and shadow distinguish him from the Venetians, and would lead us to suppose that he had been influenced by the Lombards, if we had not good reason for ascribing this effect to Antonello [2].' But here, as often, Signor Cavalcaselle's acute observation is spoiled by his less valuable generalization. He had not correctly reconstructed Antonello's personality, not sufficiently distinguished him from Alvise, not quite emancipated himself from the tradition which made Antonello the *deus ex machina* in the evolution of Venetian painting, to observe that in no *genuine* Antonello (except in such Alvisesque works as the Dresden *St. Sebastian* or the Berlin Portrait of 1478) do we find the sharp contrasts of light and shade combined with the hard porcelain tone of Cima, while we have this combination in an exaggerated form in Alvise's Venice Academy *Madonna* of 1480.

In 1480 Cima was already twenty years old, and was probably finishing his education under Alvise, for it is of the Alvise of this date, severely ascetic in feeling, transparent in colouring, sharply contrasted

[1] Cf. Alvise's *Madonna and Saints* of 1480 in the Venice Academy, or *St. Antonio* in the Correr Museum. Note, by the way, that Cima's thrones have elaborate sculptured tops, and are in general of the style in Alvise's pictures.
[2] *Painting in North Italy*, chapter on Cima.

THE VIRGIN AND CHILD, WITH SAINTS

Anderson photo]   *[Parma Gallery*

in *chiaroscuro*, that he is always reminding us, Cima having clearly had one of those temperaments which are for ever determined by the first powerful influence exerted upon them. That he at the same time saw Giovanni Bellini's works and was impressed by them, I would not for a moment deny, but if they had an influence upon him, this influence touched the artist rather than the painter—if I may be allowed to distinguish between the two. When Cima finally settled in Venice, about 1490, his relations with Alvise seem to have remained intimate. We have, it is true, not a word to this precise effect in any contemporary record, but it seems stated with unmistakable clearness in the archives of San Giovanni in Bragora at Venice [1], and in the pictures still remaining in that church. San Giovanni in Bragora, so far as I know, not only never employed the Bellini, but seems to have been a special patron of the Vivarini. To this day it contains a triptych by Bartolommeo, and not less than three separate works by Alvise. Of these, the bust of the Saviour was executed in 1493, the *Madonna* some years earlier, the *Resurrection* in 1498. Alvise seems therefore not to have lost favour with this church in the last decade of the fifteenth century, and if in 1492 the picture for the high altar was not commissioned to him, the probable reason is that he was too busy or too ill to undertake such a task. This *Baptism* was given, as we know, to Cima, and I see no explanation for it, Cima being still a comparative stranger in Venice and there being no dearth of Venetian painters, unless it be on the supposition that he was highly recommended and guaranteed by Alvise, as his pupil and friend. More convincing proof of the cordial relations between Cima and Alvise, and of Alvise's

---

[1] Don V. Botteon, op. cit., p. 210 et seq.

authority at San Giovanni in Bragora, may be gathered from the following:—On January 19, 1496, Alvise was commissioned to paint the *Resurrection*, to be placed before the Ciborium, now at the entrance to the choir. Although the picture is comparatively small, it was not ready before April 4, 1498, from which we may infer how little able to execute commissions Alvise was at this time. Now, there can be no doubt that the symmetry-loving Renaissance Venetians, when they had two such precious possessions in their church as the Body of Christ and a fragment of the True Cross, would have desired to enhance the value of both by making them *pendants* to each other, and that the better to produce this effect, they would have got the same artist, if possible, to paint the pictures for both. For the Ciborium, Alvise, as we have seen, painted the *Resurrection*, for which, be it noted, he was paid forty ducats. But on February 17, 1501, Cima was commissioned to paint the *SS. Helen and Constantine*, for which he was to be paid only twenty-eight ducats. The difference of price indicates how much more highly Alvise's work was still valued than Cima's. This, and the fact that Cima made his picture, now to the R. of the entrance to the choir, in size and predelle a *pendant* to Alvise's, allow of the inference that Alvise was intended to execute both panels, but that finally, tired of waiting, the church gave it, perhaps at Alvise's own recommendation, to Cima.

I am aware, of course, that hypotheses of the kind I have now been making have a different value according as one frames them oneself or merely has them presented to one. An infinite number of minute impressions, few of which are capable of blunt statement, a living oneself sympathetically into the situation, an unavowed but irresistible anthropomorphization of certain perhaps purely artistic qualities in a given artist, all colour the mind, determine the attitude, and strengthen the conviction of the one, while the other has only the halting statement of this conviction, which he cannot well help regarding for its value as a mere syllogism. But unfortunately the perfect syllogism cannot be our standard in art reconstruction, for it would never take us far. Our reasoning to the mere logician, or to opponents, may seem circular, and we must in all candour acknowledge that to make rapid progress we are often obliged to harvest our crops before they are ripe.

In this instance, however, I have no fear that the competent examiner of my hypothesis will find it unwarranted. We can safely assume not only that Cima was the pupil of Alvise, but that the relation between them remained cordial to the last. We thus explain not only how Cima and Lotto happen to have so many points in common, but also those more peculiarly Cimaesque traits that we have found in Lotto; the one because of the common origin of the two painters; the other because of those friendly relations between Cima and Alvise which permit us to infer that Cima, on his visits to Alvise's *atelier*, frequently saw Lotto, and that Lotto in turn, while on errands to Cima, if on no other occasions, had ample opportunity to see Cima at work. The relation, therefore, of Lotto to the painter of Conegliano was very much of the kind that existed between Lotto and Jacopo di Barbari, and not at all that of master to pupil; on the contrary, Cima himself contributes his share, as Barbari, Bonsignori, and Montagna have already done, to the proof that Alvise, and no other, was Lotto's master.

VI.—TESTIMONY OF LOTTO'S ENTIRE CAREER TO HIS DESCENT FROM ALVISE

We have now cleared out of the way everything that would tend to establish a contrary hypothesis; we have seen that the artists of whom Lotto has up to this point reminded us, far from being a mere jumble of names, were all of the following of the Vivarini, and particularly of Alvise. There remains but one other painter who has been suggested by Lotto, and that is Marco Basaiti. He need not detain us long, for his discipleship under Alvise is undisputed, and every point of striking likeness between him and Lotto, as for instance between the Magdalen in Lotto's Recanati polyptych and Basaiti's early Madonnas, we may take without further discussion as proof of Lotto's kinship with Basaiti and descent from Alvise. Lotto, therefore, at the end of this long discussion, appears to us clearly as the pupil not of Giovanni Bellini but of Alvise Vivarini, influenced, to some extent, by his elder fellow pupils, Cima and Barbari, especially by the latter.

To make perfectly sure of our hypothesis, however, let us take a rapid glance through Lotto's works to the end of his career, for the first strong influence that is brought to bear upon a person is apt to leave its traces upon him to the hour of his death. These traces may grow faint, but they do not balk the careful observer. Leonardo, for instance, never denies his origin, Andrea Verocchio; Raphael, in spite of the many and varied influences he came under, and to which he was so phenomenally responsive, proclaims his descent from Timoteo Viti in the measure that he asserts his own individuality; and Titian, sixty years after Giorgione's death, still reminds us of the companion of his youth. I have already said, in discussing the claims of Cima to having been Lotto's master, that scarcely a distinct reminiscence of him appears after Lotto's maturity, but that traces of Alvise and of his school keep on surprising us to the very end of his career.

We find, then, in the very next works that we shall have to examine, that Lotto's general tone is very blond, with blond flesh-tints, as in the Madonna in Alvise's earliest work, the polyptych at Montefiorentino; or that it is golden, as in Alvise's *Resurrection* of 1498 at San Giovanni in Bragora. In Lotto's altar-piece at San Bartolommeo in Bergamo, the highly elaborate architecture reminds us of Alvise's Berlin and Frari pictures, and in grouping it is but a variation on the latter. The ovals of his Madonnas from 1518 to 1525, with the delicacy of their features, seem but an evolution of the oval of Alvise's *Sta. Giustina dei Borromei*[1]. The hands of the same period in Lotto's career have frequently the two middle fingers pressed close together and distinctly separated from the little finger and the index, as in Basaiti's early Madonna at Berlin, and in Montagna generally; or they have clumsy fingers, thick, or broad and tape-like, with the second phalanx of the thumb very much larger than the first[2], clearly betraying their derivation from Alvise. Furthermore, as in Alvise and his pupils, but even to a greater degree, the hands are given a great deal of play, and made dramatis personae, as it were, of the action. The landscape still retains its Alvisesque character of low sky-line with hills in the distance, as for instance in the *Prothonotary Giuliano* of the National Gallery.

---

[1] Casa Bagati-Valsecchi at Milan.
[2] Striking examples in the Museo Civico portrait at Milan, the Vienna portrait, the portrait of a lady at Dorchester House, London, the Lochis *Marriage of St. Catherine*, at Bergamo, and the Ancona *Madonna*.

The feet continue to be awkwardly placed, in Alvise's manner—the Brera *Assumption of the Virgin* and the Bergamo altar-pieces offer good examples—and as a rule have the big toe much shorter than the others and separated from them [1], as we find it in Alvise and his school. In his Bergamask period, Lotto makes great use of Turkey carpets, cushions, and foot-stools, simply as decoration, putting the cushions, for example, more frequently under the Virgin's feet than on her lap. These, be it noted, are all *motifs* rarely, if ever, employed by the Bellini, but constantly by Alvise and his imitator Jacopo da Valenza. Lotto's type of Child also continues chubby and round-headed, as he derived it from Alvise. In the Dresden picture He lies across His mother's lap exactly as in the National Gallery *Madonna*; in the San Bernardino altar-piece at Bergamo He stands on her knee blessing, very much as in Alvise's *Madonna* of 1480 in the Venice Academy. The action of these two Madonnas, by the way, is so fundamentally alike, with the dramatic gesture of the arm, that one seems the rejuvenated, more articulated, and more modern reincarnation of the other. The lights and shadows, although no longer contrasted as in Alvise or in Lotto's own earlier works, attain to a delicacy and transparency, to a refinement [2], which, though rivalling such paintings as Vermeer van Delft's, were doubtless the result of the scrupulous attention devoted to *chiaroscuro* by Alvise and his school. Even the tints of Lotto's mature works, with their exquisite clearness and subtle contrasts, seem but a development, a sixteenth-century efflorescence of Alvise's and Cima's porcelain-like colouring [3]. What is perhaps most

[1] Cf. Alvise's *St. John*, the one nearly in profile, in the Venice Academy (No. 621), for a good instance; also the *Santa Giustina dei Borromei*.
[2] As for instance in the Berlin *Christ taking leave of His Mother*.
[3] Precisely the shade of very light (periwinkle) blue employed by

BART. MONTAGNA

Alinari photo.] [*Museo Civico, Vicenza*

THE MADONNA AND CHILD, WITH SAINTS

startling of all is that Lotto continues into his old age the Squarcionesque, Crivellesque use of fruit and flowers as mere bits of decoration in his pictures [1].

Coming now to the last twenty years of his life, we find almost a recrudescence of Alvisesque traits, as if, no longer possessing the force to resist them, the habits acquired in early youth got the mastery over him once more, this time never to be ousted. In the Ancona *Madonna* of about 1546, the Virgin is enthroned between two windows as in Alvise's Venice Academy *Madonna* of 1480, and in her L. hand we note a return to the form of hand in Bonsignori's earliest picture, the *Madonna* in San Paolo at Verona. In Lotto's last works particularly, although throughout his whole career as well, we find the big toe shorter, as in all the Alviseschi, but in him more marked than in any of the others. Finally, in one of Lotto's very last pictures, the *Sacrifice of Melchizedek* at Loreto, the armour is painted not with the sparkle and iridescence of the Bellineschi, but quietly, as in Alvise, Bonsignori, and Cima.

We have now seen that from youth to old age Lotto betrays the most subtle morphological connexions with Alvise and his school. We have therefore no reason for further hesitating to admit that he was the pupil and follower, not of Giovanni Bellini, as he has hitherto been considered, but of Alvise Vivarini.

VII.—ALVISE VIVARINI

'And who was Alvise Vivarini?' the reader may ask at this point. 'Why all this fuss as to whether

---

Lotto with great frequency in his middle years is found already in Alvise's Montefiorentino altar-piece, and occurs again and again in his works.

[1] Cf. the San Bernardino altar-piece at Bergamo, the Berlin *Christ taking leave of His Mother*, and the Cingoli altar-piece.

he or Bellini was Lotto's first master?' I will answer both these questions, one after the other, with all dispatch.

That Alvise Vivarini was a painter highly considered in his own time and a great figure among the Venetian masters of the fifteenth century, we have had ample chance of proving to ourselves, not only from the higher price his work fetched than Cima's, but from the fact, just established, of his having been the master of such eminent painters as Bonsignori, Montagna, Cima, and Lotto. He was not, therefore, merely a scion of the Vivarini, who, towards the end of his career, was half unwillingly dragged along in the wake of Bellini. Let us, then, turn at once to his works, and see what they reveal to us of their author's quality and evolution, and of his relation to his successful rivals, the Bellini.

The first dated work by Alvise that has come down to us is the polyptych of 1475 [1] at Montefiorentino, a lonely Franciscan monastery on the bleak spur of the Apennines overhanging the upper valley of the Foglia, at a point where the provinces of Pesaro-Urbino and Arezzo meet. The polyptych is in five panels, in a Gothic frame. In the central panel the Madonna is seated on a simple throne, with her hands clasped in adoration, while the Child lies asleep, with His knees crossed, on her lap. To the R. stand St. Paul and John the Baptist, and to the L. SS. Peter and Francis. The general tone is light and gay, as in the works of Lotto's earlier maturity, the blue on the Virgin and on SS. Peter and Paul being the precise shade found in Lotto. The flesh-tints of the Madonna are very blond, whitish brown, as in Lotto's *Pietà* of 1512 at Jesi. Even her expression, with its touch of pouting melan-

[1] This date is unmistakable, and not 1476, as given by Messrs. Crowe and Cavalcaselle.

ALVISE VIVARINI

POLYPTYCH OF THE MADONNA AND CHILD, WITH SAINTS

ALVISE'S PLACE IN VENICE 67

choly, reminds us of Lotto's Recanati and Bridgewater Madonnas. In no other work, as in this earliest one, does Alvise reveal himself so clearly as the precursor of Lotto. But if it is a prophecy of Lotto on the one hand, it reveals to an even greater degree the author's descent from his Muranese relatives, Bartolommeo and Antonio Vivarini, and his indebtedness to Padua. In mere forms [1] and mannerisms it reminds us to the minutest details of Bartolommeo's works of about the same date, particularly of the polyptych at Vienna (No. 10) of 1477, although it is true that certain details go back more particularly to Antonio Vivarini, leaving us to infer that Alvise may have been their common pupil while they were working together, as we know them to have been doing in 1450. The general construction and proportion of the figures also are Bartolommeo's, but the gay colour scheme, the carriage and action of the figures, and even some of the types are very different from his. St. Peter holds himself as proudly as any figure in Pollajuolo or Tura, too haughtily for Mantegna. St. Paul's head is distinctly Squarcionesque [2], and both he and the Baptist are only less haughty than Peter. Francis, on the contrary, is simple and natural, a figure expressive of intense devotion, as in Crivelli's St. Francis in the polyptych at Massa Fermana. Although this is the first work by Alvise that has come down to us, it is obviously

---

[1] With pose and action of the Madonna and Child here cf. the Madonna in the Bologna polyptych of 1450 by Antonio and Bartolommeo Vivarini.

[2] I mean a type of head found among the Squarcioneschi, and therefore called by their name, although coming in reality from Giovanni and Antonio da Murano. With SS. Paul and John here cf. the same saints in the polyptych of 1450 at Bologna by Antonio and Bartolommeo Vivarini. Back to the same polyptych may also be traced the Child in Alvise's Montefiorentino *Madonna*, a cross between the infants in Crivelli's earliest pictures and the Child in the Bellini belonging to Mr. Theodore Davis of Newport, U.S.A.

F 2

a work of advanced maturity. The painter has great command of his craft, has been the apprentice of Antonio and Bartolommeo Vivarini, has studied in Padua among the Squarcioneschi, and has developed a colouring and style of his own. In short, the mere fact of the existence of this altar-piece in a place so out of the way, and so far removed from Venice, permits us to infer that at the time of its execution Alvise must already have been a well-known artist [1].

In his next dated work, the *Madonna* of 1480, in the Venice Academy (No. 607), Alvise shows a great advance. The cruder Squarcionesque elements have disappeared, the draperies have become simpler, the treatment of light and shade is very elaborate, and it is evident that this, along with the problems of perspective, is of special interest to the painter. But far more striking than any mere details is the composition itself. No longer do the Madonna and saints inhabit separate niches, as in the Montefiorentino

---

[1] Alvise's date of birth still remains unknown, but, thanks to documents published by Prof. Paoletti (*Raccolta di Documenti inediti per servire alla Storia della Pittura veneziana nei Secoli XV, XVI*, Fascicolo ii, Padua, 1895), we can determine it more accurately. From a will made by Alvise's mother in 1458 it appears that he was her eldest child, and not yet of age. Now a Venetian became of age at fourteen, so that Alvise must have been born after 1444. His father, the painter Antonio Vivarini, on February 4, 1446, gives security for his wife's dower, and that would look as if they had been married but recently. Their first child, Alvise, may therefore have been born towards the end of the same year, 1446. That he was not an old man at his death, which occurred in 1502, we may infer from the fact that a daughter of his, who had a husband still living and therefore not likely to have been extraordinarily aged, made her will as late as October, 1569.

I cannot see that Alvise's birth fifteen years later than I had supposed when the first edition of this book was published, makes any material difference to my estimate of his character as an artist, or even to his importance as the head of a great school. The utmost it would effect would be to take something away from Alvise, and add something to his relatives Antonio and Bartolommeo; but the point I have been trying to establish in this chapter, the existence and influence throughout the fifteenth century of a school of painters in Venice, distinct from and independent of the Bellini, remains untouched.

ALVISE VIVARINI

THE MADONNA AND CHILD, WITH SAINTS

picture. They are brought together into one composition, each looking on, listening, or thinking over the exposition which the Madonna seems to be making of the divine Child. Awkward and stiff as the figures still are, they are nevertheless slightly in motion, as if drawn towards the Virgin, and their hands express sympathy with the eloquent gesture of the Madonna's R. arm. In the Montefiorentino polyptych the colour and tone, as well as the Madonna, reminded us of Lotto. Here, the feeling, the drama, the interpretation, and the play of hands are, perhaps less obviously but even more genuinely, Lottesque. I venture to say that in no other Venetian altar-piece of this date do we find such studied interpretation of a situation and such dramatic unity. In this work, moreover, no trace of the Bellini can be discovered: on the contrary, a distinct purpose reveals itself, less purely artistic, it must be confessed, but more expressive. Alvise shows himself here as an *expressivist*—if I may be allowed a barbarous neologism—and his relation towards the Bellini thus foreshadows the relation we shall discover later to have existed between his pupil Lotto and their pupil Titian.

Thus far, then, Alvise appears as the logical outcome of Muranese artistic endeavour. If as an artist he reminds us more of the Bellini than of his own precursors, it is because he was their contemporary, because he, too, belonged to the new generation and pulsated to its feelings. He therefore puts into the forms of the Muranese, which he scarcely varies, all those emotions of freedom, pride, and eagerness which the people who gave the tone to the age were feeling in the first flush of conscious renascence. If, then, Alvise gave up his independence, as is commonly supposed, and succumbed to the overwhelming influence of the Bellini, it must have happened after

1480[1]. But before proceeding to his later works, I must crave the reader's indulgence for a brief parenthesis.

While examining Lotto's Recanati altar-piece, we noticed that the hand of the St. Thomas there reminded us of the hand of St. Nicholas in Bartolommeo Vivarini's altar-piece of 1465 at Naples, and even more of the hand of the St. Augustine in the joint work of Antonio and Bartolommeo at Bologna, the polyptych of 1450. We are now in a position to explain this curious fact. I have just said that Alvise's forms and mannerisms remain the forms and mannerisms of Antonio and Bartolommeo Vivarini. Only a small part, a mere percentage of Alvise's work has come down to us; we are, therefore, justified in assuming that if we had his entire works we should discover in them all the forms and mannerisms we cannot find in the works that remain, but which crop up in his pupils and exist in his predecessors[2]. Lotto, we may therefore assume, did not take the hand of his St. Thomas from Antonio and Bartolommeo directly, but from Alvise himself, who, we may be sure, had it in works now lost. As this is the only explanation

[1] The five bituminous-tinted figures on gold ground, of great severity and impressiveness, in the Venice Academy (No. 621), seem to have been painted before August 2, 1471 (Paoletti and Ludwig in *Repertorium*, 1899, p. 450). They represent SS. Sebastian, Antony Abbot, two John the Baptists, and Lawrence. Recently these have been framed along with seven other panels which seem to have gone with them originally, although most of them are by greatly inferior hands. Messrs. Crowe and Cavalcaselle hesitate in ascribing these panels to Alvise, but I fail to see on what grounds, as the forms are unmistakably his, and the quality certainly does him no discredit. Should it, however, turn out that they are not by Alvise, it would affect but slightly my argument in this chapter. They are Vivarinesque beyond question, and my object here is, I repeat, to establish the importance and influence of the Vivarini.

[2] This argument may seem unfamiliar in the study of Italian art, but it is well known in philology. A number of words, for instance, exist in languages derived from Latin and Greek which are not found in the classical literature of those languages, but which we know to be Indo-Germanic, and which thus lead us to the conclusion that Latin and Greek, as spoken languages, must have had them.

possible, its evidence also goes to prove Lotto's descent from Alvise.

Returning now to the later works of the master, we next encounter a Madonna signed and dated 1483, a picture hitherto unknown, which, not long after the publication of the first edition of this book, I found in the sacristy of Sant' Andrea at Barletta. Originally it almost certainly formed part of a polyptych, but now the Madonna remains alone. She sits enthroned against a curtain, holding the Child in her arms. The colouring is bright and gay. The Child is, by anticipation, Lottesque. But the sweep of the drapery betrays, if I mistake not, the influence of Antonello, for it is of distinctly Flemish character, as in the latter's Madonna formerly at San Gregorio and now in the Museum of Messina.

The Naples *Madonna with SS. Francis and Bernardino* is also signed, but dated 1485. It is an inferior work, hastily done, yet showing a certain advance towards freedom of action and largeness of style. In the Vienna *Madonna* of 1489, however, we find already the devotional spirit, with the touch of Peruginesque pensiveness, that charms us in the Redentore *Madonna* of slightly later date. Of nearly the same time—that is to say, 1489—although probably some two or three years earlier, is the *Madonna* in San Giovanni in Bragora at Venice, which in type and pose harks back curiously to the one at Montefiorentino. The next dated work is the *Head of the Saviour*, of 1493, in the same church. This head shows a singular return of flesh-colour to the blond, whitish brown of the Montefiorentino *Madonna*, and this colouring, but more glowing and in a much more flowing vehicle, characterizes the *Resurrection* of 1498, also in San Giovanni in Bragora, and those bits of the Frari altar-piece, his last work, which Alvise may be assumed to have executed himself. Such, therefore, among the pictures, not yet mentioned, as do not partake of these characteristics of colour and vehicle and general style must belong to an earlier period—prior, that is, to 1493.

Prior to 1493, consequently, must be placed the Berlin altar-piece, the most elaborate work by Alvise now existing[1]. Messrs. Crowe and Cavalcaselle, on mere hearsay, have assigned to it the date of 1501, which would make it one of Alvise's very last works. Against this hypothesis nearly every bit of the work rises in revolt. To begin with, the general tone is still between bituminous and porcelain-tinted, the vehicle thin, the lights and shadows sharply contrasted, and the modelling hard, as in the *Madonna* of 1480 in the Venice Academy. The female figures are awkward and unarticulated, the folds of the Madonna's draperies are stiff and in straight lines, instead of having the flow and ease of the draperies in the Redentore Madonna and in the *Resurrection* of 1498, while the *putti* have not yet the chubbiness and grace of those in the Redentore or even Vienna pictures. None of that feeling for comeliness, none of the subtle beauty of the dawning sixteenth century found in Alvise's last work appear as yet in this painting. Even as a composition, it recalls the Venice Academy *Madonna* much more than the Frari altar-piece. Change the settings and take away the two *putti* in the one, and the Berlin and Venice Academy altar-pieces are almost identical in grouping. Here, moreover, if anywhere in Alvise, one feels a certain closeness of contact with Antonello. I venture, for instance, to believe that if the head of the

[1] No. 38. The Madonna sits on a beautifully sculptured throne under a splendid domed portico, with the Magdalen and St. Catherine at R. and L. on the steps, and below SS. Sebastian and Jerome, while two *putti* make music on a step in the middle, and SS. Peter and George stand at the extreme R. and L.

St. George existed as a fragment by itself, it would, like all of Alvise's portraits, have passed for Antonello's. But we have seen that the most distinct trace of Antonello's influence upon Alvise occurred in a picture painted in 1483 (Barletta). We have many reasons, therefore, to assign this Berlin work to a date prior certainly to 1489; the date of the Vienna Madonna, and I believe it to be no later than 1485.

Now the determining upon this date rather than upon 1501 for the Berlin altar-piece is of more consequence than would at first appear. If it reminds us of any one work by Giovanni Bellini it is of the San Giobbe altar-piece of about 1488, now in the Venice Academy (No. 38). If Alvise executed his work about 1485, then he and Bellini developed at a pace nearly identical; if, on the contrary, he executed it in 1501, then he was a good decade behind Bellini. Fortunately we have seen the latter date to be untenable, and Alvise therefore reveals himself in his most elaborate work as a master of less even attainment, it is true, and of less endowment, but of parallel development with Bellini, and as the possessor of great qualities of his own.

Before leaving this altar-piece, I would ask where any one can trace in it a dependence upon Giovanni Bellini. Surely not in the composition, with the figures grouped around the throne on different levels? We have a similar composition, as we have seen, in Alvise's *Madonna* of 1480, and considering that we find the same system of grouping in all his altar-pieces, while it is never found in Bellini, we have every right to regard it as peculiarly his own. In the types and figures, I am equally at a loss to find any element Alvise could not have acquired by himself, with the outfit given him by Antonio and Bartolommeo, and some contact with Antonello. As to the sentiment, it is not at all Bellinesque, but a trifle woe-begone, as in all the Muranese. Now when Bellini stood for all that was interesting in Venetian fifteenth-century painting, it was natural that the strong Venetian character of this Berlin *Madonna and Saints* should have suggested the greatest surviving Venetian name. If it had had no signature, we may be sure it would have been ascribed, as Alvise's San Giovanni in Bragora and Redentore *Madonnas* have been ascribed, to Bellini himself; but as that could not be done, Alvise was dumped in along with the general rabble of Bellini's followers, and has thus come to be considered, in the popular view, as one of the Bellineschi. But we, allowing for the great likeness there must necessarily exist between two contemporary fifteenth-century townsmen of something like the same level of genius, must either minutely distinguish between them, defining clearly the quality and describing the evolution of each, or remain as ignorant as were our fathers, not only of the history of Venetian art, but of the purpose of art history in general.

Of Alvise's paintings in the Doge's Palace, executed between 1489 and his death in 1502, we can unfortunately frame no distinct idea, as no historical composition from his hand, which might help us to reconstruct them, has come down to us. Vasari praises them especially for their perspective, which agrees with our own appreciation of Alvise's perspective in the Frari altar-piece, and enables us to understand where Lotto got his peculiar delight in this science, of which we shall have much to say when we return to Lotto's works.

Between the Berlin altar-piece and the *Madonna* at Vienna, that is to say, between 1485 and 1489, I would place in the order in which I name them, the *Madonna* formerly in the Manfrin collection and now at the

ALVISE VIVARINI

(*National Gallery, London*

THE MADONNA AND CHILD

ALVISE VIVARINI

[*Academia, Venice*

ST. CLARE

National Gallery, the elderly female Saint bearing a palm of martyrdom at the Vienna Academy, the *St. Clare* of the Venice Academy, the second Berlin altar-piece, the *Matthew*, and the *Baptist reading* of the Venice Academy again. The National Gallery *Madonna,* although not thought worthy by the present director of taking place along with his other recent acquisitions, is nevertheless a work of fine design and delicate sentiment. The Child, although more bony, anticipates the *putti* in the Vienna *Madonna*, but the Virgin's hands resemble those in the Naples triptych of 1485, and in Alvise's still earlier, but not in his later paintings. The female Saint of the Vienna Academy is a quiet but severe figure, no unworthy rival of the *St. Clare* at Venice. The last named is a powerfully conceived and ably executed bust of a firmly believing, strenuously acting old woman. Her face is one of the best studies of character that had up to that time been produced in Venice. The forms in both works, when carefully studied, persuade one that they were painted scarcely much later than the Naples triptych. The second Berlin altar-piece (No. 1165) represents the Madonna enthroned between SS. Sebastian, Augustine, Jerome, and the Baptist. It is in no too good condition, and has never attracted the attention that it deserves. The drawing of the hands and the type of the Child make it clear to me that this is a work executed between 1485 and 1489, yet it possesses a pictorial quality and a freedom which already anticipate riper Venetian art. One finds more than one note here taken up by later and more famous painters. Thus the Sebastian suggests not only Lotto's at Berlin and Loreto, but a figure in Pordenone's altar-piece at San Giovanni Elemosinario in Venice, while the R. arm and hand and the whole reposeful action of the Virgin remind me vividly of Catena's

Madonna with the Knight in Adoration, at the National Gallery. As for the *Matthew* of the Venice Academy, he is a vehement figure of more morphological and psychological interest than actual beauty. The *Baptist*, painted obviously very soon after the figure of the same saint in the second Berlin altarpiece, although less violent than the *Matthew*, its companion, is yet very emphatic as compared with the saints Bellini was already painting at this time. In structure, he is Alvise's best figure; the movement is admirably expressive of tension and brooding thought. The draperies are still angular and full of catches, but the stroke throughout, particularly in the painting of the foliage, is large and free. In conception this *Baptist* is superior to any one figure by Giovanni Bellini, and in execution it lags behind but little.

Two or three years after the *Madonna* in the Imperial Gallery at Vienna, Alvise must have painted the replica thereof—that exquisite picture still shown to tourists as a favourite Bellini—the Madonna with the two music-making baby angels in the church of the Redentore at Venice. In fullness of forms, in glow of colour, in readiness of vehicle, it anticipates the *Resurrection* of 1498. As a composition no work of the kind by Giovanni Bellini even rivals it. Behind a parapet, on a throne of the most perfect simplicity, sits the Madonna, solemnly yet pensively worshipping the Child, who lies fast asleep on her lap. Behind the throne a green curtain hangs loosely from a cord. On the parapet two chubby baby angels with little wings sit with one little leg drawn up, playing on their tiny mandolins and singing. The whole art of such a masterpiece lies in the unswerving directness, the bare simplicity with which the painter has carried out his idea of placing before us the baby Child in quiet yet slightly roguish play, and the baby Child fast asleep,

ALVISE VIVARINI

THE MADONNA AND CHILD, WITH ANGELS

Venice, Church of the Redentore

with the tender, worshipping young mother to solemnly watch and adore.

Gladly as I would acknowledge it, here also I fail to find any traits necessarily derived from Giovanni Bellini. The Madonna's oval, far from reminding us of Bellini, harks back to the ovals of Antonio Vivarini, as, for instance, in the SS. Vito and Venanzio in his polyptych of 1464 in the Lateran. Even the baby angels, Bellinesque as at first sight they seem, betray nothing in their build or action which cannot be accounted for by Alvise's natural evolution.

From the Redentore *Madonna* to the *Resurrection* at San Giovanni in Bragora, painted in 1498, it is but a step. In technique the two pictures have much in common, in colouring also, and all the faces in the latter picture have something of the childlike *naïveté* of the Redentore baby angels. But in feeling how different are the two works! In the one, devout contemplation still prevails; in the other, the painter stops just short of Correggio's ecstasy. It shows us Christ, a soft but beautiful figure, standing triumphant over His tomb, while below, on the sky-line, there is an exquisite effect of sunrise—or rather the first strong flush of pink in a sunless sky. To the L. are seen the heads of the two guards with a look of surprise in the beautiful faces, not of dismay, but as if they too were glad. What a time must this dawn of the sixteenth century have been when a man of seventy, and not the most vigorous and advanced of his age, had the freshness and youthful courage to greet it, nay, actually to depict its magic and glamour, as Alvise does in this *Resurrection*! Giorgione is here anticipated in the roundness and softness of the figures, and in the effect of light. Titian's *Assunta* is here foreshadowed in the fervour of the guards' expressions [1].

[1] The authenticity of this picture is unquestionable, even on morpho-

If this *Resurrection* anticipates Giorgione's magic, another of Alvise's pictures, painted towards the very end of the fifteenth century, anticipates not only his severe grace and refinement, but even his oval and shape of skull, even the locks of hair that fall over the necks of his female figures[1]. The picture I am referring to is the almost life-size, full-length *Santa Giustina dei Borromei* in the Casa Bagati-Valsecchi at Milan. She steps forward on a narrow platform, the whole of her figure relieved against the curling cloudlets of a bluish-grey sky. Her body is still vibrating delicately with motion, as if she were going to take one more step forward, and in sympathy with this vibration, the palm that she daintily holds out in her R. hand, takes a curve of the subtlest grace. The exquisite beauty of her oval, the almost morbid refinement of her features, the slightly trembling limbs, are in vivid contrast with the massive structure of her torso and the majestic height of her figure—contrast, but not contradiction, for the refinement and the power are here so harmonized that the one seems the essential index to the quality of the other. She wears a jewelled diadem with a string of pearls over her forehead, and pearls in her flaxen hair. A jewelled girdle confines her high waist, and her mantle, held together over her breast with a clasp of jewels and pearls, falls in natural folds over her broad shoulders, and, leaving her waist bare while clinging to her knees, is held in place by the L. hand, which at the

---

logical grounds. The documents, moreover, put the matter beyond doubt (see Botteon, op. cit., p. 212). In connexion with this *Resurrection* may be mentioned the much earlier picture in the sacristy of San Giovanni e Paolo, the solitary Christ dragging His Cross through an ominously silent world. Ruined as this picture is, its poetry is still overwhelming. Here also we are made to think of Giorgione, of his cross-bearing Christ once in the Palazzo Loschi at Vicenza.

[1] Cf. *The Trial of Moses* in the Uffizi, and the *Judith* at St. Petersburg, there ascribed to Moretto, but if not an original Giorgione, at least an old copy after him.

ALVISE VIVARINI

[Milan, Galleria Bagatti-Valsecchi]

SANTA GIUSTINA

same time supports a book on her hip. From this point it falls like a maniple over her figure, and from under the elbow it descends in an almost straight but beautifully swung line nearly perpendicularly to the skirts of the mantle, which lie in quiet folds on the R., diagonally balancing the arm with the palm to the L. In no other figure by any Italian known to me has the drapery been so successfully studied to bring out the rhythm, vibration, and dignity of the figure, and its relation to the space containing it, as in this panel by Alvise. As a composition altogether I scarcely know its rival, unless, indeed, it be Raphael's *Granduca Madonna*[1].

Yet, supreme though this Santa Giustina be in composition, tender and refined in sentiment, great as a creation, it is not possible to overlook the fact that her author seems never to have mastered the nude, that he cannot properly articulate the human figure, that he has no precise idea of its proportions. To him the human form is not an interest apart, and its construction is not an almost all-sufficing end. To him it is something to drape and to fit in as a composition —a solid, majestic, human-shaped *herma* upon which to place a head of the greatest loveliness. Take away the head, think away the arms and the draperies, and you have left a figure almost as unnecessarily massive, as unarticulated, as ill-proportioned, as any in Alvise's own earliest works, or in those even of his predecessors. In structural problems he had made only such advance as was necessary to give the figure movement and swing, while Bellini, at the same moment, was learning to construct the human figure in such wise that, even during his own lifetime, his pupil, Giorgione, could paint a nude like the Dresden Venus, the most beautiful

---

[1] Of nearly as late a date as this Santa Giustina is the full-length figure of a female Saint holding a monstrance, in the Vienna Academy—an inferior but unquestionable work.

in Italian art. Expressivist and linealist, rather than structuralist, by nature, Alvise's development lay chiefly along the line of expression and lineal effect; hence such a creation of beauty as this Santa Giustina, so refined, so modern in feeling, that she makes us think of Giorgione rather than of Bellini (in whose works she finds no parallel), of Giorgione and of that brief moment in Italian art when the evolution of form and craftsmanship were at such a point that they could give adequate but not opulent or riotous expression to ideals of beauty already perfectly modern, but as yet unexploited, unhackneyed, and unspoilt.

This Santa Giustina, one of his very latest works, seems at the same time Alvise's artistic biography and his testament. She is his autobiography, because she shows us so well where her author began, what experiences he met with, and to what he attained. To any one acquainted with Mantegna's works, Alvise's Santa Giustina immediately suggests the Santa Eufemia in the Brera polyptych. The action and pose are practically identical, but Mantegna's figure is better constructed, while Alvise's is a world more beautiful, more subtle, more artistic. We have already noted how like Alvise's earliest works the Santa Giustina is in build. She has the massive chest, the disproportionately long thighs, and the deep curve inwards between hip and knee, that we have found in all the Vivarini and in their followers. The drapery on the R. arm and in the mantle under the waist has the characteristic straight parallel folds, joined by a short straight line, and to the R. of the knee the folds are huddled together, parallel and close, but curved. The oval, wonderfully new as it is in refinement, is after all but a slight variation on Alvise's early SS. Lawrence and Sebastian, the which, in turn, are themselves but slightly varied from the SS. Vito and Venanzio in Antonio Vivarini's Lateran altar-piece.

Even the refinement is half that well-known pensive melancholy which we have found in Alvise's Madonnae. Of this Santa Giustina it may be said almost literally that her author has done nothing but pour new wine into old bottles—put a new spirit into old forms. And that is why Alvise and his pupils, even the young Lotto, have something archaic about them, in spite of their greater expressiveness and greater consciousness of the psychological problem.

In this sense the Santa Giustina is Alvise's artistic autobiography. She is his testament as well, because all that is most exquisite in her was at once absorbed by Giorgione, the subtle, although unconscious combiner of all that was best, no matter how divergent, in the art which preceded him; because she left an indelible impression upon the mind of the one painter who continued into the sixteenth century the traditions, the habits, and the ideals of Alvise, upon the mind of Lorenzo Lotto. Lotto, up to the point we have followed him thus far, seems to have lacked either the craftsmanship or the mental qualities to paint a face so refined as Santa Giustina's, although many of the faces in his early works, particularly that of the angel in the Recanati altar-piece, have suggested hers. But all of a sudden Lotto goes back to her, and, allowing for the modifications introduced by his own personal qualities, it is this type, with the great, almost morbid, refinement, delicate mouth, soft lids, and beautifully braided, silken, jewel-enwoven hair, that we have in his Dresden *Madonna* of 1518, and in nearly all his female figures up to 1530. In the *St. Catherine* of 1522, in the Leuchtenberg collection at St. Petersburg, we find not only nearly the same sentiment, nearly the same *coiffure*, but the palm branch identical in curve and swing with that of the *Santa Giustina*.

The qualities that we found in the *Santa Giustina*, beauty of composition and of face, balance and rhythm, we find again in the splendid work that Alvise did not live to finish, particularly in those parts of it in which Basaiti's clammy touch is not too distinctly felt. The Frari altar-piece, begun probably early in 1502 [1], represents St. Ambrose enthroned under the elaborately coffered vaulting of a broad, deep apse. By the throne with him stand SS. George and Vitale—archangels rather than saints for comeliness and matchless beauty of manly youth—in full armour, George with drawn sword. On a lower level to R. and L. stand six saints, among them Gregory, with his crozier composing finely with the crook of Ambrose and the sword of George. On a step under the throne two angels are playing on mandolins [2]. In the foreground to R. and L. stand SS. Jerome and Sebastian. Over the arch, behind a balustrade, Christ is seen crowning His Mother, while two angels are holding a curtain behind them. In grouping [3], this is the most successful altar-piece of many figures that had yet been painted in Venice. Essentially the composition of the 1480 *Madonna*—two figures nearly on a level and close to the principal one, with the others on a lower plane—the task here is much greater, the attempt more ambitious. Barring the Jerome and Sebastian, the eight other saints are grouped around Ambrose with the greatest possible naturalness and unity of interest compatible with severe architectonic composition. Jerome and Sebastian are so detached from

---

[1] Alvise seems to have died before March 20, 1502 (Paoletti and Ludwig in *Repertorium* for 1899, p. 275).
[2] With these, cf. the two angels in Montagna's great altar-piece in the Brera (No. 167).
[3] I mean the lower group regarded by itself. It should be remembered that the coronation must have been ordered as part of the altar-piece, and that Alvise had no choice in the matter.

ALVISE VIVARINI

Alinari photo.] [*Venice, Church of the Frari*

ST. AMBROSE ENTHRONED

the other figures, so out of harmony with them, that I feel more than tempted to believe that Alvise did not so much as even lay them in, but that they are an addition by Basaiti, who could ape Alvise's forms, but understand neither his composition nor beauty. The architecture is very elaborate, with projecting cornices and an absence of detail which anticipate the actual architecture of a whole generation later. The perspective is treated as by a specialist delighting in his craft. The architecture, the perspective, the grouping, in this altar-piece, and probably in others very much like it, must have produced a great impression upon Lotto, for, as we shall see, in the first crowded altar-piece that he had to paint, the one now in San Bartolommeo at Bergamo, he gives us what is in all the points just mentioned, nothing but a variation of this last work by his master.

Although there can be no doubt that the execution of a considerable part of this altar-piece is due to Basaiti—hence its inferiority in detail to the *Santa Giustina*—yet the work as a whole can be counted as Alvise's, not only in its composition, but in the forms and draperies; for in these details here, and so late even as in his *Calling of the Children of Zebedee*, painted in 1510, Basaiti differs from Alvise only in quality. I have therefore, in previous sections of this chapter, spoken of the hands and ears and draperies as wholly Alvisesque, since they are unmistakably such, even where they were not actually executed or finished by Alvise.

I trust that by this time enough has been said to bring out Alvise's great qualities as an artist, and his independence of Bellini, inferior in essentials to his great rival though we must confess him to be. But thus far I have taken no account of his portraits, having purposely avoided them, wishing to treat of them together. Unfortunately the only perfectly authenticated portrait [1] is so repainted that, striking and powerful as it still is, it does not do Alvise all the credit that it would otherwise. It is the bust of an oldish, smooth-shaven man, in a blue cap, seen behind a parapet on which he rests his L. hand. It is signed and dated 1497, and has the glowing, almost golden flesh tone of Alvise's other works of about this time. But although the only authenticated one, the Bonomi-Cereda bust is by no means the only indication we have of Alvise's talents as a portrait painter. Formerly in the Cavalli collection at Padua, and now in the gallery of that town [2], is the almost life-size bust of a man of about forty. His look is vehement, as in Antonello, from whom, however, it is not derived, occurring already in the saints in Bartolommeo Vivarini's polyptych of 1464 in the Venice Academy. His auburn hair falls down from his purple cap to his shoulders. He wears a purple coat, has brown eyes, marked features, with a strong beard just sprouting. The modelling is hard but careful, the flesh-colour between porcelain and ivory. In this respect, and in all morphological details, this bust is so nearly identical with the figures in Alvise's Venice Academy *Madonna* of 1480, that there cannot be a serious doubt about its authorship. Messrs. Crowe and Cavalcaselle already noted its great likeness to Alvise, and only a momentary indecision seems to have prevented their ascribing it to him. As a portrait, as marked individualization, it is certainly one of the strongest ever executed up to that time—about 1480—in Venice, not excepting even Antonello's great achievements in this art. Somewhat later in date than this Paduan portrait

---

[1] Formerly in the Bonomi-Cereda collection at Milan, and now Mr. George Salting's.
[2] Legato Cavalli, No. 1381, attributed to Antonello.

ALVISE VIVARINI

[*Salting Collection, London*

PORTRAIT OF A MAN

ALVISE VIVARINI

Anderson photo.] [*Padua Gallery*

BUST OF A MAN

is the small bust (25 × 18 cm.) in Lady Layard's collection at Venice, where it is still attributed to Antonello, although Morelli long ago recognized it for an Alvise. But as this little painting does come remarkably close to the kind of portrait usually ascribed to Antonello, it is worth while to note precisely wherein it is distinguishable from the works of the Messinese, and how much closer is its connexion with Alvise.

The upper eyelid, then, is never so raised in Antonello as in this bust, where, as frequently in Alvise, it almost forms a right angle; in Antonello, on the contrary, it is a very shallow curve, the whole eye being more almond-shaped and much less wide open. In Antonello's *paintings*—in his drawings, he is a better observer—the pupil is always a full circle, even if in contradiction with the movement of the eyes. In the bust before us, the pupil is seen slightly sideways, in perfect harmony with the movement of the head. In Antonello, moreover, the pupil is always sharply defined as a little disk, distinct from the rest of the iris. Here, on the contrary, the division is not marked in any peculiar way. As in Alvise, but not as in Antonello, the nose is slightly hooked and the nostril inflated. The mouth, as very frequently in Alvise [1], but never in Antonello, is distinctly turned down at the L. corner (L. from the spectator), and rather turned up at the R., and has altogether more movement and sensitiveness than in Antonello. The cheeks are, for the type of face, fuller in this Layard portrait than in Antonello, and the modelling smoother. The general tone is neither the brick-red of Antonello's earlier nor the pale greenish-blue of his later years, but a subdued turquoise, coming much nearer the general tone of Alvise between 1480 and 1490. As a rendering, it is

[1] A good example is the *St. Clare* of the Venice Academy.

distinctly analytical and psychological, in this respect also being much more in harmony with what we already know of Alvise than with the almost brutal impersonality of Antonello's portraits.

With Lady Layard's bust stands or falls a small portrait of the same technical and morphological characteristics, although representing a different kind of person. It is the portrait of a boy of fifteen or sixteen at the utmost, a little defiant or shy, yet frank in look, with a *zazzera* of blond hair cropped short over the eyebrows, wearing a coat of pale turquoise blue. It now belongs to Mr. Salting of London, but formerly it was in the Duchâtel collection at Paris, where it was seen by Messrs. Crowe and Cavalcaselle, who pronounced it to be not by Antonello, to whom it is still ascribed, but by Andrea Solario. This attribution, although interesting[1], cannot be taken seriously. As a matter of fact, the authorship of this portrait does not lie between Alvise and Antonello, or Solario, but between Alvise and his fellow pupil, Jacopo di Barbari. To prove to what a remarkable degree it is Alvisesque, would simply be repeating the proofs I had to give for ascribing the Layard bust to Alvise. Such repetition is unnecessary, but I must allow myself a word to justify the attribution of this portrait to Alvise rather than to Jacopo di Barbari. That they become almost indistinguishable at times we have already noticed in discussing Barbari's superior claims to a head in red chalk in the Uffizi. The bust we are now considering is almost equally ambiguous. But the colour-scheme, of a rather low turquoise tint, is, to my knowledge, not at all Barbaresque, but distinctly characteristic of Alvise. Peculiar to the latter also rather than to the former, is the slight

---

[1] It will be remembered that Solario was in Venice towards 1495.

ALVISE VIVARINI

Alinari photo.] [*Lady Layard, Venice*

PORTRAIT OF A MAN

ALVISE VIVARINI

[Hanfstaengl photo.] [Salting Collection, London

PORTRAIT OF A YOUTH

turn of the pupil and its lack of sharp division from the iris, Barbari's pupil and iris being much more like Antonello's than Alvise's—that is to say, a perfectly circular black disk within a larger circle. Finally, the look is too direct for Barbari—the painter has made more of an attempt at the interpretation of the sitter's character than I find in any of Barbari's works, at least in those of his earlier years. So, all considered, I feel safe in placing Mr. Salting's bust among the list of Alvise's portraits.

Other painted portraits by Alvise are the magnificent life-size busts, one in the Louvre and the other at Windsor, both attributed by certain critics to Savoldo, and a smaller bust in Paris, belonging to the Comtesse de Béarn, who attributes it to Antonello. The Louvre portrait is of Bernardo di Salla [1], a smooth-shaven man just turning to middle age. The glow on his face is even more golden than on the *Resurrected Christ* in San Giovanni in Bragora. The oval, with the slightly swollen look to the cheek, is distinctly Alvise's, as in the Christ just mentioned. The cut of the eyes, the vivacious look, almost a twinkle, and the modelling under the lower lid are all peculiar to Alvise. The mouth, with one corner turned down and the other tending to curve up, mobile yet controlled, recalls the mouths in the Layard and Bonomi-Cereda portraits, and in the *St. Clare* of the Venice Academy. The nose has the sharply outlined inflation of Alvise. The setting of the eyes, the deep shadow between the brows and lids, and the direction of the look, resemble, more or less, all Alvise's mature works, but particularly the *St. Clare*. Even the folds on his dark green coat, where we should scarcely expect it, have the curves, the swiftness of line, that we find in the drapery over

[1] Louvre, No. 1519. He holds a letter with this name written on it, a not unusual way of labelling a portrait.

the knees of St. Ambrose in Alvise's Frari altar-piece, and the loops and catches found in all his works. In short, in this portrait we have before us a work which marshals itself unquestionably among Alvise's last achievements. It is already mentioned as such in Habich's *Vade Mecum,* and even its present attribution to Savoldo, and its ascription by Messrs. Crowe and Cavalcaselle to Buonconsiglio, are indirect proofs of my thesis. Buonconsiglio was, as is well known, the pupil of Montagna, and therefore of Alvise's school. As to Savoldo[1], if he did not actually begin his career under Alvise, he began it under Alvise's pupil, Bonsignori. The Alvisesque character of the Louvre head has therefore, even if unwittingly, been acknowledged by everybody, and among the Alviseschi of the very beginning of the sixteenth century[2], none but Alvise himself could have produced a work of such matchless glow of colour and of such subtle characterization. I venture to say that from whatever point of view we consider this bust, it ranks with the most fascinating portraits ever painted in Italy.

Scarcely inferior to the Louvre portrait is the one in Windsor Castle of a smooth-shaved man feeding a hawk. At a distance this head seems but a replica of the one in the Louvre, so identical are they in pose, movement, and all morphological characteristics. But the sitters were very different. The Windsor man is quick-tempered, passionate, almost sinister, with none of Salla's merry twinkle. In colour-scheme the Windsor bust is bituminous, and having darkened, its effect is remarkably Savoldesque. It is interesting

---

[1] This theory of Savoldo's descent, which I cannot stop to prove here, is based upon a careful study of his technical and morphological characteristics.

[2] That the portrait dates from precisely this time is sufficiently proved by the dress and *coiffure*.

ALVISE VIVARINI

Braun photo.] [Louvre, Paris

PORTRAIT OF SALLA

not only because of its great qualities, but also as revealing a phase of Alvise's colour which makes us understand whence Savoldo derived his, it being a not over rare occurrence that a pupil was all his life determined by the one phase, even if momentary, in which he happened to find his master.

The bust belonging to the Comtesse de Béarn, if it had not suffered so much from scrubbing, would be the most interesting of the series [1]. The personality represented is barely saved from ferocity by the look of calculating cruelty. Proofs for the attribution of this bust to Alvise are scarcely necessary after all that has been said about his characteristics, which, by any one acquainted with them, can scarcely fail to be recognized at sight; in the cutting of the eyes and mouth, in the lines on the face, in the oval, and in the pose [2].

Since the publication of the first edition of this book I have had the good fortune to discover several other portraits by Alvise. The earliest of these belongs to the Misses Cohen of London, who attribute it to Antonello. It is a bust half the size of life, of a noble Venetian. He is smooth-faced, wears a dark cap over his brown *zazzera*, and a dark coat. He is seen against a green curtain, and to the L. is a twilight grey landscape, with low hills on the horizon, and above them a fascinating stretch of sky. The general character and all the morphological details, such as the eyes and the mouth, for instance, amply establish Alvise's authorship. Indeed I should be at a loss to name a work in which Alvise's style was more

---

[1] The eyes turn a little to L. The hair is brownish auburn, the cap dark, the coat, if I remember, a dark shot tint, the age of the sitter about forty-five.
[2] Of less importance is the life-size bust of a clean-shaven man of about thirty, in the Stanza del Patriarca of the Seminario at Venice, which seems to me to have most of the characteristics of Alvise's last works.

clearly manifested. It must have been painted after Mr. Salting's portrait, and before the one belonging to the Comtesse de Béarn.

Somewhat later than this portrait is the splendid life-size bust of a Venetian senator, in the Stuttgart Gallery (No. 257), there ascribed to Jacopo di Barbari. The confusion is pardonable; for one thing, because, thanks to Morelli's efforts, Barbari is now an object of keen study in Germany. Then here Alvise really is so close to Barbari that it requires more than usual insight and knowledge to see that after all it is by Alvise. The outline of the face, the eyes, and the mouth establish this amply. Perhaps nothing, however, will so help to convince the student that here we are dealing with Alvise and not with Barbari as a comparison with a work by the latter which is singularly close to this head. I refer to the splendid bust of an ecclesiastic at Naples (Sala degli Olandesi e Tedeschi, 51), where it is still ascribed to Holbein, although recognized long ago by Morelli as a Barbari. But I must not leave the Stuttgart head without a reference to its dignity, its power, and its beauty of colouring.

The life-size bust of a smooth-faced man of about fifty, in black cap and coat, which I found at Lord Wemyss' place, Gosford House in Scotland, belongs to the period of the Louvre and the Windsor portraits. It has the same character, and the same clayey, bituminous colouring. But, though powerful, it is not quite as fascinating.

Passing by, as of less interest because of its bad condition, the bust of an elderly, smooth-faced man in the Sterbini collection at Rome, I must draw attention to a very small bust at Modena (No. 319). It is of a mature, smooth-faced man, of fine, alert presence. In every respect it is a characteristic work

ALVISE VIVARINI

[*Contessa de Béarn, Paris*

PORTRAIT OF A MAN

by Alvise, and of a quality which assures its being attributed to Antonello. Thus far, I believe, it has attracted no attention whatever.

Besides these painted portraits that we can safely ascribe to Alvise, several drawings for life-size heads remain to be spoken of, and if we can persuade ourselves that they also are by Alvise, we shall not only have made an important addition to the scanty list of his works, but shall be confirmed in the opinion we already have of his great qualities as a portrait painter. The first of these heads [1] is known to me only in the trustworthy reproduction of Messrs. Braun et Cie., who photographed it when it was exhibited at the Beaux Arts in Paris in 1879 [2]. It is the bust of a smooth-shaven old man, slightly turning to the R. He wears a cap from which his hair falls down in ringlets, and over his tunic he wears a fur-trimmed mantle. The look is a little worn, and the eyes, although wide open, have a pensive, almost absent look. In conception this is so different from Gentile Bellini's well-known portraits that not even for a moment is one tempted to ascribe it to him. Giovanni is almost as rapidly excluded, and then, with the knowledge we have just acquired, the name of Alvise at once suggests itself as the only remaining candidate for the authorship of a head of this character.

Now let us see whether the morphological characteristics that we have found in his other works, particularly in such as are most authenticated, occur in this drawing—for this is the only method whereby we can identify the authorship of drawings. The mouth strikes us at once as being of the character of Alvise's Bonomi-Cereda portrait, and also of the

[1] Both these heads were known to Morelli, who believed them to be by Alvise.
[2] *Beaux Arts*, 198.

Louvre head. The upper eyelids and the brows have deep shadows along the line where they meet, and from this line of coincidence they diverge at a sharp angle, as nearly always in Alvise[1]. The setting of the eyes is nearly the same as in Alvise's *St. Clare*. The outlining of the nose, the prominent nostril, and the line marking the inflation are equally close to the last-named figure. With the same work also must be compared the many lines, furrows, and modellings along the cheeks, the striking likenesses of which a mere glance at the photographs of both will reveal. I call particular attention, however, to the furrow coming from under the cheek-bone, and in part of its course almost parallel with the furrow coming from the nostril and curling around the mouth. These furrows are not mathematically identical in the drawing and in the *St. Clare*—mathematical coincidence is not known in art—but they reveal the same will to observe certain characteristics, the same alertness of attention on the part of the artist. (And this kind of identity, by the way, and not machine-tests, is what we deal with in searching for the author of a work of art.) It is to Alvise, therefore, that we can unhesitatingly ascribe this powerful head, so masterly in execution and so intimately observed. We can even safely date it as a work of about 1495, some years later than the *St. Clare*, than which it is considerably larger in style.

Another head, in charcoal, in the library of Christ Church, Oxford, need not detain us long, partly because it is in bad condition, and therefore less valuable, and partly because the proofs we have found for Alvise's authorship of the Beaux Arts drawing hold true for this one as well. It is the bust of an old man wearing

---

[1] Cf. particularly the *St. Clare* of the Venice Academy.

ALVISE VIVARINI

[Windsor Castle Library

CARTOON FOR HEAD OF AN OLD MAN

a cap over his grey *zazzera*, and an embroidered coat on which occur the letters I M N V. His look is alert and decided. The eyes are even more distinctly Alvisesque than in the last drawing. The hair along the side of the face is treated as in the Layard portrait. But in this Christ Church head, the likeness with Bonsignori becomes almost as confusing as elsewhere in Alvise we have found the resemblance to Barbari. Bonsignori is, however, much more purely lineal in his effects, and very different in minor details, so that he does not seriously interfere in our attribution of this drawing to Alvise; but the fact of its reminding us of Bonsignori points to an earlier date than the Beaux Arts head, to some time in the period between 1480 and 1488, when Bonsignori had just branched off from Alvise, and when they were still close to each other.

Of earlier date than the last two are two other cartoons for life-size busts, both of even more striking quality, and of even clearer Alvisesque character. One, at Windsor, is a rapid sketch, done at a short sitting with powerful charcoal strokes, and telling dabs of white. It is of a smooth-faced, self-assertive, determined man of about fifty, and is ascribed to Lorenzo di Credi. Yet surely I have talked in vain if the student who has followed me thus far fails to recognize in this division of masses, in these eyes, and in this flexed mouth, the spirit and hand of Alvise (Photo. Braun, Windsor, 138). The other cartoon, the ablest perhaps of Alvise's drawings, belongs, or at least, several years ago, did belong, to Monsieur P. Mathey of Paris. Again a smooth-shaved, wide-awake, determined Venetian. It would be little less than an insult to the competent reader to attempt proving that this also was by Alvise. It is so obvious!

Alvise, then, at the end of our study of his works,

reveals himself to us as an artist of great poetical and interpretative power, endowed with a peculiar feeling for beauty and for composition, a careful observer of the human face, because it is so important as a vehicle of expression, a careful student of light and shadow and perspective, because the one is indispensable in composition and in producing effects of grandeur and noble surroundings, and the other is almost the only means whereby a painter may hope to introduce magic into his pictures. Such studies as were not necessary to the interpretation of the face, or to its beauty; such as were not necessary for harmonious and noble composition and for the effects of light which colour and determine our moods, Alvise neglected. He belongs, therefore, to that great class of painters, all of them second-rate, when severely judged, who are poets and thinkers expressing themselves in form and colour—who at times tempt us to believe that they have not chosen the best vehicle for their expression; for, on the one hand, they overload their art with what it carries reluctantly, and, on the other, they fail to make use of its best potentialities. In a word, they are fundamentally illustrators—great and sublime as you please—and only by accident, as it were, are they painters. But inferior to the Bellini as we must grant Alvise to have been, we must insist upon his independence of them, and perhaps in the eighties of the fifteenth century, when he was in the full activity of his genius, surrounded by pupils and assistants, the head of the school of painting which continued the deep-rooted traditions of Muranese art, the inferiority was not so striking as it now appears. We have seen that around him centre such important and interesting figures in Venetian art as Jacopo di Barbari, Francesco Bonsignori, Bartolommeo Montagna, and Cima da Conegliano. It has not been my purpose to write a treatise

ALVISE VIVARINI

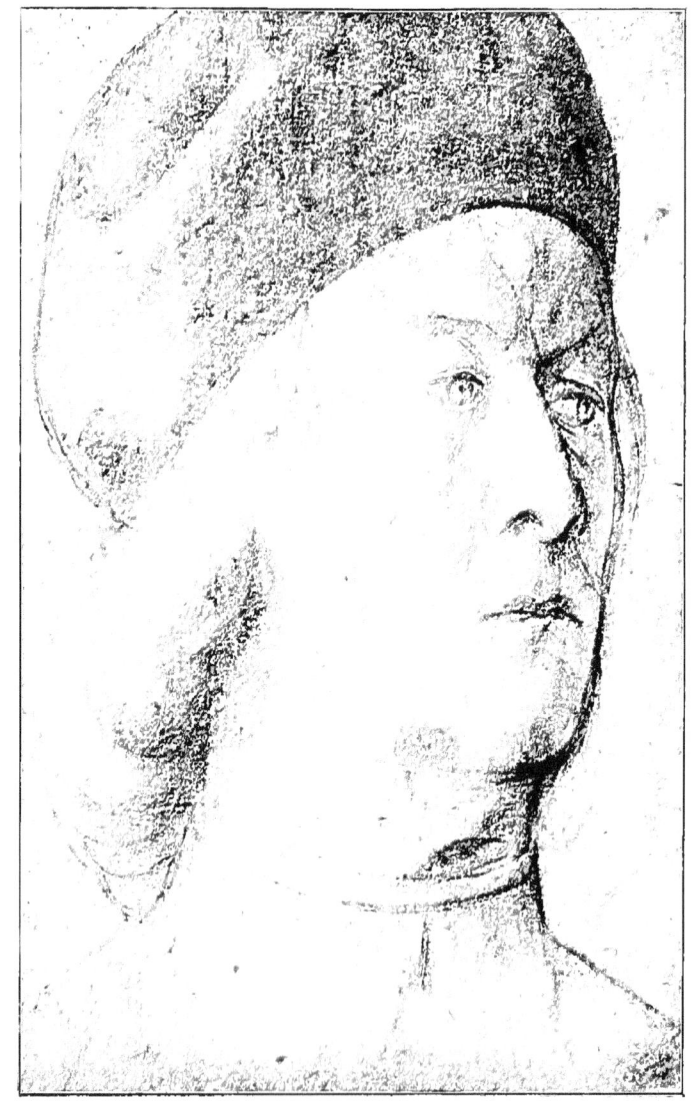

[*P. Mathy, Paris*

PORTRAIT OF A MAN

THE ARTIST AND HIS ANTECEDENTS

on the school of Alvise, or I should have had other artists, such as Boccaccio Boccaccino[1] and Andrea Solario, to discuss, and still other questions to consider, such as the sympathy that seems to have existed between the pupils of Alvise and those of Gentile Bellini. My intention has been only to prove how flourishing the school of the Vivarini still was at the end of the fifteenth century, and what kind of a man was at the head of it, so as to remove all apparent incongruities, all important objections to my connecting Lotto with the same school.

VIII.—THE PURPOSE OF KNOWING THE ARTIST'S ANTECEDENTS

That all such objections have been cleared away, that I have established Lotto's descent from Alvise Vivarini, I trust I may at this point take for granted. It now remains for me to justify all the pains I have taken in demonstrating this thesis, and all the patience I have required on the part of my readers, by answering the question: What difference does it make whether Giovanni Bellini or Alvise Vivarini was Lotto's first master?

In the beginning of this long chapter on Lotto's

---

[1] In the *Santa Conversazione* by Boccaccino in the Venice Academy (No. 600), the hand of the Baptist is taken with scarcely a change from Alvise. As to Solario, the oval of his *Madonna* of 1495, painted in Murano but now in the Brera, is Alvisesque. His *Madonna with the Music-making Angels*, belonging to Dr. J. P. Richter of London, is almost as Alvisesque as any other picture not actually by Alvise himself that we have mentioned in connexion with him. Solario's *Cross-bearing Christ*, in the Museo Civico at Modena, has been attributed to Bonsignori also. Finally, in both of Solario's portraits in the National Gallery, the mouths are Alvisesque, and, as in Alvise, the nostrils are prominent with the inflation firmly outlined, and the cheeks a trifle dewlapped. A further proof of Solario's close connexion with Alvise may be seen in the fact that Messrs. Crowe and Cavalcaselle could mistake the one for the other, as they have done in Mr. Salting's portrait.

descent, part of this question was already answered. We there decided that it was not conceivable that Lotto, if he had been under Bellini, the fellow pupil of Giorgione, would have been able to resist the influence of Giorgione, which, as we granted, neither Palma nor Titian had been able to resist. We came to this decision because the mere power of reaction it would presuppose on Lotto's part would necessitate the hypothesis that physically and intellectually Lotto was far more robust, that he was far more insensitive to influence, to his surroundings, than Titian—an hypothesis in flagrant contradiction with what we already know of Lotto, and even more with what we are still going to find out about him. 'If Giorgione had such an overwhelming influence on his fellow pupils,' it may be asked, 'would he not have exerted it on outsiders as well?' My answer is that he did not. The rivalry, and I must add enmity, between the Alviseschi and the Bellineschi remained unchanged—we have no reason for thinking otherwise—until Alvise's death; and it is not likely that the apprentices of the one had much intercourse with those of the other. And that Giorgione for some time remained confined to a narrow circle is evident from the fact that Dürer on his second visit to Venice, in 1505, makes no mention of him. Indeed, it seems as if it were only his death that drew universal attention to his genius, and as if, there being no longer a dread of his rivalry, every one was eager to be acknowledged his heir, and to have the inheritance estimated at its full value.

But by this time, in 1510, Lotto was no longer in Venice, and had been away, as we have seen, most of the time since 1503, at any rate. That he had been absent from Venice even before this date and so far south as Recanati, the archives of that town afford every reason to believe. On the hypothesis, therefore, of their not having been fellow pupils, there is nothing strange in the fact that as a young man Lotto was uninfluenced by Giorgione.

A similar difficulty, even if smaller, would remain if we left Giorgione out of the question. To be so independent of Giovanni Bellini as Lotto was, and yet to have been his pupil, would imply not only a greater power of reaction on Lotto's part than we can credit him with, but a conscious archaistic purpose, such as it would be startling, if not incredible, to suppose to have been cherished by any painter born in 1480. But all such difficulties are removed; we need not ascribe to him gigantic powers of reacting against influences, when we know that in his youth Lotto had little, if any, close connexion with Bellini and his school. All that otherwise would seem strange and marvellously original in Lotto takes a more natural aspect when we have seen how much he owes to Alvise Vivarini.

Now, one of the principal objects of the kind of criticism that we are pursuing is the discovery of the data that will enable us to form a fair estimate of the artist we are studying. This end we can accomplish only when in the work of art we have unmasked the artist. Every work of art that our eye can light upon is a combination of elements: some of them the artist gets from the outside; others he himself contributes. Our estimate of the artist is largely determined by his manner of acquiring the outside elements, by the proportion in his work of outside to personal factors, and by the kind of assimilation that has taken place between them. Certain artists suffer rather than acquire outside elements, and these are of course the artists of the least personality and the least interest. Others, endowed with greater powers of assimilation, pick and choose from the motives in favour in their youth all that they can assimilate and make their own ; and these artists, in whose works there is scarcely an element, as such, which has not come from the outside, are, if not positively the greatest, at least the most delightful, the Raphaels and Giorgiones. Others still are irreconcilably personal. They too cannot dispense with outside elements, but they choose them from far as well as from near, from the past as well as from the present. This is the class which comprises a few of the very greatest artists that have ever existed, artists of the stamp of Donatello and Michelangelo, and also—different though they are—all those artists who lacked the Titanic power necessary to give body to an entirely personal vision of the universe, and therefore remained fanciful, suggestive, sympathetic, but never great.

To this last category we should have to relegate Lorenzo Lotto, if, while lacking Michelangelo's power of persuading people of its reality, he yet had had a way of seeing and of registering his vision as personal as Michelangelo's. And that it was as idiosyncratic we should be constrained to acknowledge if we were bound to believe that Lotto, as the pupil of Bellini, was as uninfluenced by his master's teaching as Michelangelo by Ghirlandajo's.

Happily we are under no such constraint. We have seen that as a painter Lotto was the pupil of Alvise Vivarini, and that this theory of his descent accounts for the great divergence between his art and the art of Giorgione and Titian. As we pursue our study of him, we shall see more and more clearly to what an extent Lotto continued the habits, the traditions, the views of the Muranese artists into the sixteenth century, not slavishly, not even as Alvise himself would have done had he lived on another half-century, but as a man born in 1480, who formed his artistic habits under Alvise and took his first view of life from him and his like.

'But, having granted,' it may be said, 'that Lotto was not great, you are now at the pains to prove that he was not even supremely original. Why bother our heads about him then?' Because, being, as he was, the product of a school of art, distinct from the Bellinis' and not quite so much in touch with the dominant tendencies of the time, yet active and popular, and therefore representative of certain other tendencies of the time, we may be sure that he continued to appeal to the spiritual descendants of the people to whom his master had appealed, and that his works therefore were not a mere caprice, a mere accident, but representative, they also, of certain prevailing although, it is true, not dominant tendencies in his own times. If neither supremely original nor supremely powerful, Lotto was at the least representative, and my claim for him is that he was, as we shall see by-and-by, the representative of a very interesting minority.

Having established Lotto's descent from Alvise Vivarini, seen whence he got his first start, what habits of visualizing and painting, what ideals went to mould him as an artist, we are now prepared to pursue our study of the rest of his career, and we shall be able to advance all the faster for the encumbrance of false traditions that we have thrown over, and for the knowledge we have gained of the direction his art comes from and must tend to continue.

CHAPTER III

THE TRANSITION

1508–1517

1508-1512. EXCEPT for a pregnant notice presently to be mentioned, the years between 1508, the date of the Recanati altar-piece, and 1512, the date of the Jesi *Entombment*, form a gap in Lotto's career which no existing work of his helps us to bridge. But he emerges at the end of these three or four years with his manner of painting surprisingly changed. From comparative dryness and sallowness, he has passed to a fluid vehicle and a gay, blond, almost golden tone, so that the works of 1512–1516 have, both in colour and vehicle, every resemblance to Alvise's last paintings, particularly to the *Resurrection* in San Giovanni in Bragora at Venice. The change in Lotto is therefore to be explained as one necessitated by inherent tendency. It seems by no means to have come in a flash, for we have seen, in the Asolo and Recanati altar-pieces, Lotto's vehicle becoming more fluid and his colouring blonder. The real difficulty is to explain why he did not come to this manner sooner. I would suggest that he acquired his rudiments from Alvise before this master himself changed to the manner of his last paintings, and that Lotto could not keep pace with this advance either because of his own mental or manual immaturity, or because that at a date so early as 1497 he was already shifting for himself at Recanati.

A few years ago, when poetical similes borrowed 1508–1512. from popular botany seemed amply to explain all the casualties of artistic development, it would have sufficed to say that in such and such a year Lotto, who had hitherto remained shut up like a bud, blossomed and ripened into the Lotto of the Bergamask period. The trouble with the vegetable analogy is the fact that a man has a much larger number of possible moves than a plant. Of a plant we can say that, if it matures at all, it must become precisely such and such, but of a man we can make no such prediction. All we can say is that given a certain temperament *plus* a certain mental, emotional, and manual training, the product (the artist) will *tend* to act and to express himself in a way that is determined. But his training does not cease; he keeps coming in contact with other influences, each one of which tends to modify the product that was the adolescent artist. And the nature of the new influences that will be brought to bear upon the adolescent, the young man, the mature man who has not yet woven about himself the web of habits which makes him impervious to all newness, is what we cannot possibly foresee. Sympathetic forces, such, that is, as are sufficiently like to be easily assimilated and sufficiently unlike to be complementary, may be beneficent and promote healthy growth; on the other hand, overwhelming forces may overtake the young artist and make him a mere satellite; other forces still may simply blight him, or call out and favour certain sides of himself that keep him in a backwater and prevent him from pushing out into the full current of the life of his day.

Lotto might, as well as not, have fallen under influences which would have counteracted his inherent tendencies, but he seems to have escaped such, for

1508–1512. after losing sight of him for a few years, we find him again with all these tendencies developed and ripened.

It is conceivable of course that he remained quiet somewhere in the Marches, thus escaping all influences. It is a temptation also to believe that he returned to Venice and there devoted himself to the study of Giorgione's works. But I find no convincing reminiscence of Giorgione in those of Lotto's pictures that we are now to consider, and it is more than questionable whether Giorgione would have permitted, not to say encouraged, the ripening of Lotto's own tendencies, Giorgione's vehicle and scheme of colour being very different from Lotto's[1].

Now it seems that Lotto's inherent tendency towards a slow vehicle and a blond, golden tone not only could have met with no interference, but must actually have received distinct encouragement, and such encouragement he could have got only from one of two sources: either from Perugino directly, the Perugino of 1508–1512, be it remembered, a painter of a golden tone, employing a slow medium, or the still Peruginesque Raphael of the *Stanza della Segnatura*.

Such an hypothesis would seem preposterous if Lotto had been a painter chained to the Rialto, never moving from it, but it becomes less startling when we realize that the very contrary was the case. We know that in 1506–1508 he was at Recanati, a town already within the range of Umbrian influence, and we know even more (here comes in the one notice which we have about Lotto for the years between 1508 and 1512)—

[1] That Lotto would have felt the difference and tried to bridge it, we must believe, considering that a little later, in the Alzano altar-piece, we find him trying to imitate the Giorgionesque vehicle and colour schemes as they were understood by Palma.

we know that in *1509 Lotto actually was in Rome, and there not merely as a pilgrim or sightseer, but as a painter employed in the Vatican, where Raphael at the selfsame time was painting the Stanza della Segnatura.* 1508-1512.

The notice in question is a document in the Corsini Library in Rome, which states that on March 9, 1509, Lotto received a hundred ducats in prepayment for frescoes to be executed in the upper floor of the Vatican[1]. Whether Lotto did or did not execute these frescoes, is by itself no longer a question of interest, seeing that no trace of them remains. But we are greatly concerned to know whether he did or did not remain in Rome, not only because we then should know where to place him at an important period in his life, about which, hitherto, we have known nothing, but also because if he did remain, the hypothesis that he was encouraged in his own tendencies by the example of Raphael would be fully confirmed. Documents are silent on the subject, but fortunately these are not our only sources of information. The work of art itself must be compelled to tell us much, if not all, of what we want to know about its author. Let us then consult Lotto's works next in date to 1509, and others even later, to see whether in them we do not discover Raphaelesque reminiscences, and, if we do discover them, and trace them back to definite bits of Raphael's works, we shall, from our knowledge of the dates of these, be able to tell just how long Lotto remained in Rome. March 9, 1509.

Turning, then, to Lotto's next dated work, the *Entombment* of 1512 at Jesi, we notice that the landscape, one or two of the figures, and the little angels in the sky are Peruginesque in the way 1512.

---

[1] Lermolieff, *Galerien zu München und Dresden*, p. 62, note. Cavalcaselle e Crowe, *Raffaelle* (Italian Edition), vol. ii, p. 11.

1512. that Raphael still is in the *Stanza della Segnatura*. The *Transfiguration*, the fresco of *St. Vincent*, and the little *St. James* at Recanati, all of the same date, bear unmistakable traces of Raphael's influence. In the *Transfiguration* the cherubs are obviously Raphaelesque. In the *St. Vincent*, the *putti* nestling close to the saint are not only clearly Raphaelesque, but recall the various *putti* in the allegorical and historical subjects of the ceiling in the *Stanza*. St. Vincent's drapery has folds in loops ending not in one, but in two small curves, a distinct peculiarity of the Umbrians. In all these pictures the mouths, the hands, and even the poses recall the *Disputation* and the *School of Athens*. Lotto, therefore, could not have left Rome before the last fresco was finished; but we may, indeed, safely assume that he was in Rome to an even later date, up to some time in 1512. The reason for this supposition is the fact that only in 1512 did Raphael execute the *Expul-
1524. sion of Heliodorus*. Now in a fresco of about 1524 at Credaro, near Bergamo, Lotto painted a horseman so very similar to Raphael's celestial horseman in the *Expulsion* that he must have been not only acquainted, but intimately acquainted, with Raphael's figure. This acquaintance Lotto could not have acquired (he catches the spirit too well to have taken the figure from a drawing copied by some one else) except at the time of its execution. Allowing for the possibility that Lotto returned from Recanati to Rome for a short visit early in 1513, he could not have visited Rome again before painting the Credaro fresco; for in May, 1513, he was already at Bergamo, a neighbourhood which he did not leave for any length of time for more than ten years. It is highly probable, therefore, that Lotto remained in Rome until the *Expulsion of Heliodorus* was finished, or, allowing for the fact that he

could not have helped knowing Raphael personally, until the drawings for it were ready.

The years, then, from 1508 to 1512 cease to be a blank. Lotto must have spent most of this time in Rome in the midst of an artistic activity which has scarcely been paralleled since. Raphael was painting in the *Stanza*, Michelangelo in the Sixtine Chapel, and Bramante building St. Peter's, while surrounding them were a hundred architects, painters, and sculptors, all men of talent, and some, like Sodoma and Sebastiano del Piombo, themselves men of nearly Lotto's own level, and touching him closely on certain sides of his nature. But much as he may have come in contact with most of the artists then in Rome, and known their work, he yet, on the whole, keeps his independence. Although in his frescoes at San Michele and in the intarsias at Bergamo of 1524-1527, we find distinct reminiscences of Michelangelo. Michelangelo seems to have been to him suggestive as illustration merely. But Raphael, on the contrary, encouraged Lotto's own inherent tendencies, and even made them go a trifle too far on his, Raphael's, own road, so that Lotto soon recoiled, ceasing to be so golden in tone as he is in the works of 1512. Hence the works of about this year have in them an obvious element of unnaturalness, as if while painting them the artist was not quite himself, and had tried to take hold of more than he could carry. Let us now examine them one by one:

1508-1512.

JESI, LIBRARY. ENTOMBMENT (from San Floriano).

Inscribed: LAVRENTIVS LOTVS MDXII. On wood, 2·90 m. h., 1·98 m. w.

The movement is not only dramatic, but passionate to the last degree. The colouring is light and flowing,

1512.

1512. and the tone golden, almost as in Perugino's works of the same time, although Lotto, it must be added, is much blonder. The feathery trees on the sea-cliff and one of the Marys in the middle distance are more than accidentally Peruginesque, and do, in fact, betray the influence of Raphael. The St. John, although a Lottesque type, has also a touch of the Raphaelesque superimposed. Distinctly reminiscent of Raphael are the baby angels in the sky.

RECANATI, MUNICIPIO. TRANSFIGURATION (from the church at Castelnuovo).

Of the signature only LAVRENTIVS is legible. On wood, arched, 3 m. h., 2·03 m. w. Life-size figures. Darkened by candle-smoke, and repainted.

Mentioned by Vasari, who describes three *predelle* which have disappeared.

Photographed by Anderson, Rome.

1512–1513. The treatment is identical with the *Entombment* at Jesi, but the profuse gilding and the stunted figures, here appearing for the first time, but characteristic of Lotto's less careful work, spoil the picture. John is the same as in the *Entombment*. The great, even exaggerated play of hands, not surprising in a pupil of Alvise Vivarini, is due to the encouragement given to this tendency by Raphael's example in the *Disputa*. Even in shape, the hands of John, Peter, and Elijah tend to assimilate themselves to the Raphaelesque type. Elijah has a suggestion of the Ambrose, and of still other figures in the *Disputa*.

RECANATI, SAN DOMENICO. SECOND ALTAR L. ST. VINCENT IN GLORY.

Fresco, life-size.
Photographed by Anderson, Rome.
This fresco is identical in treatment with the *Trans-*

[*Jesi Library*

THE ENTOMBMENT

figuration, so that there can be no doubt about its being 1512-
of the same date; but it is a much happier work—on 1513.
the whole, the best of this series, well composed, and
well constructed. The little angels trumpeting in the
sky are Alvisesque, as in Alvise's Frari altar-piece; but
Vincent himself, and the *putti* playing around him,
betray the influence of Raphael. His features and the
modelling of his face recall faces in the *Disputa*, as of
the Stephen, for instance. He points upward with the
gesture of the first figure on the R. in the *Disputa*,
or the Plato in the *School of Athens*. The *putti*
have a distinct resemblance to those in the allegories of
Poetry and *Justice* on the ceiling of the *Stanza della
Segnatura*.

RECANATI, ORATORIO DI SAN GIACOMO. ST. JAMES.

St. James, dressed as a pilgrim, stands in a pretty
landscape, holding an open book in his R. hand, and
a staff in his L. He seems to be searching for something. At his feet lie his hat and his scrip. Same
characteristics as the last works.

On wood, 22 cm. h., 16 cm. w.

Photographed by Anderson, Rome.

MILAN, BRERA, PINAC. OGGIONO, NO. 16. ASSUMPTION OF VIRGIN.

On wood, 29 cm. h., 59 cm. w. Evidently part of
a *predella*.

Photographed by Marcozzi, Milan.

The Madonna is but slightly changed from the one
in the Asolo *Assumption* of 1506. The figures of the
Apostles are stunted, as in the Recanati *Transfiguration*, and the St. James in both is identical. The play
of hands is very remarkable, and, on the whole, natural.
The outlines of the landscape and the feathery trees

1512-1513. have much in common with the Jesi *Entombment*—a distinct Umbrian look. The colouring and the drapery also bring this little panel close to the pictures of 1512. It probably formed part of an altar-piece of about this date.

Even before the first edition of this book went to press I was convinced that a half-ruined portrait bust of a smooth-faced man in the Doetsch collection was by Lotto. I also knew that the person represented was the one who passes for Piero Soderini, the Gonfaloniere of Florence, famous for his political incompetence. I cannot now understand why I failed to speak of this in the first edition.

LONDON. DOETSCH COLLECTION (formerly). BUST OF PIERO SODERINI.

Life-size.

A number of versions exist, all of them copies, as in the Uffizi (a very poor one), in the Panciatichi and Bartolommei Collections at Florence. The last two are attributed to Leonardo. Even this attribution is not without significance, for it amounts to a confession on the part of the old connoisseurs that the portrait was not Florentine. That it is by Lotto I decide from the conception of the whole and the drawing of every feature, as well as from what appears of the ear, and the greyish tone of the colouring. That it really is a portrait of Soderini we may believe on the strength of an old tradition. Thus in the official life of Piero, written for his descendants by Silvano Razzi and published in Padua in 1737, the Doetsch version is reproduced without a change in the head.

It may be asked, how did Lotto, a Venetian, come to portray the Gonfaloniere for life of Florence? The

[Formerly in the Doetsch Collection

PORTRAIT OF PIETRO SODERINI

answer is easy. Without knowing who the sitter was, the Alvisesque character of his portrait would have led me to believe that Lotto could not have painted it much after 1512. Now we know that a day or two after the sack of Prato, Soderini, having timidly given up his office, went to Siena, and then to Loreto, and Ancona, whence, towards the end of October, 1512, he embarked for his exile at Ragusa. What more natural than that his friends demanded his portrait before he left them, perhaps never to return! Lotto was then, as we know, near Ancona, and there was no other painter in those parts to put beside him. To whom else under the circumstances could Soderini have sat as well? Lotto thereupon painted the bust that used to be in the Doetsch collection, and very likely more than one version. As a portraitist no Florentine except Leonardo of those then active was a match for Lotto. No wonder therefore that his effigy of Piero Soderini became the standard one.

1512–1513.

The original black chalk cartoon for this head, cut down to its outlines and much effaced, is now at Chatsworth in the Duke of Devonshire's Collection.

Photographed by Braun, Chatsworth, 84.

Lotto makes a contract with Alessandro Martinengo, the grandson of Bartolommeo Colleoni, to paint for five hundred gold ducats the altar-piece now in San Bartolommeo at Bergamo. The document is reproduced as an appendix to vol. i of Locatelli's *Illustri Bergamaschi*, Bergamo, 1867.

May, 1513

In the Church of Santo Spirito at Bergamo is the tomb of Luigi Tasso, Bishop of Recanati, assassinated while on a visit home to Bergamo in September, 1520. It is a temptation to connect this bishop with Lotto's going (perhaps directly) from Recanati to Bergamo. But unfortunately Luigi Tasso was not made Bishop of Recanati before January 16, 1516, when Lotto was already well established at Bergamo. The bare possibility of such a connexion remains, however, but it would take me too far away from our subject to discuss the question here. The curious are referred to Moroni's *Dizionario di Erudizione Storico-Ecclesiastico*, Venice, 1846 *circa*, articles 'Macerata' and 'Parenzo.'

Although the contract for the San Bartolommeo altar-piece was signed in May, 1513, the picture itself was not executed before 1516, the date which it bears. Large and elaborate as this work is, it could not have occupied Lotto for three whole years. As a matter of fact, four other works (if no more) were executed in the interval. A *St. Jerome* painted in 1515, formerly in the Mündler Collection[1] in Paris, and now not traceable, I have never seen. I also have not seen the sketch for the San Bartolommeo altar-piece, but according to Morelli[2] this sketch, on wood, four feet high, and two wide, bore the inscription 'LAV. LOT. IN 10. PAV. PINXIT': 'Lorenzo Lotto painted in San Giovanni e Paolo.' It is certain, therefore, that between signing the contract for the altar-piece and executing it, Lotto visited Venice. (It also follows, by the way, that he no longer could have had close family ties at home, or he would not have been living in a monastery). But did he go to Venice at once after signing the contract? To answer this question, we must examine all the works that appear to have been painted between 1513 and 1516.

Let us first take up the picture dated 1515 in the National Gallery, which contains the portraits of Agostino and Niccolò della Torre. In 1515 Agostino was professing medicine at Padua and Niccolò was

---

[1] Lermolieff, *Galerien Borghese und Doria*, p. 391.
[2] Id., *Galerien zu München und Dresden*, p. 68, note 2.

living in Bergamo. No one with a feeling for composition can doubt for an instant that Agostino was originally intended to be alone on the canvas, as he occupies all of it that a well-composed single bust ought to occupy, while Niccolò is ungracefully crowded into the background. Morelli's inference seems thus to be well founded that Lotto, on his return from Venice to Bergamo, stopped at Padua and painted the portrait of Agostino, which he brought to Niccolò at Bergamo, who thereupon had his own portrait added. If this inference is correct, then Lotto did not return from Venice to Bergamo before 1515. On his return he must have gone to work at once upon the San Bartolommeo altar-piece, needing all his time to finish so huge a work for 1516. The style of this altar-piece and of the Della Torre portraits also confirms the supposition that they were executed the one immediately after the other, for they betray an unbroken continuity of artistic purpose. Now there is still another work which critics have always assigned to a date prior to 1516, and, as it is a picture not only too large to have been crowded in between the two works we have just been discussing, but of an altogether different style, different technique, and entirely different purpose, it follows that it must have been painted some time during the interval between 1512 and 1515. If my hypothesis about Lotto's not leaving Rome until 1512 is correct, and if we allow for the time it must have taken to paint the works of that date at Jesi and Recanati, he could scarcely have come to Bergamo before 1513. The time Lotto must have spent in Venice, makes it probable, on the other hand, that he left Bergamo in 1514. At some time, then, in 1513–1514, he must have painted for Alzano the picture which is now going to engage our attention; and it was this work, in all probability, that occupied him

1513–1516.

1513-1516. between the date upon which he signed the contract for the San Bartolommeo altar-piece and his journey to Venice.

We remember that in the pictures of 1512, Lotto makes the impression of a man who was not quite sure of himself. The influence of Raphael had made his own equilibrium a trifle unstable, and, although he was sufficiently self-centred to make it certain that he would in the end completely recover himself, he was meanwhile in a state of oscillation, which made him more than ordinarily sensitive to other attractions, and more than ordinarily ready to make new experiments. The experiment that we find him trying in the Alzano altar-piece is the technique and methods of painting as well as the artistic ideals of Giovanni Bellini, as they were kindled into an intenser activity by Giorgione and struggling for existence in the slow, placid, and somewhat rustic temperament of Palma.

ALZANO, NEAR BERGAMO, PARISH CHURCH. ASSASSINATION OF ST. PETER MARTYR (formerly in San Pietro Martire).

On wood, arched, figures life-size.
Photographed by Alinari.

1513-1514. The general tone is rich, with the colours fused, the *impasto* thick, and the vehicle fluid, exactly as in Palma. Even in conception the picture lacks Lotto's usual vivacity and psychological grasp of a situation. The assassins are almost as placid as Palma's *Jacob and Rachel* (Dresden): the Martyr has a Palmesque pose, and the infrequent folds of his heavy drapery are in Palma's manner: while the God the Father, the cherubs, and the angels are, even in type, scarcely to be distinguished from Palma's, and the landscape, with its

Alinari photo.] [*Bergamo, Cathedral of Alzano Maggiore*

ST. PETER MARTYR

dense green foliage, the fig-tree in the foreground, and the soft slope of the mountain range in the distance, suggests Palma in every touch [1]. It is a beautiful picture as pattern and structure, but the spectator cannot help feeling a certain chill before it, occasioned by the artist's state of mind while painting it. A lack of clear purpose, an empiricism without great confidence in the result, seem to have overtaken Lotto at the moment. But fortunately he swung back from this disturbing influence almost at once, for, although later on we shall find him making another approach to Palma—this time very slight—distinct traces of that master's influence are otherwise scarcely to be perceived in Lotto after the Alzano picture.

That the extraordinary approach to Palma, visible in the *Assassination of Peter Martyr*, took place before the painting of the San Bartolommeo altarpiece, rather than at any later time, we can ascertain not only from Lotto's probable state of peculiar sensitiveness at the moment of rebound from Raphael, but even from more indisputable facts. In the first place, Lotto's evolution from 1515 to 1527 is continuous, undetermined by any outside influences, and leaves no room for such an anomaly as the *Peter Martyr*. In 1527, when there is another approach to Palma, it is not only slight, but it approaches another Palma, the painter of peculiarly blond Madonnas and courtesans. The Palma, on the contrary, whose influence is manifest in the *Peter Martyr*, is the Palma who is just emerging from his first into his second manner, who is nearly in the stage at which we find him in the *Santa Barbara* panels at Santa Maria Formosa in Venice. We have, in further proof of our hypothesis,

1513-1514.

---

[1] The woodmen cutting down trees in the forest suggest the Bellinesque *Assassination of Peter Martyr* in the National Gallery, a picture which Lotto may have had in mind while painting his.

1513-1514. the fact already noticed by Morelli, that in pictures of Palma's middle manner, such as the Naples *Santa Conversazione*, the Louvre *Nativity*, and the Dresden *Holy Family with St. Catherine*—to mention only striking cases—the counter-influence of Lotto is visible not only in the greater contrasts of light and shade and in certain peculiarly Lottesque colours (the violet, for example), but also in the more delicate types and in the subtler feeling. As all these pictures must have been painted soon after 1514, they go to prove that Palma had come in contact with Lotto at about this time. Finally, a picture comes to our aid, not by Lotto himself, but a copy of an original by him, now lost:

ROME, VILLA BORGHESE, No. 157. SANTA CONVERSAZIONE (Copy).

The Madonna sits under an orange-tree, with SS. Christina and Barbara to the R. and L., the one recommending a female and the other a male donor.

Canvas, 1·35 m. h., 1·91 m. w.

Photographed by Anderson, 4381.

That the original of this picture must have been by Lotto, is attested by the still Alvisesque oval of the Madonna's face, by the resemblance in pose and dress of the St. Barbara to the St. Vito in the Recanati altar-piece, by the bit of landscape between St. Barbara and the Madonna, so like, as Morelli already pointed out, the landscape in the Asolo *Assumption*, by the Madonna's L. hand, identical in form with the hand held out by the St. Catherine to receive the ring, in the Munich picture, and, finally, by the purely Lottesque character of the female donor, who anticipates such portraits as that of a Lady, in the Carrara collection at Bergamo, or the Elizabeta Rota, in the Berlin picture representing *Christ Taking Leave of His*

BORGHESE 'SANTA CONVERSAZIONE' 115

Mother. Even the carving on the pedestal of the Madonna's seat recalls Barbari and Alvise, and, like the heir of Murano-Squarcionesque traditions that he was, Lotto puts an orange and its leaf in the foreground. But the composition—the Madonna under a tree, with the figures arranged as in a *Santa Conversazione*—is not natural to Lotto but to Palma, and the Child is not only purely Palmesque in type, but has a movement of drawing back, such as Palma not infrequently gives Him[1]. Now, as the comparatively early character of this work is sufficiently established by its obvious relation in essentials to Lotto's other early works, and as its having been painted later than the pictures of 1512 follows from the comparatively advanced character of the portraits (the donors), we are obliged to assign the original of this *Santa Conversazione* also to the period between 1512 and 1515. But it has more affinities with Lotto's early works than are found in the Alzano altar-piece, and consequently must have been painted earlier. The Alzano picture, we remember, was as Palmesque as a work by Lotto could possibly be. In the picture we are now considering, only the general arrangement and the Child are Palmesque. The original of this Borghese copy must have been painted, therefore, when Lotto first felt the influence of Palma, and as it is clear that it just antedates the Alzano altar-piece, it follows that the first close contact between Lotto and Palma occurred at the same time—that is to say, at some time in the year 1513[2].

1513-1514.

[1] Cf. *Putti*, in Palma's Venice Academy *Assumption* (No. 315), and in most of his *Sante Conversazioni*, particularly the one at Naples.

[2] While the original of this admirable work is lost, the original sketch thereof remains, and is now in the collection of Lord Pembroke at Wilton House. It is a drawing in black chalk heightened with white (reproduced as plate 11 in Messrs. P. and D. Colnaghi's publication of Lord Pembroke's drawings). It is hasty, and, as usual with Lotto, of small value as draughtsmanship. The differences are significant and even

1513-1514.
The question still remains where this contact took place. I am inclined to think it must have been at Bergamo itself. Palma was not only a Bergamask, but seems to have made a longish visit home in the middle of his comparatively short career[1]. The Alzano altar-piece, moreover, is on wood, and not likely to have been painted far away from the spot.

But wherever Palma and Lotto first exerted a strong influence one upon the other, it could not have been much later or earlier than the spring of 1513. Now as the Alzano *Assassination of Peter Martyr* is not only thoroughly Palmesque, but has no other Palmesque works following it, we may safely assume that it came at the end of a close intercourse with Palma; and that the intercourse must have lasted a number of months we can infer from the thoroughness of the Palmesque saturation in the Alzano picture. This work, therefore, was probably painted early in 1514.

Since the publication of the first edition of this book I have come to the conclusion that the splendid bust of a man of about thirty, ascribed to Giovanni Bellini in the Naples Gallery, is a work that Lotto must have painted between the Alzano altar-piece and the Della Torre portraits.

NAPLES. BUST OF MAN OF ABOUT THIRTY, wearing a four-cornered white hat, and a white coat.

Life-size.

Photographed by Alinari, Florence.

The proportions of the face, the drawings of the eyebrows and eyelids, the inflated nostrils, the cut of

amusing. Thus in the sketch both the Virgin and the Child devote their entire attention to the donor, while in the painting his wife gets the best of it. Of course, the elaborate costuming is absent from the sketch.

[1] Palma's Polyptychs in the Bergamask mountain villages, Serina and Peghera, in every probability painted on the spot, are in his style of about this time.

[Alinari photo.] [Naples Museum.

PORTRAIT OF A MAN

the mouth are all Alvisesque and Lottesque. More 1513-
especially characteristic of Lotto at just this period is 1514.
the golden flesh-colour, and the rather slow vehicle in
which the work is painted. In conception it is in every
way Lottesque and worthy of the master. Original,
searching, yet a dreamer's is the character presented.
Its next of kin among Lotto's other works is the
drawing of a young man, in the Uffizi, and the Berlin
portrait, No. 320.

The thoroughly Palmesque character of the Alzano
altar-piece, surprising as it is, and revealing to what
a remarkable degree Lotto was sensitive to influence,
is yet not so startling as is the absence of even the
slightest trace of Palma in Lotto's next work, the
Della Torre portraits in the National Gallery, which
I have already mentioned:

LONDON, NATIONAL GALLERY, No. 699. PORTRAITS OF
AGOSTINO AND NICCOLÒ DELLA TORRE.

Inscribed: L. LOTVS. P. 1515. On canvas, 85 cm. h.,
69 cm. w. Figures life-size, more than half length.
Photographed by Morelli, London, and by Braun.

Neither in conception nor technique is there in this 1515.
canvas a trace of Palma. The vehicle is the Alvisesque
one, and the flesh-colour blond brown, as if Lotto had
never been in contact with Palma. And, although he
must have painted the portrait of Agostino while
returning from Venice, where he could not have helped
seeing Giorgione's pictures, it contains no suggestion
of Giorgione. Agostino has not in the least that
look of perfect self-possession, either unconscious or
distinctly militant, which we are accustomed to find
in the Giorgionesque portrait. He is posed and
visualised in a way that clearly recalls Alvise, and his
mouth is Alvisesque; but he is interpreted—we catch

1515. the man's character by his manner of drawing breath—as Lotto alone among the Venetians of this time could interpret.

Of the same date, because of the same technique, and of the same strictly Alvisesque character, must be the excellent portrait recently acquired (1901) by Prof. R. von Kaufmann.

BERLIN.   PROF. RICHARD VON KAUFMANN.

Bust of a jeweller seen behind a parapet against the sky and trees, holding in his L. hand a box full of rings, and in his R. a single specimen. He is a cheerful, genial, shrewd townsman.

Canvas, 73 cm. h., 63 cm. w.

This work is not signed, and needs no signature, bearing as it does Lotto's sign mark on every square inch of its surface.

Still of exclusively Alvisesque character are two further portraits, which therefore shall find mention here, and as they are of slight importance that mention shall be brief.

MILAN.   SIGNOR B. CRESPI.

Small bust, scraped down nearly to the panel, of Niccola Leonicinio of Lonigo.

LONDON.   DOETSCH COLLECTION (formerly).

Bust of a man with a close-cut beard, holding open in his left hand a partition of music.

Canvas, $18\frac{3}{4}$ in. h., $17\frac{1}{4}$ in. w.

Reproduced in catalogue of Doetsch Sale, June, 1895, plate 36.

In 1515, then, Lotto had completely recovered his

[*National Gallery, London*

PORTRAIT OF AGOSTINO AND NICCOLÒ DELLA TORRE

balance, having cast away all foreign elements that
he could not keep house with; and, as happens frequently when we have expelled from within ourselves
the unassimilable outsider, he must have felt his
personality re-established, and his faith in himself and
in his training and habits confirmed. Hence we find
him in the National Gallery *Double Portrait* more like
the Alvise of 1498-1503 than he had ever been before.
But in the great undertaking which he carried out
immediately after, we shall have occasion to note that
the Raphaelesque and Giorgionesque had not passed
over him without leaving a trace, no matter how faint.
We are never so much our old selves as at the
moment of asserting our independence of *something*.
A little later, we find that that *something* has, after all,
left its thumb-mark upon us.

The undertaking in question was the one for which
Lotto had signed the contract with Alessandro Martinengo in 1513. Sometime in 1514, while at Venice in
the monastery of San Giovanni e Paolo, he made the
large sketch for it that was known to Morelli. Sometime in 1515 he got to work on the altar-piece itself,
and toward the end of 1516 he must have finished it,
since that is the date he himself placed, along with his
name, on the Madonna's throne, while the donor's
dedication[1] attached to the original frame bore the
date 1517.

Painted for Santo Stefano, this altar-piece was in
1561 transferred, with the transfer of the Dominicans,
to San Bartolommeo[2]. In its original blue and gold
frame, with *predelle*, pediment, projecting columns, and

---

[1] Given in Tassi's *Vite de' Pittori, Scultori e Architetti Bergamaschi*, vol. i, p. 118. Part of the dedication was as follows: 'Imaginem hanc Coelesti potius quam terrestri manu Depictam.'

[2] Locatelli, *op. cit.*, vol. i, p. 66.

1516. delicate carvings, it must have been one of the most resplendent works of art in Italy. But in 1749[1], when the church of San Bartolommeo was given its still existing wash of *rococo* architectural decoration, the monumental frame was handed over to a carpenter for the trouble of destroying it, and the painting in the pediment was thrown in to boot[2]. The *predelle* were transferred to the sacristy, and the central panel was given a Louis Quinze frame. Fortunately the carpenter, not being so crass a barbarian as were the sons of St. Dominic, saved the angel in the pediment, which has recently been purchased by the Buda Pesth Gallery. The *predelle* have at last found a resting-place in the municipal gallery of Bergamo, and the central panel still remains in its trivial frame in the church of San Bartolommeo.

BERGAMO, SAN BARTOLOMMEO. HIGH ALTAR. MADONNA AND SAINTS.

The Madonna enthroned, with SS. Sebastian, John, Stephen, Augustine, and Catherine to R., and Alexander, Barbara, James, Dominic, and Mark to L. Two angels, poised in air, hold a crown above the Virgin, and two other angels lean over a round balustrade at the top, decking it with banners, while two *putti* spread a carpet at the foot of the throne. The throne stands at the meeting of the transepts and choir of a vast church.

Inscribed: LAVRENTIVS LOTVS MDXVI. On canvas, about 5 m. h.

Photographed by Alinari.

Mentioned by the *Anonimo* (edition Frizzoni), who

---

[1] Tassi, *op. cit.*, vol. i, p. 118.
[2] Locatelli, *op. cit.*, vol. i, p. 71 note. It will be noted that it was a layman who had this work of art created, ecclesiastics who did their best to destroy it. The case is typical.

[*Herr R. von Kauffman, Berlin*

PORTRAIT OF A JEWELLER

saw it in Santo Stefano. Ridolfi speaks of it as being 1516. at San Bartolommeo.

This altar-piece is full of Alvisesque elements. As a composition, with the figures grouped around the principal one, towards which their looks and movements converge—with the magnificent hypethral transept and deep, elaborately vaulted choir—as a composition it is, in these respects, but a variation upon Alvise's Frari altar-piece. Speaking merely of the extent to which the grouping is Alvisesque, we may compare the composition before us with Cima's *Madonna with Six Saints* in the Parma Gallery (No. 360). In both the Madonna looks and inclines her head at the same angle to the L. In both she holds out her R. arm in protection of the group on the L., while the Child, facing in the opposite direction, blesses the group on the R. In both there is great variety in the play of the hands, and great unity of interest; and such fervour of feeling that most of the figures have their mouths open as if ejaculating, while some have their bodies inclined towards the Madonna, as if irresistibly drawn to her. In both, therefore, the movement of the figures jars with the severe lines of the architectural setting. In Cima, who was twenty years older, the discord between the architecture and the figures only begins to be felt, while in Lotto, in 1516, it is already strident. But the seeds of this discord were contained in Alvise himself. He was, as we remember, an arduous student of perspective and light and shade because he realized their value as factors in the impression he wished to make: and this impression, we also remember, was apt to be one appealing more directly to our sense of poetry in the abstract than to our delight in painting by and for itself. In order to express all that he wished to say, he himself began to give his figures

1516. movements which make their whole bodies intensely eloquent, but tend at the same time to put them out of harmony with the lines of the architecture. His pupils developed both tendencies, but, as it were, separately, making the architecture more and more magnificent, and at the same time giving the figures more and more movement, until at last, in the altar-piece by Lotto before us, the two elements are so distinct that they can be thought of apart, nay gain in being thought of apart, and lose when they are taken too seriously as one composition. Lotto, after completing the picture before us, may have felt this antagonism as clearly as we do, for it is a fact that to our knowledge he never again painted an altar-piece with an architectural setting of this splendid, columnar kind.

With an architecture of the grandeur and sweep of the choir in this San Bartolommeo altar-piece, we should have had statuesque, hieratic figures, subduing the vast arch and making it seem like a mere frame to give them unity. Instead, Lotto has given us saints who are no longer objects of worship, as in the Quattrocentist Venetians, nor a parade guard and escort for the Madonna, as in Giorgione and the young Titian, but pious souls, in whose faces and gestures we discern the zeal, the fervour, the yearning, the reverie, or even the sentimental ecstasy peculiar to the several temperaments most frequently occurring among the children of Holy Mother Church. So well has he analysed and re-created these types, so well has he made their minds intelligible to us, that, do what we will, their bodies also cannot be thought of as other than merely human; and, being very sensitive and refined, they appear even more than usually frail and delicate. Now, putting these frail and delicate bodies, none of them six feet high, against pillars which ought to measure at least thirty, but only rise by a third or

Alinari photo.] *[Bergamo, San Barto*

THE VIRGIN ENTHRONED, WITH ANGELS AND SAINTS

two-fifths of their height above the figures, produces
an effect of perplexity of the kind we feel in a panorama. That is not the worst: against the pillars are
placed, on one side, a sentimental St. Sebastian, in
a wriggling attitude occurring among other Alviseschi,
with his L. foot at right angles to his unnaturally
twisted R. foot[1], and on the other side a lovely
St. Alexander leaning, with one foot on his helmet, on
the staff of his pennon, and looking up at the Madonna
with eyes in which yearning and reverie mingle.
Worst of all: the pillars are some distance away
from the spectators, and, although the heads of these
two saints are leaning towards us, yet they are almost
flat against the pillars, while their feet are only a foot
or two away from us. Instead of being in the same
plane, therefore, their bodies are really leaning back
a distance of some ten feet. To lean back ten feet
with bodies not measuring six and yet remain perpendicular sounds like a tale from *Alice in Wonderland*,
but is a miracle performed even nowadays by painters
of the best standing, so that we must not be too severe
on Lotto. It is clear, however, that his architecture
and his figures do not stand close examination as
a connected whole.

1516.

Against the figures themselves there is but little
reproach to be made. They are not, it is true, remarkably well constructed, but attention is not drawn
to their structure one way or the other; the painter
has arranged for us to see nothing but the beautiful
expressive faces, and the fascinating, subtle, transparent tints. The least happy in beauty and expres-

[1] Cf. St. Sebastian in Montagna's altar-piece in the Venice Academy
(Sal. Pal., No. 13). Nothing can be more instructive than these two
figures by pupils of the same school, belonging to different generations.
Deduct what they have in common, and you have on one side the real
Montagna, and on the other the real Lotto. But how very much they
have in common—everything but the feeling!

1516. sion is the Madonna herself. The Child is not much changed from the one in the altar-piece at Santa Cristina, near Treviso. St. Stephen, with his look of sentimental ecstasy, reminds us of St. Basil in the Asolo *Assumption*. The *putti* spreading out a carpet before the throne are still Alvisesque, recalling the baby angels in Alvise's Redentore *Madonna*, and their presence and action are only to be explained by the fact that Lotto belonged to a school in which Murano-Squarcionesque tradition lingered on long after it had been abandoned by the Bellini and their close followers. That Lotto should have thought of putting so fanciful a pedestal to the Madonna's throne, and of ornamenting the balustrade with flags and banners, and olive and palm branches, also betrays the lingering on in his mind of Murano-Squarcionesque usages. But, although the idea occurs to him at all because of the old usage, how he changes it, how indicative he makes it of his own spirit! Let us take the decoration of the balustrade alone. There are no heavy garlands and corals symmetrically arranged, but a feeling such as the Japanese, and many artists of to-day have, that *this* will be charming here, and *that* delightful there, that just such a touch of colour will add to the lyrical effect desired. Fancy, then, and not geometry, was the inspiration of Lotto as a decorator; and on this account, and because he was a person who was wont to project his own states of feeling into the inanimate things about him, we can never quite tell just where in his decoration ornament or trimming ends and symbolism begins. He was too delicate and too true an artist to have felt the division strongly himself, still less to let us feel it.

Returning once more to the architectural setting, we cannot but acknowledge that in no other painting existing has the choir of a church so vast, so buoyant,

and so rhythmical, been represented. This is the 1516.
reward of all the architectural painting in which Lotto's
precursors had been pre-eminent; yet we may question
whether Lotto himself would have attained such grandeur if the influence of none but his Venetian masters
had been brought to bear upon him. The only architecture in painting which rivals this, and, as architecture merely, even surpasses it, is in the *School of
Athens*, the space-feeling, arches, and vaultings of
which were certainly inspired by Bramante. Now,
although Lotto might never have painted such a choir
as the one before us if he had not been the pupil of
Alvise, I believe, on the other hand, that he would
never have had a conception so airy and vast had he
not been to Rome and come in contact, directly or
indirectly, with the greatest space-composer the world
has yet had. (And, as if to strengthen us in this
belief, we note that in the spandrils he has put two
medallions, one containing a (painted) mosaic of
St. Mark and the other of St. John the Evangelist,
the latter not only having a distinctly Raphaelesque
face, but wearing his mantle over one shoulder, a practice almost universal among the Umbrians, rare in
Florence, and rarer still in Venice, where, after Antonio
da Murano, it scarcely ever occurs.) But having given
us an arch that uplifts by its airiness, Lotto, more than
half conscious (as we shall later find him to be) of the
value of space-effects in determining our moods, has
placed the angels who are crowning the Virgin not
directly over her (where of course they would have
choked the space), but flower-like and flame-like high
above, whence, as our eye suddenly looks down, we
get an effect of unexpected sheerness of depth, which
for the first time makes us fully aware of the vastness
of the choir.

From the architecture in this San Bartolommeo

1516. altar-piece we turn naturally to the examination of the painting as painting, because it is peculiarly admirable in the execution of the choir. The purity of the colours and the transparency of the shadows are such that through the shade of the deep choir we see not only the deep darkness on both sides outside the colonnade, but the whole depth beyond the choir of the long-stretching apse and the effects of light and shadow within it. The same transparency and purity characterize the rest of the painting. The colouring is dainty and gay, not so golden as in the pictures of 1512, but of a delicate ivory tint, with the *patina* a trifle enamelled. In the vehicle, this work shows as little trace of Palma as we have found in the composition and figures, the medium being as slow as in 1512. It is noticeable, finally, that the brush-work of the angels on the balustrade is much larger than in the lower part of the picture, for no other reason than that they were placed so much farther away from the spectator. For a similar reason, the brush-work is even bolder in the figure of the angel originally in the pediment.

BUDA-PESTH, MUSEUM. ANGEL.

An angel with streaming yellow hair, and fluttering pink draperies with folds like the line of the iris flower, seems to be flying downward, holding in one hand a crystal globe and in the other a sceptre.

Photographed by Taramelli, Bergamo, and Lotze, Verona.

But as if to show us what technique Lotto worked in, when left to himself, untrammelled by a public, then, even more than now, regarding the well known as the only beautiful, we have fortunately preserved for us the first sketches for the *predelle* of the altar-piece we are still engaged upon.

BERGAMO GALLERY, LOCHIS COLLECTION (ATTRIBUTED 1516.
    TO SCHIAVONE).

No. 32. ST. STEPHEN PREACHING. On wood, 22 cm. h., 31 cm. w.

No. 33. STEPHEN EXPELLED FROM THE SYNAGOGUE. 22 cm. h., 28 cm. w.

No. 34. MARTYRDOM OF STEPHEN. 22 cm. h., 31 cm. w.

Photographed by R. Lotze, Verona.

That these sketches first ascribed by Signor Frizzoni to Lotto are by him is put beyond a doubt by the movement of the figures and the forms of hand. But as brush-work, and as a colour-scheme, they are modern, as modern as Delacroix, to whose technique, indeed, they bear a striking resemblance. We thus see that an artist of Lotto's age and kind was not unaware of certain methods employed so delightfully since, but that either his own taste or that of his patrons forbade the employment of these 'modern' methods.

In unfavourable contrast to these spirited and surprisingly modern sketches stand the *predelle* finally executed for the San Bartolommeo altar-piece;—not that these are in themselves despicable, but that the slow vehicle and the blond, brownish golden tone seem tame after the juicy, herb-like quality of the sketches.

BERGAMO, CARRARA GALLERY, PREDELLE TO SAN BARTOLOMMEO ALTAR-PIECE.

ST. DOMINIC RAISING NAPOLEONE, THE NEPHEW OF CARDINAL FOSSANUOVA.

THE STONING OF STEPHEN.

THE ENTOMBMENT.

On wood, each 48 cm. h., 93 cm. w.

Photographed by Alinari.

In the first and second, the figures are not in proportion to each other, nor to the composition as a

1516. whole. The *Entombment*, however, is one of the most romantic treatments of the subject in existence. The effect of light here recalls Alvise's *Resurrection* at San Giovanni in Bragora at Venice. Just as in the central panel itself we found, in contrast to the purely Alvisesque character of the Della Torre portraits, faint traces of Raphael and of Lotto's Roman residence in general, so in these *predelle* we find elements, such as the costumes and the effects of light, that it would be easy to pronounce Giorgionesque, if we did not know that the lights are Lotto's own, as developed from Alvise, and that the costumes were the costumes of the day, for which Lotto, as we have already seen in the St. Vito at Recanati, had, to say the least, no less liking than the rest of his North Italian contemporaries. In the *Stoning of Stephen*, however, there is one figure, an officer in white and purplish grape colours, which, I believe, Lotto never would have painted had he not been acquainted with works by Giorgione. But reminders of Raphael and Giorgione, faint even as we have found them in this San Bartolommeo altar-piece, are scarcely to be met with again[1]. From this date, 1516, for ten years, Lotto's art develops continuously, evenly, on the whole, and unaffected by other methods of style or technique. Before we turn to these pleasantest years in his career, we must briefly note three other pictures belonging to the transitional period, and consider a certain question which will interrupt us least at this point.

The three pictures are the following:

BERGAMO, SANT' ALESSANDRO IN CROCE, SACRISTY. THE TRINITY.

1517, circa. Christ, nude but for a waist-cloth, a mild, inade-

[1] The guards and some of the elders betray the baleful influence of contemporary German and Dutch engraving.

quate conception (as Christs painted by psychological painters are apt to be), floats over a landscape, the Dove hovering above Him, and a mystic shadow, God the Father, just discernible behind. The *idea* once grasped by our own minds, and then translated into our own vague visual imagery, is sublime, but it cannot be said that Lotto has succeeded in making it artistic. In his picture it remains in the 'symbolical' stage, and distinctly anticipates the Bolognese phantasms of a century later.

[margin: 1517, circa.]

On canvas, 1·70 m. h., 1·15 m. w.

Mentioned by the *Anonimo* who saw it in its original place, the church of La Trinità. Mentioned also by Ridolfi.

Ivory tinted and a little hard; obviously just after the altar-piece in San Bartolommeo. The landscape, although peculiarly rural for this date, yet recalls Alvise, and particularly Cima, in such a picture as the *Madonna with Six Saints* in the Venice Academy (No. 36).

The second picture of about this date is so washed out that it is not worth dwelling upon.

BERGAMO, SANT' ALESSANDRO IN COLONNA. THE DEPOSITION.

Tempera, on linen, figures under life-size.

Mentioned by the *Anonimo* as 'most touching,' and by Ridolfi as 'most pitiful'; but modern feeling will here also find a sort of anticipation of the taste formed by that ingenious steam-incubator of contrition, the 'Exercises' of St. Ignatius Loyola.

The third picture is one that has suffered from multiple cleanings and restorations, to such an extent that, to any but a practised eye, it is almost unrecognizable. It is more than usually difficult, therefore,

1517, circa. to date it with precision, but as it has many traits in common with the San Bartolommeo altar-piece, and, at the same time, certain features that suggest the works of 1521, I think we may place it at the end of this transition period, and no later, because it is peculiarly Alvisesque in composition.

LONDON, COLLECTION OF THE LATE MR. HENRY DOETSCH. MADONNA AND SAINTS.

On wood, 1·52 m. h., 1·19 m. w.

Under an arched trellis supporting a rose-tree, whose branches cross behind the green draped throne, sits the Virgin, with the naked Child standing uneasily on her L. knee offering a rose to Catherine, who kneels in profile to the R. To the L. kneels the Magdalen, holding daintily a rose in one hand, and in the curved palm and fingers of the other her ointment-box. To R. and L. of the Virgin stand St. Jerome and the Baptist.

On wood, $59\frac{3}{4}$ in. h., $46\frac{3}{4}$ in. w. Reproduced in catalogue of Doetsch sale, plate 37. In 1900 this picture was in the hands of M. Sedelmeyer, of Paris.

The composition is almost mechanically simple, with two storeys of saints, so to speak, as in Alvise's compositions. The trellis reminds us vividly of Cima's earliest work, the Vicenza altar-piece, the only other Venetian picture in which such a setting occurs. The pointing index of St. John is Alvisesque, and the Magdalen's curved palm and finger are found in Alvise's Berlin altar-piece, and in Bonsignori's San Paolo *Madonna* (Verona). The roses occurring here and frequently elsewhere in Lotto's works are probably a survival of the rose-garden in the backgrounds of Lotto's Muranese predecessors. Of the colouring little can now be said, Lotto being recognizable only in touches of red in the Magdalen's robe, and in touches of heliotrope in John's mantle. Elsewhere 1517, Lotto is seen most clearly in the Child, who suggests the one in Signor Piccinelli's *Madonna* of about 1522, and has Lotto's peculiar ear. The Madonna's R. hand is identical with the hand of St. Catherine in the San Bartolommeo altar-piece.

The question which, I said, we could best consider at this point, regards the supposed likeness between Lotto and Correggio, of which altogether too much Lotto has been made.

If we compare the San Bartolommeo picture, upon which we have dwelt so long, with Correggio's first important altar-piece, the *Madonna with St. Francis* (Dresden, No. 150), we cannot fail to be struck with certain marked resemblances between them. In both, the Madonna leans over holding out her R. hand in protection of the group to her R. In both, the figures are too much in movement for an architectonic composition, this fault being caused, in each case, by a desire to express great fervour and demonstrative feeling. In both pictures, finally, the pedestal of the throne is already baroque, and the St. John is represented as pointing at the Child. In these elements, then, the pictures resemble each other; but Correggio's chiaroscuro is far less contrasted, his flesh-painting is of an altogether more life-like texture, and his structure is more solid. Let us, however, shut out the difference for the moment and devote our attention to the resemblances. How are these to be accounted for? Correggio was in his native town, painting his picture, while Lotto was, in all probability, at San Giovanni e Paolo planning out his, and that one should have borrowed from the other is therefore wellnigh out of the question. We have accounted, moreover, for nearly everything in Lotto's painting, and seen how he came by each element, and that he certainly owed

K 2

1517, circa.

none to Correggio, who, by the way, was only twenty years of age in 1514, while Lotto was already thirty-four. Is it likely, on the other hand, that Correggio knew Lotto and was influenced by him before this date? Not if our view of Lotto's residence in Rome and the Marches up to 1513 is correct. Morelli, it is true, conjectured that Correggio actually studied for a while in Venice, and that there he met Lotto, or at least studied his works[1]. But Lotto could not have had a studio of his own at this time. His absence from Venice throughout 1512 is attested by the number of works of about that date in Recanati and Jesi; part of 1513 he certainly spent at Bergamo, and we have seen how probable it is that he visited Venice only after the spring of 1514. It is barely possible, of course, that Correggio was in Venice at this time, but I doubt whether he would, even so, have made the acquaintance of a man who was not established there as a painter, but a mere visitor to his native town, without a home of his own, working in a monastery. That Correggio might, while in Venice, have been influenced by Lotto's works, we cannot allow, except as the merest conjecture, for we have no knowledge of the existence of pictures, other than portraits, by Lotto in that town prior to 1529, the date of the Carmine altar-piece. Furthermore, although contact with Lotto at this date, just before painting the *Madonna with St. Francis*, might account for the Lottesque character of this altar-piece, it would not account for the Lottesque traits in Correggio's earlier works; and there is no less logical connexion between Correggio's *Madonna with St. Francis* and his own earlier productions, than there is

---

[1] Morelli, *Galerien zu München und Dresden*, p. 73; *Galerien Borghese und Doria*, p. 292.

between the San Bartolommeo altar-piece and Lotto's earlier works. 1517, circa.

But is there really anything in the *Madonna with St. Francis* that Correggio could have acquired only by contact with Lotto? Let us return to the resemblances between this picture and Lotto's at San Bartolommeo. It is true that in both the Madonna holds out her hand protectingly, but in Lotto, as in Cima, she holds it out from her elbow, while in Correggio she holds it out from her shoulder, and her whole body moves, supple and graceful, with the movement of the arm. This movement and gesture, therefore, have only the roughest resemblance to Lotto and to Cima, whose picture (now at Parma) Correggio might have seen at the neighbouring Carpi. But in so far as movements rendered by great artists, inspiring, but not slavishly copying one another, can be identical, the action of Correggio's Madonna is, in fact, identical with the action of Mantegna's *Madonna of Victory*, now in the Louvre[1], from which picture Correggio undoubtedly took it. Lotto and Cima took their action, we may be sure, from Alvise, who already gives the arms and hands considerable play in his Venice Academy *Madonna* of 1480, and Alvise, in turn, took it from the common Murano-Squarcionesque artistic activity going on between 1440 and 1460 at Padua, whence also Mantegna derived all that he had to learn from others. In speaking of the pedestal

---

[1] That Correggio spent some time in Mantua under Costa, looking at the works of Mantegna and coming in contact with Dosso Dossi, from whom he probably got all the distinctly Venetian elements discoverable in his works, can, I think, be proved by a detailed study and comparison of his earliest pictures with the paintings of Francia, Costa, Mantegna, and Dosso. 'Some Comments on Correggio in connexion with his Pictures at Dresden,' first published in the *Knight Errant* (Boston, U S.A.), for April, 1893, and reprinted in *The Study and Criticism of Italian Art* (London, Bell, 1901), by the present writer, deals in part with this subject.

1517, circa. hung with beads and corals in Lotto's picture, in speaking also of the *putti* spreading the carpet, we referred both features back to the Murano-Squarcionesque tradition still comparatively vivid in the mind of Lotto, a pupil of Alvise, while the Bellini had dropped it fairly early in their careers, so that no trace of it remains in *their* pupils. Well, the barroque throne in Correggio can be referred back to the same tradition, for he took it from Francia and Costa, who, in turn, derived it from Ercole Roberti, an artist who not only had himself probably studied at Padua, but was the pupil of Cosimo Tura. Now Tura had certainly studied at Padua, and he may, in fact, be counted among the Murano-Squarcioneschi quite as much as Mantegna and Bartolommeo Vivarini. At Padua between 1440 and 1460 all the founders of North Italian schools of painting were present, acquiring forms in common, *motifs* in common, and habits in common. Of this common store, each took what he could make the best use of, what was most in harmony with his own temperament and native tendencies, and dropped all the rest. But although each dropped a good deal, and the Bellini took another path almost from the moment they were established at Venice, yet such of the founders as Mantegna, Tura, and Bartolommeo Vivarini do, to the last, continue to have many usages and mannerisms in common. This, be it noted, accounts for the fact that many of the 'peculiarities' we called 'Vivarinesque' are peculiar to the Vivarini and their school only as distinct from the Bellini and their following, but are of not infrequent (although, compared to the Vivarineschi, comparatively rare) occurrence outside of Venice, particularly among the Ferrara-Bolognese painters. It is this common inheritance of usages which may have made Raphael—in his most rooted habits a descendant, through

Timoteo Viti, Costa, and Francia, of Tura—seem so intelligible and adoptable to Lotto. And it is this same common inheritance of habits which makes Lotto and Correggio, persons of similar temperament, express themselves with such remarkable likeness. Both were sensitive, emotional, lyrical natures, to whom painting was not chiefly an affair of architectonic composition or structure, but a vehicle for the expression of feeling. The forms which their predecessors took from a common source had meanwhile undergone parallel developments, so that in spite of their being sixty years away from the common origin, these forms were still remarkably alike in Raphael, Correggio, and Lotto. Besides, Lotto, being on one side of his nature very close to Correggio, and wishing, like him, to express fervour, devotion, and even rapture, puts his figures in movement, and employs *putti* very nearly as Correggio does, and gives a gaiety and delicacy to many of his paintings of the period between 1515 and 1530, which, because it is Correggio's *dominant* quality, we call Correggiesque. Thus far and no farther goes the resemblance between them.

1517, circa.

In reality too much has been made of the likeness between Lotto and Correggio. Even Morelli was guilty of seeing Correggio in Lotto where he is not at all to be found, as, for instance, in the Borghese *Santa Conversazione*, where the peculiarly Palmesque Child, and the decoration on the pedestal of the throne, really of the kind found in Crivelli, Bartolommeo Vivarini, Cima, Jacopo di Barbari, and the Lombardi[1], struck him as Correggiesque. Where Lotto and

---

[1] Instances in Crivelli need not be mentioned, as almost any of his enthroned Madonnas will serve to illustrate the point. But cf. B. Vivarini's Naples altar-piece of 1465 and Frari tryptych of 1487; Barbari's frescoes at Treviso and in the Frari; Cima's *Coronation of the Virgin* in San Giovanni e Paolo.

1517, circa. Correggio are not temperamentally alike, the likenesses are due, as I have suggested, to a common, if distant, origin[1], and, as I have already said, Lotto is like Correggio only on one side of his nature. In so far as he is analytical, in so far as he is contrite in religious expression, in so far as he is a great portrait painter and even a humorist, he is very different from Correggio, whom, moreover, he never for a moment resembles in the subtler considerations of technique.

[1] How close to one another Lotto's master, Alvise, and Correggio's master, Costa, could approach appears in a Madonna belonging to the present writer. His first impression on seeing it was that its author was Alvise. This was the experience of nearly every connoisseur who has seen it. Some have even found difficulty in persuading themselves, although all have ended by recognizing that its real author was Costa.

CHAPTER IV

THE BERGAMASK PERIOD

1518–1528

THE ten years in Lotto's career to which we are now going to devote attention, were the years in which he was in the fullness of his manhood—when, as his works of this period show, he began to feel himself complete master of his style and to take pleasure in it. He had freed himself from all unsympathetic influences, and his own life during these years must have run smoothly and happily. It is probable, too, that his analytical, humorous, and bizarre temperament felt itself at home and with friends among people like the Bergamasks, who, if we may trust the accounts of Bandello[1] and other contemporary writers, seem to have been endowed with plenty of caprice and humour, and to have been, at any rate, so far interested in the analysis of character as to have acquired a reputation for it. It may also have been well for Lotto that he spent the greater part of this fruitful period of his life among provincials, probably sympathetic, of whom, as a native of the *Inclita Dominante*, as the subject towns soon began to call Venice, he is not likely to have stood in awe. Being without a rival, the more cultivated Bergamasks could scarcely have helped employing him when they

1518–1528.

[1] *Novelle*, part i, xxxiv.

wished to show off their wealth in ornamenting churches, and their stylishness in having their portraits done by a painter from the capital. Being alone, he could impose his own tastes on his public, as he could not have done in Venice, where there was a choice of painters for all kinds of cultivated amateurs. Lotto, therefore, in these years expanded his genius in every direction, enjoying the benefits of perfect independence, but, we must also add, suffering from the disadvantages of not rubbing up against superiors, or at least equals. Many a careless or archaic touch, tending to spoil works of art otherwise great and remarkably modern, he might easily have got rid of had they been pointed out to him by a competent critic.

But even this decade cannot quite be treated as a unit. Only the first five years of it seem to have been spent constantly at Bergamo. In December, 1523, we find Lotto in Venice, apparently established and receiving commissions. But that he must have spent most of the year 1524 in or near Bergamo is attested by frescoes, and also by documents of this date. The same documents speak of him as being still at Bergamo on February 25, 1525, and it is possible that he spent the end of this year in the Marches, his presence at Jesi, in 1526, being witnessed to by a couple of works of considerable size *on wood*. Most of 1527, we know, Lotto spent in Venice, and although we have no distinct records of 1528, it is probable that he did not long absent himself from Venice in that year. The object of following him in his wanderings is not only that we may have some notion of what were our artist's successive environments, but also that we may convince ourselves that up to some time in 1526, Lotto could have spent but little time in Venice, and that he therefore had about ten years in which he came but slightly, if at all, in contact with Venetian painters of his own rank. Thus we are not surprised to find that in these 1518–1528. years the pupil of Alvise expresses himself in a way which betrays his origin, and that he continues steadily to beat out the path begun in his first score of active years—a path from which nothing yet has made him seriously turn away. Perhaps the artist who was continuing and developing the Bellinesque and Giorgionesque tradition, as Lotto was continuing the Muranese and Alvisesque, perhaps Titian, who in this same decade was advancing from one triumph to another, would have changed Lotto's course, but happily Lotto did not come in contact with him until the end of this period, and then he was already forty-eight years old, and, as we shall see in our next chapter, no longer capable of being radically influenced.

Meanwhile we shall turn to his works of 1518–1528, examining each, and determining, when possible, its precise date, or at any rate marshalling it in line with its fellows. We can afford to be brief, now that we have settled Lotto's descent and have become fairly well acquainted with his character and qualities, and fortunately we have no misleading traditions for this period, and no unintelligent criticisms to clear out of the way. We can be all the briefer, too, because a number of the pictures we are now going to consider will be touched on again in the closing chapter of this book, when we come to define the impression Lotto has finally left upon our minds. Here, therefore, we shall at times limit ourselves to questions of morphology, technique, and date.

The work with which this series opens is one that, 1518. until two years ago, did not bear Lotto's name, but was catalogued as by an unknown North Italian master 'who without doubt had known Leonardo da Vinci and Correggio.' It is a work, therefore, in which the

Venetian character, that is to say, the character of the followers of Bellini and Giorgione, was not recognized, and, as we know, for a good reason, its author having had little, if any, connexion with the school which, when every other Venetian school had been forgotten, came to be considered as synonymous with 'Venetian' in general. Its subtle treatment of light and shadow, its delicate, refined colouring, a certain sweetness in the mouth of the Madonna and softness in her eyelids—all characteristic of Lotto as we know him already, or presently shall know him—suggested Leonardo and Correggio. Signor Frizzoni, however, had already recognized it as a Lotto in 1889, but this attribution probably would not have received the official seal if Mr. Charles Loeser had not since then, in the autumn of 1891, discovered the signature and date.

DRESDEN, No. 194A. MADONNA AND CHILD WITH INFANT ST. JOHN.

The Madonna, in a lilac dress and blue mantle, sits in front of a red curtain looking at the Child in her lap, who embraces the infant John. To the L. over a parapet is seen a landscape with low hills in the distance and a river in the foreground.

Inscribed in script on the parapet: Laurentius Lotus 1518.

On wood, 52 cm. h., 39 cm. w.

Photographed by Braun under the name of Vincenzo Tamagni, and also by R. Tamme, Dresden.

The composition recalls the National Gallery's Alvise, with the difference that in the one we have for a background a wall and a view through a window, and in the other a curtain and the open air, with the addition, moreover, in the Lotto, of the infant John. The *motif* of the two holy children embracing each other is, I

Hanfstängl photo. *[Dresden Gallery*

THE MADONNA AND CHILD, WITH ST. JOHN

believe, not to be found in any work earlier than 1518 1518. executed by a purely Venetian painter, and it is not at all improbable that Lotto took it from some Milanese Leonardesque painting seen by him at Bergamo itself, or in the closely neighbouring Milan. Such a *motif* could not have helped appealing to him, taking, as we shall see, the interest that he did in child-life, but the mere fact that he adopted it does not of course affect the essential character of his art. Both the children, for instance, remain the chubby, pug-nosed *putti* that we found in Alvise's Redentore *Madonna*, and the Christ-child lies across His mother's lap in a way that vividly recalls the Alvise just mentioned. The Madonna herself, more winning even than beautiful—a type, by the way, which occurs again and again in Lotto's works during the next twenty years—is anticipated by Alvise's *Santa Giustina dei Borromei*. Like her, she has a peculiarly graceful and refined face on a disproportionately large and badly articulated torso. The softness of her lids, the sweetness of her mouth, and the daintiness of her silken hair remind us equally of the *Santa Giustina*. Of Alvise we are still further reminded by the landscape, and by the long thick fingers of the Madonna's R. hand.

But analysing a work of art into its elements and showing how the author came by them, does not account for its quality and value. All the formal elements become in the author's temperament fused into something which is very different from the rough materials; and in this *Madonna*, although much of it, much even of the sentiment, was anticipated by Alvise, we feel the contact, through its gay, lilac colouring, through the grace and daintiness of the Madonna and the sweetness of the children, with a refined, gay personality, and feelings much like our own, in an age which we are too apt to think of as one devoid of

1518. humane sentiments and wholly given over to men and women of only heroic passions.

1518-1521. There is no picture by Lotto known to me that we can safely place between the Dresden *Madonna* and the San Bernardino altar-piece dated 1521. But we may be sure that he was not idle during these years. Documentary notices[1] exist of a number of works executed at about this time which have disappeared; and as these notices are themselves waifs that have reached us by the merest chance, we may feel certain that even they represent scarcely a percentage of the works Lotto was painting in these years. Five-and-twenty years later, when he was already an old man, we happen to know that he turned out dozens of pictures each year, and it is far from likely that he was less industrious in this, his most vigorous period.

It may be asked how we are to ascertain that he spent these years from 1518 to 1521 at Bergamo rather than elsewhere. Our chief reason for believing that they were spent in or near Bergamo arises from the fact that we have no records of him elsewhere at this time, and that in the works of 1521 we find his style, his quality, so unchanged from what we found them in the Dresden *Madonna*, that he could not have come in contact during the interval with other noted artists; least of all could he have been much in Venice and have remained utterly untouched by Titian's *Assunta*. The cause of our having no works of this date is probably the simple one that he was painting chiefly for private persons, works in private possession being much more liable to be destroyed or lost than important compositions for churches such as he executed in 1521.

---

[1] *Sunto de li quadri facti de pictura per mi lorenzo loto a miser Zanin Casoto*, published in Locatelli, vol. i, p. 463. It is interesting to note that Lotto charges not by the picture, but for each figure separately.

Alinari photo] [*Bergamo, San Bernardino*

THE MADONNA AND CHILD, WITH SAINTS

BERGAMO, SAN BERNARDINO. MADONNA AN SAINTS.

The Madonna, sitting on a partly draped high 1521. pedestal, with her feet on a cushion, eloquently expounds the blessing of the Child standing on her R. knee, to the bystanding saints, Antony Abbot, John the Baptist, Bernardino, and Joseph. On the lowest step of the pedestal, powdered over with roses, an angel crouches over a book in which he is writing down the Madonna's words. Two angels floating in the air hold up a green curtain behind her, and two others spread it out into a canopy over her head.

Inscribed: LLOTVS MDXXI. On canvas, 3 m. h., 2·75 m. w.

Photographed by Alinari.

Mentioned by the *Anonimo*, and Ridolfi.

Modern, and full of feeling and movement as this altar-piece is, it yet has elements which still recall Alvise. The Madonna's eloquent gesture, for instance, is but an advance on the movement of the Madonna in Alvise's picture of 1480 in the Venice Academy. The Baptist is pointing up at the Child as he always does in Alvise and his school. Even the spreading of the curtain behind the Madonna we have already—but how differently!—in the *Coronation* in Alvise's Frari altar-piece. The roses are, of course, a reminiscence of the Murano-Squarcionesque fruit and flower decoration. But as the figures and the draperies have from sculptural become supple and alive, so these roses are not metallic or in lacquer, as in Crivelli, but moist and dewy as if just plucked.

In type, although much more eloquent and spiritual, the Madonna is not far removed from the one in Dresden. The forms and the draperies show but little change from one picture to the other. Having all

1521. the purity and transparency of the San Bartolommeo altar-piece, the one we are now considering is more fused in colouring, and more dewy in the shadows. Lotto's peculiar scarlets, light blues, and heliotropes occur here in large masses for the first time. The sky, one of the finest in any Italian picture, could have been painted only with a brush as clean as was Lotto's at this period. The four angels above are bathed in opaline shadows, and startlingly foreshortened, the one in the upper R. corner being as daring as any figure in Correggio.

Faults this picture has, but, Lotto once granted, they are slight. For a work in which the touch is so dainty, and where there is so much movement and feeling, the arrangement is still too architectural, the pedestal too massive; and unfortunately the canopy and the angels supporting it make the composition a little top-heavy. In structure, also, the figures leave much to be desired, and the snail-shaped coil of drapery over the Baptist's L. arm is scarcely to be excused. Yet in few other pictures is an idea conveyed to the spectator so directly and through such flower-like line and colour.

The picture to which we now turn is in many ways but a variation on the last; as a composition, it avoids the mistakes of that one, but it has neither its freshness nor its depth of feeling:

BERGAMO, SANTO SPIRITO. FOURTH ALTAR R. MADONNA AND SAINTS.

The Madonna, with the Child sitting on her lap, is enthroned on a pedestal hung with a Turkey carpet, with a cushion under her feet. She seems to be haranguing the surrounding saints, Antony Abbot,

Alinari photo.] [*Bergamo, Santo Spirito*

THE MADONNA ENTHRONED, WITH SAINTS AND ANGELS

SANTO SPIRITO ALTAR-PIECE 145

Sebastian, Ambrose, and Catherine, while two nude baby angels hold a crown over her head, and the infant John, at the foot of her throne, sprawls on the ground, hugging a lamb. The sky is filled with a host of angels flying, dancing, and making music, who form a sort of rainbow under the Holy Spirit, which is hovering down in the form of a dove.

Inscribed, in script: L. Lotus. 1521. On canvas, 2·87 m. h., 2·69 m. w.

Photographed by Alinari.

Mentioned by the *Anonimo*, and Ridolfi.

The Madonna, instead of leaning forward with a look of awe in her face, pityingly eager to persuade, sits back haughtily, talking loudly and demonstratively, as if impatient and even contemptuous of ordinary human understanding. Certainly Lotto cannot be accused of having produced this effect intentionally. He probably thought of nothing but avoiding a repetition of the San Bernardino *Madonna*, and the result is as unfortunate as the fruit of the mere desire for variety is apt to be. The St. Sebastian also is a little too fervid, almost *Scicento* in movement, and the St. Catherine, on the other hand, is a trifle worldly[1]. But the composition as a whole is freer and better spaced, while the choir of angels is without a rival in art, excepting, of course, Correggio's cupola at Parma. In the episode of the infant John hugging the lamb too closely for its comfort, we have an instance of Lotto's pleasure in child-life.

In technique, this picture differs but little from the one in San Bernardino, and would differ even less if the latter were not over-cleaned. In Santo Spirito, and in one or two other works of this period, Lotto makes considerable use of saffron yellow. Here, for

[1] Her being a portrait would account for this, and for her looking, not at the Madonna, but out of the picture.

1521. the first time, perhaps, he outlines in a way which became extremely characteristic of his middle and later years, giving his contours a sort of brownish shadow, interrupted frequently by little spots, as if done with a soft brush which had stopped and blotted.

In another phase so different that were the picture not dated we should scarcely ascribe it to the same year with these last two works, and, being obliged to give it the same date, we are left wondering at the artist's versatility—in another phase, we see Lotto in a work mentioned by Ridolfi as being in Casa Tassi at Bergamo, and by Tassi as belonging, with its *pendant*, to G. B. Zanchi of the same town, but which is now in Berlin:

BERLIN, No. 325. CHRIST TAKING LEAVE OF HIS MOTHER.

In a vaulted Renaissance hall, opening at the back upon an Italian garden, Christ kneels with His hands crossed on His breast before His mother, who sinks fainting into the arms of John and one of the Marys, while St. Anne, behind them, clasps her hands in silent grief. To the L. Peter and Judas [1], the latter putting out his hands in surprise. In the foreground to the R. a lady kneeling with an open missal in both her hands, and a little dog playing with the ample folds of her skirt. Tassi [2] affirms that this lady was Elizabetta Rotta, the wife of Domenico Tassi. In the extreme foreground lie a cherry-branch and an orange.

---

[1] In the *Sacre Rappresentazioni* it is nearly always Judas who with Peter accompanies Christ in this scene, and it is Judas to whom the Virgin specially entrusts the care of her son. As the sacred performances and painting were closely dependent the one upon the other, it is probable that the figure with his hands out was intended for Judas.

[2] *Vite*, vol. i, p. 125. The *pendant*, by the way, a 'Nativity,' contained the portrait of Domenico himself. Of this picture no trace remains.

Inscribed, in script: Mo. laurenttjo Lotto pictor 1521. 1521. On canvas, 1·26 m. h., 99 cm. w.

Photographed by Hanfstängl.

This is an unequal picture, the bad qualities of which are accentuated by the retouching it has suffered. Perhaps nothing more wonderful as painting of architecture, with subtle play of cool shadows and varying lights, exists elsewhere in Italian art; but in contrast to this magnificence, painted with the subtlety of Vermeer van Delft, we have the mean-looking Christ, and the meaner-looking, stumpy Judas. The group of the fainting Virgin is rendered with great realism, the silent sorrow of the old being well contrasted with the more noisy grief of the young. The realism of a scene like this reminds us of a man who in many things was Lotto's fifteenth-century parallel, Carlo Crivelli, and, as if to assure us that we are not seeing likenesses where they do not exist, the purely decorative cherry-branch again reminds us of Crivelli, and the Murano-Squarcionesque school, from which they both sprang. If we had the portrait alone, and the architecture, this picture would be a great piece of *genre*. As it is, we need only think away the other figures, and the loving execution of the different effects of light, the peep into a bedroom at the end of a colonnade, a frightened cat in a corridor, all make us feel that the painter's intention must have been largely to produce an effect of *genre*.

The two following works, although not dated, can be safely ascribed to the same year, because they are nearer to the pictures of 1521 than to those of any other date.

BERGAMO, SIGNOR PICCINELLI. MADONNA AND TWO SAINTS.

The Madonna, her amber-brown hair entwined with pearls, sinks down upon two heavy cushions, with her

1521. feet drawn up and her head bending over the Child, who sits back in her lap, looking out of the picture and blessing. To R. an almost nude, very blond, curly-haired St. Sebastian, and to L. St. Roch, leaning over with his R. hand held out, as if pitying and interceding for the worshippers, whom the arrangement of the pictures implies as being at some distance below, looking up at the Madonna, whose foreshortening is thus explained.

Signed: L. Lotvs. On wood, 80 cm. h., 1·07 m. w. SS. Roch and Sebastian knee-length. Photographed by R. Lotze, Verona.

Mentioned by Ridolfi as being in Santa Grata at Bergamo.

In type the Madonna resembles both the one at Dresden and the one in Santo Spirito, but her build and action suggest the latter only. In movement the Child recalls the Child in Santo Spirito, and in type both the Holy Child and the infant John in the same picture. The tone is exceptionally blond. St. Roch is one of Lotto's tenderest and least affected figures. The L. hand of the Madonna has considerable resemblance to the L. hand in the following work:

BERGAMO GALLERY, CARRARA COLLECTION. BUST OF A MIDDLE-AGED WOMAN.

She looks straight out of the canvas. She wears a turban-like hat, a string of large pearls on her hair, several strings of smaller pearls around her neck, as well as a chain and other jewels. To the L. a moonlit landscape.

On wood, 51½ cm. h., 42 cm. w.

Photographed by Alinari.

This portrait has a certain resemblance in features to Elizabetta Rotta in the Berlin picture, but the

[Hanfstängl photo.] [Berlin Gallery

CHRIST TAKING LEAVE OF HIS MOTHER

difference between profile and full face renders it difficult to make sure of the identity. The eyes, rather genial and kind, are not in character with the mouth, which is a little acid and cruel. May not this be due to Lotto's tendency to see the sitter's mouth through his Alvisesque habits of visualization, and his consequent tendency to draw it after the pattern learned under Alvise? A mouth like this may be a sort of compromise between the reality and the artist's habits of visualizing and painting, and this may account for the fact that it is not altogether in harmony with the rest of the face.

1521.

The year 1522 is represented by three dated works, all of the same peculiarly dainty type, in which the Madonna or female saints are beautifully dressed, lovely women, treated in a way bordering on highly refined *genre*. The most charming of the three is the following:

1522.

CASTELLO DI COSTA DI MEZZATE (near Gorlago Station). MARRIAGE OF ST. CATHERINE.

Inscribed in script: Laurentius Lotus, 1522. Figures half life-size and rather more than half length.

Mentioned by Tassi (*Vite*, vol. i, p. 125) as being in Casa Pezzoli at Bergamo.

The Madonna leans back as if she were a little tired, and watches the play between the Child and the beautiful St. Catherine. The Madonna herself is more beautiful still. She has golden-brown hair and soft brown eyes, and in type is halfway between the *Madonna* of 1521, and the one in the *Marriage of St. Catherine* of 1523, to which we shall come presently. St. Catherine wears pearls and jewels in her amber-brown hair, and is wreathed with laurel and periwinkle. The colouring is bright and clear.

1522. The same Madonna occurs in a picture that has suffered considerably and been restored in water-colours, but still remains pleasant:

LONDON, MRS. MARTIN COLNAGHI. MADONNA AND SAINTS.

The Madonna is seated against a green curtain, with a quiet landscape opening out to the L., between St. Jerome and St. Anthony of Padua, who is dressed in grey and holds in his hand a long-stemmed white lily.
Figures knee-length, half of life.

But even daintier and more refined—a Simone Martini or Crivelli acclimatized to the sixteenth century—must be a *St. Catherine*, known to me only through an engraving:

ST. PETERSBURG, LEUCHTENBERG COLLECTION. ST. CATHERINE.

The saint, wearing a jewelled crown and pearls in her hair, her head inclining a little to the R. and her figure a little to the L., folds her hands over her wheel, which barely shows over the parapet behind which she is standing. In her R. hand she holds a palm-branch, as slim and graceful as in Alvise's *Santa Giustina*.
Inscribed, in script: LAURENTIUS LOTUS, 1522. Half length.
Engraved by N. Muxel in his work on the Leuchtenberg Gallery. Joseph Baer, Frankfort, 1852.

1522 (?). Of the same year possibly is the following bust, remarkable at the same time for its modernity and for the number of Alvisesque traits that reappear in it:

Alinari photo.] [*Bergamo, Carrara Gallery*

PORTRAIT OF A LADY

London, National Gallery, No. 1105. Portrait of
the Prothonotary Giuliano.

A smooth-shaven old man with a face that one would 1522 (?).
not be in the least surprised to see to-day anywhere,
and least of all in England, is seen from the waist up
between a wall hung with a green curtain and a table
covered with a Turkey carpet. He turns slightly to
the L., looking quietly out of the picture. To the L.
on the table lies a large volume which he keeps open
with both his hands. Over it, a window discloses
a view of a range of hills on a low horizon. On the
table lie two letters addressed to the sitter.

On canvas, 94 cm. h., 70½ cm. w. Life-size, half
length.

Photographed by Morelli, London.

The drawing of the face is remarkably Alvisesque,
as we see in noting the following points: The deep
shadow between the base of the upper lid of each eye
and the brow; the high light on the ridge of the nose;
the outlined inflation of the nostril; and the modelling
of the face and chin. The landscape, also, is scarcely
varied from one existing in a work from Alvise's
atelier—the *Madonna* at Piove del Sacco, near Padua.
The L. hand, however, is peculiar to Lotto alone, the
thumb and forefinger being almost the same as in the
L. hand of St. Roch in Signor Piccinelli's *Madonna*.

As a portrait, it is the quietest of all those by Lotto
known to me, and—if I may be allowed the word
here—the most 'gentlemanly.'

The year 1523 is represented by two dated works of 1523.
such widely diverse character as the *Marriage of
St. Catherine* in the Bergamo Gallery and the *Bride
and Bridegroom* at Madrid, the one dainty and lovely,

1523. both in feeling and in technique recalling the works of 1522, and the other humorous and even ironical in conception, almost monochrome in colour and grey in tone, in these points, and in general handling, anticipating Lotto's style of ten years later. We should have hesitated long in ascribing these two pictures to the same year, and we are thus warned how hazardous it is to attempt to affix to Lotto's works dates too precise, although it is true that with sufficient circumspection we may hope to attain to satisfactory, if not final, conclusions. Lotto was not like Titian, whose development had a momentum as constant as it was, so to say, mechanical. Our painter at times made leaps forward, as if on trial experiments, into styles which became characteristic of him only a decade later, and occasionally, as we shall see, he tended to revert to ways of painting which it seemed as if he had already left behind him.

We will now examine these two dated pictures, and, having examined them, see what undated works can safely be classified along with them. We turn in the first place to:

BERGAMO GALLERY, CARRARA COLLECTION, No. 66. MARRIAGE OF ST. CATHERINE.

The Madonna is sitting in front of a parapet hung with a Turkey carpet, bending over a little to the R., and holding with both hands the Child, who also bends over toward the devoutly kneeling St. Catherine, on whose finger He puts a ring. To the R. stands an angel with his hands crossed over his breast; to the L. behind the Virgin, a man of about forty-five, looking straight out of the picture.

Inscribed, in script: LAURENTIUS LOTUS 1523. Full-length figures, almost life-size.

National Gallery, London

PORTRAIT OF PROTHONOTARY GIULIANO

'MARRIAGE OF ST. CATHERINE' 153

Photographed by Alinari. 1523.

Seen by the *Anonimo* in the house of Niccolò di Bonghi, whose portrait, according to the same contemporary authority, we have here. Ridolfi relates that the blank space above the parapet originally contained a view of Mount Sinai so beautiful that, during a French occupation of Bergamo, a soldier cut it out and carried it away.

This is a picture of rare charm. Catherine's features are not remarkably beautiful, but the Madonna is one of the loveliest women ever painted. The grace of their movements, the Madonna as she leans forward, and Catherine as she kneels and bends over, is so simple and natural that we shall scarcely find elsewhere in Italian art anything better. They are both dressed in ample robes, with a great deal of shining white damask silk, producing a dazzling effect. The Madonna makes so little pretence to be more than a beautiful young woman, that she is even elegant, dressed—one is tempted to say—in the height of the fashion, without being spoiled by it. St. Catherine has pearls in her hair, and is clad altogether as a lady of her time: her features, indeed, lead us to suspect a portrait. The Child, with His 'grown-up' way of ceremoniously placing the ring on Catherine's finger, is a trifle comic.

This otherwise perfect composition is somewhat marred by the too obtrusive presence of Niccolò di Bonghi, who evidently insisted on being placed where he could be well seen, and, to make sure of not being overlooked, probably insisted on having his head painted on a larger scale than the other figures. Even Lotto cannot interest us—and perhaps he did not wish to—in this stupid man.

The colouring is perhaps a trifle too dazzling, the scarlets and flashing whites being both too highly

1523. pitched for each other's comfort. The vehicle is thin, as in the works of 1521 and 1522.

Of a very different technique and colour-scale is the other dated picture of this year:

MADRID GALLERY, No. 288. A BRIDE AND BRIDEGROOM.

The Bridegroom sits back a little, and the Bride leans toward him, while he takes hold of her hand, upon which he is about to place a ring. At the same time, Cupid, curly-haired and laurel-crowned, flies up behind them, and with a roguish, amused look at the Bridegroom, puts a laurel-wreathed yoke upon their necks.

Inscribed, in script: Lotvs pictor 1523. On wood, 71 cm. h., 84 cm. w. Figure nearly knee-length.

Photographed by Laurent, Madrid.

Locatelli, in his *Illustri Bergamaschi* (vol. i, p. 463), publishes a bill to which we have already had occasion to refer, made out 'per mi lorenzo lotto a Miser Zanin Casoto,' one of the entries of which is as follows: 'El quadro delli retrati, cioè miss. Marsilio et la sposa sua con quel Cupidineto rispetto al contrefar quelli habiti di seta seu ficti e collane . . . £30.' There can be no doubt, of course, that this is the picture described[1].

The scheme of colour is almost a grey monochrome such as we frequently find in Lotto ten or fifteen years later. But in spite of this, and of the handling, which is unusually large for the date, the drawing of Marsilio's face has much in common with the portrait of Agostino Della Torre, painted, we remember, in 1515. Cupid also betrays close kinship with the infant John in the Santo Spirito altar-piece of 1521. His arms, by the way, are of an impossible length.

[1] For a mention of this work in the seventeenth century see Campori's *Raccolta di Cataloghi*, p. 453.

Alinari photo.] [*Bergamo, Carrara Gallery*

THE MARRIAGE OF ST. CATHARINE

This is perhaps the first positively humorous interpretation of characters and of a situation that we have in Italian painting, and we never again have it so well done. The characters are presented to us as distinctly as in a modern psychological novel, and in our minds no more doubt is left than in Cupid's as to which of the two will be master of the new household.

1523.

The same psychological spirit reveals itself in a Family Group in the National Gallery, but, as if to convince us that Lotto was ironical only when the characters and the situation forced it upon him, as they did in the Madrid couple, and that he was not, as certain people looking at that picture might be tempted to think, a precursor of Schopenhauer, always on the watch for the contrast between the individual's wishes and Nature's intention, we have in the Family Group no touch of irony, although possibly one determined to discover 'the bitterness of things,' might find a trace of it here also.

LONDON, NATIONAL GALLERY, No. 1067. A FAMILY GROUP.

Near a window opening on a sea with a hilly coast, sit to R. and L. of a table covered with a Turkey carpet, a man of about forty, and his wife, a little younger. On the table is a plate of cherries, from which the father has taken a couple, holding them just beyond the grasp of an almost nude boy of two, who is reaching out for them, while his sister, only twice his age, but dressed in as 'grown up' a way as her own mother, clambers on to the table, putting one hand into the plate, and with the other taking some cherries from her mother's hand. The man and the woman are, it is true, both looking out of the picture, but nevertheless the feeling we have is that the group before us is not, as is

1523. usual in Italian family pictures, a mere collection of portraits, but that it is composed of people who are intimately related to each other, constantly acting and reacting one upon the other, and that it is presented in a way which, while giving the individuality of each, makes it hard to think of them except as conditioned, and even determined, by each other's presence.

Signed: L. LOTTO. On canvas, 1·15 m. h., 1·40 m. w. Photographed by Braun, and by Morelli, London.

The woman suggests the Portrait in the Carrara Collection at Bergamo: the man is painted in a somewhat larger style, but nevertheless is close to the portrait of Bonghi in the *Marriage of St. Catherine* in the same collection. The colouring is even more transparent than usual, and as modelling, the figure of the woman is exceptionally well done. The man's hands are even clumsier and stiffer than the hands of Alvise or Cima, which they recall.

Dec. 11, 1523. The first two of the three pictures just described were executed at Bergamo, but the last may have been painted at Venice, where Lotto must have spent some time at the end of this year, seeing that on December 11th we find him residing on the ' Spiaggia delle Case Brucciate,' and receiving commissions[1]. But the *St. Lucy* which he then undertook he did not complete for a number of years, because he must have been called back to Bergamo almost at once.

1524. The year 1524 was one of Lotto's fullest and most successful. Dated works, and others that we have every reason to believe he executed at the same time, reveal him to us not only in the phases which we already know, but as a great decorator, as an admirable fresco painter, and as a profound interpreter of sacred story and legend. In the works of this year we come

---

[1] See Hugo von Tschudi, ' Lorenzo Lotto in den Marken,' in vol. ii of *Repertorium für Kunstwissenschaft*.

A BRIDAL COUPLE

perhaps at times in more naked contact with the *man* than is advantageous to the *artist*: I mean that some of the subjects and some of the decorative allegories and symbols among the intarsias in Santa Maria Maggiore at Bergamo are so suggestive that we do not enjoy them to the full for their qualities of composition and functional line, but lose ourselves either in the reveries they induce in our own minds, or in wonder as to precisely what were the contents of the painter's mind while he was engaged upon them.

The work I shall mention first is one I have never seen, but which has been enthusiastically described by Mündler[1], Crowe and Cavalcaselle, and Morelli. I place it early in this year, because it seems to be only an enlarged replica of the *Marriage of St. Catherine* of the last year, without the donor, and with the addition of several other figures.

ROME, QUIRINAL[2]. MARRIAGE OF ST. CATHERINE, WITH SS. JEROME, GEORGE, SEBASTIAN, ANTONY, AND NICHOLAS OF BARI.

Inscribed: L. Lotu. 1524. Life-size figures.

This seems to be the picture mentioned by Lotto in the bill published by Locatelli: 'el quadro per la camera de miss. Marsilio et nel mezo la Madona con el figliolo in brazo . . £15. Dala parte drita S. hieronimo . . £8. S. Zorzo . . £6. S. Sebastiano computando et leon de S. hieronimo . . £4. Dala parte sinistra stã Catrina . . £10. Sto Antonio . . £6. S. Niccolò di Barri . . £4.'

But so much of this year seems to have been

---

[1] *Beiträge zu Burckhardt's Cicerone.*

[2] Repeated inquiries have failed to discover the present whereabouts of this picture. Apparently it is no longer at the Quirinal. I shall not be surprised to see it turn up some day in the Lateran or Vatican.

158   THE BERGAMASK PERIOD

1524. devoted to fresco painting, that we may call it Lotto's Fresco Year. We must not expect from these, I hasten to say, the qualities of Florentine fresco, which was so great because so strictly subordinated, as composition, and as colour, to the architecture it decorated. Venetian fresco, as a whole, was too impatient of this restraint with regard to colour, and as to Lotto's frescoes in particular, we know him too well by this time to expect of his eager, quick *tempo*—I beg to be allowed this word, supposed to apply to music only—a becoming respect for architecture. But let us now turn to the frescoes, and first to those which are dated:

TRESCORRE, NEAR BERGAMO.   ORATORIO SUARDI.

On the L. wall is the story of St. Barbara, related not in distinct compositions (as, for instance, in Andrea's frescoes in the Annunziata at Florence, or Sodoma's at Monte Oliveto), but in more archaic fashion like a panorama unfolding itself continuously along the length of the wall, broken only in the centre by a colossal figure of Christ. From the fingers of His outspread hands stretch vine-stalks, which, along the top of the wall, twine into frames, each enclosing two or three half-length figures of male or female saints. At each end of the wall giants, symbolizing heresies, who attempt to scale the vine, are hurled down from their ladders. At the feet of Christ are the bust portraits of the three donors, and over His head is a nearly effaced inscription, part of which only need be quoted here: 'Baptista Suardus, Ursolina uxor, Paulina soror, Laurentio Loto pingente hic exprimi pro voto curarunt, anno salutis MDXXIV.'

Towards the choir end, the composition becomes more united, and it is here that Lotto is seen at his best. The variety of motives, the animation of the groups in the market-place, the differences of class and character, the sunshine, and the gaiety, turn it into a scene of *genre* to be compared not so much with anything else in Renaissance painting as with certain scenes in Goethe's *Faust* or *Egmont*. It is interesting, by the way, to place such a scene beside the ceremonious *genre* of Gentile Bellini and Carpaccio; we then realize what an advance in the rendering of actual life was made by Venetian painting in a quarter of a century.

1524.

On the R. wall, and on part of the west wall, are episodes from the legend of St. Clare, with single half-length figures of prophets and sibyls in the medallions above. Lotto has turned the scene of Clare taking her vow into the picture of a family at mass, with the female members on the R., and the male on the L., all with portrait features. This forms in itself a complete picture, and is to be reckoned among the most valuable of Lotto's works. The officiating bishop takes us back to the bishop in the Borghese *Madonna* of 1508. The little boy held back from plucking at his mantle is a characteristic touch, betraying the painter's interest in children.

The remaining part of the entrance wall is taken up with the Communion of the Magdalen.

The simple wooden roof is decorated with *putti* sporting in a trellis of grape-vines.

The entire work has been carefully described by Dr. Gust. Frizzoni in vol. iv of the *Giornale di Erudizione Artistica*, Perugia; and at even greater length by Signor Pasino Locatelli in a splendidly illustrated work entitled, *I Dipinti di Lorenzo Lotto nell' Oratorio Suardi*, Bergamo, 1891. All the frescoes have been photographed by Taramelli, Bergamo.

This series of frescoes, in part ruined, shows Lotto at his best and at his worst. His weakness and carelessness are almost revolting in the figure of Christ.

1524. On the other hand, excepting the intarsias, there are few works in which his graphic talent, his sense of beauty, his humour, his tenderness, his power of giving the very vibration of movement, and catching the character of entire groups of people have had such free scope. He reveals himself here, furthermore, as an extraordinary improvisor, endowed with an exquisite sense for decoration, not of the architectonic, monumental sort, but as we have already observed, of the more personal, Gothic, or Japanese kind.

We will now enumerate Lotto's other frescoes in or near Bergamo which, having, in so far as place and subject would permit, the characteristics of those at Trescorre, were almost certainly executed in this same year.

Not far from Trescorre is the village of Credaro, the old church of which had an open chapel attached to it, dedicated to St. George, which Lotto decorated with frescoes. This chapel it pleased the ecclesiastics of some time later to turn into a sacristy, entered from the church, and for this purpose a door was broken through the principal side of the original chapel, and the paintings on it were partly ruined.

CREDARO, SAN GIORGIO. SACRISTY.

Vaulting: God the Father, a powerful figure reminiscent of Michelangelo's in the ceiling of the Sistine Chapel, which Lotto could have seen while in Rome.

Principal Wall: St. Joseph eloquently expounds the new-born Child to SS. Sebastian and Roch, while three shepherds look in through the shed. This fresco is now a mere ruin, but was originally a fine composition.

Right Wall: St. Stephen with two saints above him.

Left Wall: St. George, with St. Catherine and 1524. John the Baptist above him. The Catherine, with her crown and jewels, must have been very beautiful.

Over the Entrance: The Annunciation, a mere ruin.

On the Outside, Right Wall: St. George and the Princess. St. George is nearly effaced, but his horse, better preserved, has exactly the action of the horse in Raphael's *Expulsion of Heliodorus* in the *Stanze* of the Vatican.

Left Wall: St. George leading up his horse to the Princess and telling her of his victory.

From the bits still remaining—and some of them are curiously well preserved—we can judge what a fascinating work this must have been[1].

The frescoes at San Michele in Bergamo are in a scarcely more happy condition:

BERGAMO, SAN MICHELE DEL POZZO BIANCO. CHAPEL TO L. OF CHOIR.

Vaulting: God the Father in the midst of *putti*, distinctly Michelangelesque, as at Credaro.

Outside Wall: The Visitation.

Inside Wall: The Marriage of the Virgin.

Right Wall: The Presentation of the Virgin.

The Marriage of the Virgin, although half effaced, still has great beauty. The Presentation anticipates Tintoretto's treatment of the same subject in Santa Maria dell' Orto at Venice. All these frescoes, except the vaulting, are badly repainted.

We have finally to mention a couple of mere fragments:

---

[1] Ridolfi and Tassi mention a number of other frescoes which have now completely disappeared.

BERGAMO, SIGNOR ANTONIO FRIZZONI.   TWO ANGELS.

1524. Two angels, one seated, playing on a lute and looking up with a sweet, rapt expression, the other swinging a censer; fragments from some fresco of about this date.

Transferred to canvas, each 51 cm. h., 34 cm. w.

Lotto's brush seems to have got so much into the habit of aiming for the large, rapid effects required by fresco, that we find him executing in the same way a small panel which he must have painted in this year:

MILAN, SIGNOR FRIZZONI.   BUST OF ST. CATHERINE.

As pose and composition, this is identical with the one of 1522 in the Leuchtenberg Collection, but the features, the drawing, and the touch are close to the female saints in the medallions at Trescorre.

On wood, 33 cm. h., 27 cm. w.   A copy at Celana.

We can now turn to the Intarsias:

BERGAMO, SANTA MARIA MAGGIORE.   INTARSIAS OF CHOIR STALLS.

1523-1530. The qualities that attracted and repelled us in the frescoes at Trescorre, we find again in these pictures inlaid in wood, executed for the most part by Capodiferro; and, as at Trescorre, but to a higher degree, the attractive qualities prevail. A great deal of our admiration is due to the *Intarsiatore*, who, to materials, and with means so widely different from pencil and paper, has been able so faithfully to transfer Lotto's quality of line, that the eye acquainted with it recognizes it in the better preserved intarsias almost as if

INTARSIAS

they were Lotto's own cartoons. The most interesting are the principal panels, obviously the earliest, and executed at about this time (1524), which represent the *Story of David, Judith and Holofernes*, the *Crossing of the Red Sea*, and the *Flood*. Of almost equal interest are also some of the smaller panels, such as the *Creation of Man*, and a number of the allegorical and symbolical bits of decoration. A *Creation of Eve* contains an Adam so reminiscent of Michelangelo as to leave no doubt that Lotto was acquainted with the ceiling of the Sistine Chapel. So full of thought and feeling are a number of these intarsias, and, regarded even as mere illustrations they are of such an order, that had Lotto been an engraver and scattered these designs through the world, instead of squandering them upon the church of a provincial town, it is likely that he would have come down to us as the acknowledged rival of Dürer. Lotto, indeed, seems to have been not unconscious of their value, for he had thirty of his cartoons returned to him, and he treasured them up to his last years, making special mention of them in his will of 1546:

'Li quadri del Testamento vecchio, che fu modelli del Coro di Tarsia di Bergamo; et sono pezi n. 30 in tutto, 26 piccoli e pezi n. 4 grandi' (G. Bampo, 'Il Testamento di Lorenzo Lotto,' Archivio Veneto, vol. xxxiv).

Messrs. Crowe and Cavalcaselle quote extracts made from the archives of Santa Maria Maggiore by Dr. M. Caffi, from which it appears that Lotto received payments for these cartoons on May 18, 1523, again in June, 1524, and finally in February, 1525, when he was still in Bergamo. It also appears that further payments were made him for cartoons on January 27, and in August and September, 1527, and in June, 1530, all of these in Venice. From Tassi (*Vite*, vol. i,

1523-1530.

1523-1530. p. 120), we know that the cartoons were coloured, and that Lotto got nine *lire* for each.

I shall now enumerate the intarsias, putting in a word of comment when necessary. The subjects represented are as follows:

The Screen: Crossing of the Red Sea; Flood; Judith and Holofernes; Story of David [1]. Each 70 cm. h., 1·03 m. w. The coverings contain allegories appropriate to the subjects.
The Choir Stalls, Ends: R., Sacrifice of Abel. L., Annunciation.
Seats: 1. Incest of Amnon.
   2. Susanna and the Elders.
   3. Moses and the Tablets of the Law.
   4. Jonah and the Whale.
   5. The Brazen Serpent.
   6. Death of Amnon, containing a figure evidently suggested by the second figure on the R. in Giorgione's *Trial of Moses* in the Uffizi, or, it may be, by Carpaccio's drawing (also in the Uffizi), from which Giorgione himself may have taken it.

The above are among the very best, and are probably the first of the series.

   7. The Family who preferred Death to eating Pork (from the Apocrypha).
   8. The Queen of Sheba. One of the best.
   9. The Vision of Elijah. A fine landscape.
   10. Joab killing Amas. The architecture is excellent, but the figures scarcely seem to be after Lotto at all.
   11. David mourning over Absalom. Possibly not Lotto's design.
   12. Death of Absalom.

---

[1] These last two photographed by Alinari.

INTARSIAS

13. Story of Achitophel. Rather hasty. 1523–
14. David choosing Soldiers. 1530.
15. Samson and Delilah.
16. Samson drinking from the Ass's Jawbone.
17. Samson and the Foxes.
18. Parents of Samson offering a Sacrifice.
19. Selling of Joseph.
20. Sacrifice of Isaac. One of the best.
21. Lot and his Daughters.
22. Sacrifice of Melchizedek. Anticipates Lotto's treatment of the same subject at Loreto, painted thirty years later.
23. Drunkenness of Noah.
24. Cain and Abel. Abel, reclining, recalls Michelangelo.
25. Creation of Eve. Adam is Michelangelesque.
26. Temptation and Expulsion from Eden.
27. The first Sacrifice.
28. Creation of Man and the World. In Lotto's most profound and imaginative mood.
29. Cain slaying Abel.

The numerous bits of allegory and decoration escape description. Of all attempts known to me at symbolism in art, these come nearest to being profoundly suggestive without ceasing to be artistic.

The year 1525 has no dated work to offer us, and 1525. there is none that we feel obliged to assign to it, in spite of the temptation to have something to show for each year. It is to be supposed that in the first months of 1525 Lotto was busy drawing the cartoons for the intarsias, for he gets a payment for them in February. At this time he was still at Bergamo, but he seems to have gone away soon, and, for all we know, for good. We shall find works of later date

1525. near Bergamo, and up to 1530, as we have already noted, he continued to supply cartoons for the intarsias, thus proving that he continued in pleasant relations with the Bergamasks [1]; but none of these commissions were of a kind that he could not have executed in Venice and sent on to their destination in or near Bergamo. Where he passed the rest of the year 1525 we do not know, although, if we may trust Ricci, he spent it in or near Recanati.

July, 1525. Ricci (*Arte nelle Marche*, vol. ii, p. 106) makes an extract from the *Libri di Riformanze del Municipio di Recanati* to the effect that on July 17, 1525, the monks of San Domenico demanded a subsidy for an altarpiece of great price to be painted by Maestro Lorenzo Lotto, and that the Commune granted 100 florins on condition that the altar-piece should contain the figures of the patrons of the city, SS. Flavian and Vito. Unfortunately, Ricci is not to be trusted, even when he is quoting documents. In this instance, particularly, it would seem that the document in question must have referred to the altar-piece of 1508 in which these saints occur, for it is not likely that another elaborate altar-piece containing the same saints would have been required for the same church while the first was still in existence. I have referred to Ricci's statement because we do as a matter of fact find in the Marches pictures by Lotto which belong to this period, and, as they are on wood and fairly large, we have every reason to think that they were executed on the spot. One of them is dated 1526, but the other seems to me to

---

[1] Bergamo did not cease to appreciate Lotto after he left it. Before long, he was even claimed as a son, a claim, by the way, given up to-day in Bergamo only with great reluctance. In 1591 the monks of San Bernardino seemed inclined to sell their altar-piece to outsiders, and the town decreed that rather than let it be taken away, the Commune itself would buy it (Tassi, vol. i, p. 121).

precede it in style. Lotto may have executed the July, latter, an *Annunciation*, in the autumn of 1525, and 1525. begun the former at once, which he then would have finished early in the following year, dating it 1526.

JESI, LIBRARY. THE ANNUNCIATION (originally in San Floriano).

The subject is painted on two separate panels. The Madonna wears the transparent scarlet found frequently in Lotto's Bergamask works. The angel is posed as if suddenly arrested in the midst of rapid downward flight. The flesh is very blond and the shadows Murillesque. The Madonna looks somewhat too startled, and the exaggerated movement of the angel almost takes one's breath away.
Each panel 80 cm. h., 41 cm. w.
Photographed by Alinari.

JESI, LIBRARY. MADONNA AND SAINTS (from San Francesco in Monte).

The Madonna is enthroned between SS. Jerome 1526. and Joseph. In the lunette, St. Francis is represented as receiving the stigmata, while St. Clare kneels to R. holding a monstrance.
Inscribed : LAVRENTIVS LOTVS. MDXXVI. On wood, 1·47 m. h., 1·52 m. w. The lunette is considerably ruined.
Photographed by Alinari, the lunette by Houghton, Florence.
The colouring is clear and clean. The folds resemble those in the *Santa Conversazione* in Vienna, to which we shall come later. The glimpse of landscape in the lunette and the rosebuds and rosepetals scattered at the foot of the throne are characteristic.

1526. Of the same year we have another dated work, a portrait which recently passed from the Sernagiotto Collection into the Treviso Gallery:

TREVISO, PINACOTECA, SALA SERNAGIOTTO-CERATO, No. 20. PORTRAIT OF A DOMINICAN STEWARD OR PRIOR.

Inscribed, in script: Laurentius Lotus 1526. On canvas, 77 cm. h., 67 cm. w. Half length.
Photographed by Alinari, Florence.

He is seated against a green curtain at a desk, making up his accounts. He looks up as if pausing in his calculation to think of another item. We have here a careful study of character which misses nothing of the temperament of the sitter, even while representing him in his monastic garb at his book-keeping. The execution is somewhat, but only a very little, harder than in the *Andrea Odoni* of 1527. The drapery of the sleeves is characteristic. The hands are somewhat repainted. May not this have been a prior or steward of San Giovanni e Paolo? This is perhaps the portrait mentioned by Ridolfi as belonging to Agostino Onigo of Treviso.

The possibility that this Prior was known to Ridolfi, and his presence in the Veneto in this century, make me think that he was painted in or near Venice, and consequently that Lotto returned to Venice before the end of 1526. In January of the next year we find him certainly there, receiving payments for the Bergamo intarsias.

At about this date, that is to say before the end of 1526, Lotto in all probability executed two portraits which, on the whole, have more resemblance in morphology and technique to the Treviso portrait than to any other work. As one of them has a view of

A FAMILY GROUP

[*National Gallery, London*

PORTRAITS

the Venetian *Molo*, we may be reasonably sure that it was painted in Venice: 1526.

Berlin, Gallery, No. 320. Portrait of a Young Man.

A young man, of about thirty, with close-cropped hair and short beard, wearing a cap on one side of his head and a dark coat which shows the frilled white shirt, is posed against a scarlet curtain which is slightly drawn aside to expose a view, from above, of the lagoon, with Venice in the distance. 1526 (?).

Inscribed: L Lotus pict. On canvas, 47 cm. h., 39 cm. w. Half length.

Photographed by Hanfstängl.

The ear is naturalistic. The folds on the coat are almost the same as in the Vienna Portrait of about the same date. The energetic folds of the curtain also belong to this time.

This portrait may be called Lotto's *Homme au Gant*. It has the masterly directness and simplicity of that great Titian, but is not so impersonal, is more sensitive, more intellectual—an Italian of the first half of the sixteenth century, who belongs to neither of the varieties catalogued by Stendhal and all the other writers, with Taine and Symonds at their head, who have copied him or each other. The young man before us is neither cut-throat nor artist.

Not later than the last in date, and possibly even a little earlier, is the portrait in the Museo Civico at Milan:

Milan, Museo Civico, No. 85. Portrait of a Youth.

A smooth-faced youth, of eighteen or nineteen, bends over with his whole body a little to the L. and looks

1526 (?). out to the R. His hair is cropped close, and the cap on one side of his head shades the R. eye. His look is a little cruel and contemptuous, but his mouth is peculiarly sweet. He is seen against a green ground, dressed in a coat of greyish lilac stuff, striped with broad stripes of black, holding a book with both hands.

In composition and colour this is 'artistic,' in the French sense of the word, and unexpected as a work of the Renaissance. The character is presented with great clearness.

On wood, 34 cm. h., 27 cm. w.

Photographed by Alinari and Brogi.

1527. I have already referred to the fact that Lotto was certainly in Venice in January, 1527. The same source of information, the archives of Santa Maria Maggiore at Bergamo, tells us that he was there in August and September also. We may take it for granted, therefore, that Lotto spent most, if not the whole, of the year 1527 in Venice. His portrait of Andrea Odoni of this date proves that he came in contact with that amateur, one of the first private 'Collectors' of select works of art (not of mere price or curiosity) of modern Europe. At the same time Lotto seems to have renewed his intercourse with Palma, who at this date was certainly in Venice, already ill with the disease that in the next year was going to carry him off. I infer this renewed contact between the two painters from such works of this year by Lotto as the Celana *Assumption*, the Ponteranica Polyptych, and the Vienna Portrait, in all of which, in the *impasto*, in the modelling, and even in the types, there are certain unmistakable traces of Palma's influence. On the other hand, Palma's portrait of a Querini, in the Querini-Stampalia Gallery (Sala

Berlin Gallery

PORTRAIT OF A YOUNG MAN

XVII), at Venice, painted at about this time, is 1527. peculiarly Lottesque in conception.

We will first devote our attention to the works with the slight Palmesque trace:

CELANA, NEAR CAPRINO, PROVINCE OF BERGAMO. ASSUMPTION OF THE VIRGIN.

In a valley, enclosed by wooded hillocks, which frame in a view of the sea, the Apostles are gathered around the tomb of the Virgin. A spectacled old Apostle looks into the tomb, surprised to find it filled with roses. The Virgin soars heavenward, with her blue mantle fluttering in the wind. Two angels, dressed in pink, accompany her, and two *putti* float under the edge of her robe. Most of the Apostles reach after her, stretching out their arms, and leaning upon each other in their instinctive endeavour to rise from the ground.

Inscribed, in script: Laurentius Lotus, 1527, pinxit. On canvas, 2·36 m. h., 1·92 m. w. Well preserved for the most part, although dust has eaten into it in places, and here and there tiny bits have peeled off.

Mentioned by Ridolfi as '*molto lodata.*'

The composition is pyramidal, the Madonna with her fluttering mantle forming the apex, and the Apostles the base. The *putti* complete the sides. The angels are close to the Gabriel in the Recanti *Annunciation* of the next year. The group to the L., containing St. Paul, is in a more vigorous style than usual. The group to the R., anticipated, as composition, in the small *Assumption* of the Brera (1512 *circa*), has a figure which resembles the St. Sebastian in the altar-piece of 1521, in Santo Spirito, Bergamo. One of the *putti* resembles the Cupid in the Rospigliosi picture (1528 *circa*), and the wooded hillocks recall the San Bernardino altar-piece at Bergamo (1521). It would be no easy matter, therefore, to date this *Assumption* exactly, if the painter had not spared us the task. Most of the painting is, however, more solid than in earlier works, the vehicle more as in Palma, the lights and shadows (in which Lotto's progress is constant) are more advanced, and the sea-view already suggests the altar-piece of 1529 in the Carmine at Venice. The sky behind the Virgin and over the sea looks like the apse of some cosmic, air-built temple.

One cannot help comparing this *Assumption* with Titian's and Correggio's. It is certainly not so overwhelming as the one, nor so jubilant as the other, but it is far more personal than either. The Virgin looks too grateful for her bliss, can scarcely believe it as yet, and therefore cannot be rapturous and ecstatic. Here, as usual, Lotto, aside from his qualities as a painter, is in the first place an interpreter.

The style of the following work leaves no doubt that it must be of exactly the same date:

PONTERANICA, NEAR BERGAMO. ALTAR-PIECE IN SIX PARTS.

Upper middle panel: The Redeemer with the Blood spurting from all His wounds into a chalice at His feet[1].

R. upper panel: The Virgin kneeling at her *prie-dieu*.

L. upper panel: Gabriel and the Dove.

Lower middle panel: St. John the Baptist carrying a lamb.

---

[1] This subject occurs in Italy, I believe, only in Venetian painting, and, excepting this instance, only in the young Giovanni Bellini in the National Gallery (No. 1233), in Crivelli in the Poldi Collection at Milan, and in Antonio Vivarini in San Zaccaria at Venice.

R. lower panel: St. Paul. 1527.
L. lower panel: St. Peter.

On the lower middle panel the inscription, partly effaced: L. LO . . . 152 . . . Figures somewhat under life-size.

Photographed by Taramelli, Bergamo.

Peter and Paul are almost identical with two of the Apostles in the Celana *Assumption*, and the manner of painting is practically the same. John the Baptist in attitude is like Palma's Baptist at Vienna, and the landscape, also, resembles the landscape in that picture. The vehicle in this work is much less fluid than is usual with Lotto at this date—laid on more thickly and solidly, as in Palma.

Gabriel is the loveliest angel Lotto has left us. He is like the spirit of one of those roses the artist loved to paint, and a reader of Shakespeare may be tempted to compare him with Ariel.

The *execution* of this work is not Lotto's throughout. Perhaps the entire figure of Christ is by an assistant, and St. Peter's drapery is certainly by another hand. The *predelle* are obviously by Cariani.

The modelling and the vehicle in the following portrait, as well as the colour-scheme, are identical with what we have found in these last two works:

VIENNA, IMPERIAL GALLERY, No. 274. PORTRAIT OF A MAN.

A man of about thirty-five, with light brown hair and short beard, leans against a table covered with green, holding his R. hand against his breast, and in his L. a golden claw. He stands in front of a scarlet curtain, and wears a flowing dark mantle. The pose and gesture suggest Lotto's portrait of Odoni. It is characteristic of Lotto to make us feel, as he does

1527. in this splendid portrait, that we know the precise measure of the sitter's pulse and just how he draws breath.

On canvas, 98 cm. h., 76 cm. w., life-size, knee-length.

Photographed by Löwy, Vienna.

I am inclined to think that the portrait of Odoni was painted after the above works, because the lights and shadows are treated more subtly. It contains, by the way, no trace of Palma. Lotto must have quickly found out, after a first enthusiastic contact with his old friend, that his own manner was too fixed to suffer rapid change, or, if needing change, that it could not advantageously change in Palma's direction:

HAMPTON COURT, No. 148. PORTRAIT OF ANDREA ODONI.

He stands by a table covered with a green cloth, and holds a statuette in his hand. Other antique fragments surround him.

Inscribed in script: Lavrentivs Lotvs. 1527. On canvas, 1·03 m. h., 1·17 m. w. Life-size, three-quarters length.

Engraved by Cornelius Visscher for the series made after the Van Reynst pictures.

Mentioned by the *Anonimo*, who saw it in 1532 at the house of Andrea Odoni in Venice, and by Vasari, who also saw it there.

As a portrait, this is by no means one of Lotto's most sympathetic, but as a work of art it is one of his finest achievements, not only for its beautiful tone, but for the treatment of lights and shadows.

1527-1528. Excepting a statement to the effect that on November 20, 1528, Lotto had not yet finished the

Lowy photo.] [*Vienna Gallery*

PORTRAIT OF A MAN

PORTRAIT of ANDREA ODONI

(Milan, Museo Civico (Castello)

PORTRAIT OF A YOUTH

picture of *St. Lucy* for Jesi, we have no mention of 1527-
him in that year. But between the *Andrea Odoni*, 1528.
executed toward the end, probably, of 1527, and the
Carmine altar-piece, which once was dated 1529, Lotto
must have painted four of his most successful works,
all of which obviously belong to this, and not to the
next period, but could not have been painted earlier
than any of the works thus far enumerated, because
they have certain characteristics indicating a decided
advance upon those works. In the Santo Spirito
altar-piece of 1521, we already observed a tendency
to outline in brown. In the four pictures now before
us, a sharp brownish outline accompanies all the
shadow sides of the figures. The draperies are more
billowy and vigorous in movement of line than in
earlier works, the structure is more solid, the tone
constantly tending toward grey, and the brushwork
larger. Lotto, now in his forty-eighth year, was, as
we shall see, far from exhausted. Indeed, he was still
advancing, still realizing himself, and a feeling for
beauty, a grace and a humour reveal themselves in
the pictures to which we now turn, which do not
indeed surprise us, but which we have not before
found so completely harmonized.

VIENNA, IMPERIAL GALLERY, No. 273. SANTA CON-
VERSAZIONE.

The Virgin is seated under a thick-stemmed, spreading tree, holding the Child, who makes a gesture of
blessing, while He touches with His other hand the
book of the kneeling St. Catherine. Behind the
Madonna stands an angel holding over her head
a wreath of blossoms. To the extreme R. kneels
St. James the Elder. A landscape with low hills
stretches in the background.

176 THE BERGAMASK PERIOD

1527-
1528.
On canvas, 1·12 m. h., 1·48 m. w.

Photographed by Löwy, Vienna, and by Hanfstängl.

This is, to my knowledge, the only original work by Lotto in existence composed as a *Santa Conversazione* in Palma's fashion. The Madonna recalls in type the Madonna of San Bernardino, and at the same time the Venus of the Rospigliosi. The character of St. Catherine's features, and the fact that they are turned, at the cost of dramatic unity, in a way to expose them, her fashionable green dress and jewelled cross, make it seem highly probable that she is a portrait. Indeed, she suggests the Holford *Lucretia*. In features the lovely, flaxen-haired angel resembles the one at Ponteranica, while his movement and drapery we shall find matched in the Recanati and Rospigliosi pictures. The light blue of the Virgin's robe is subtly harmonized with the greyish flesh tints. The lights and shadows playing over the figures and the landscape are suggestive of coolness and breezes on a summer day.

RECANATI, SANTA MARIA SOPRA MERCANTI. ANNUNCIATION.

The Madonna turns away from her *prie-dieu*, surprised and awed by the announcing angel, who has alighted on the terrace just outside her bedroom. A green curtain hangs over her snow-white bed, and on the wall at the back runs along a book-laden shelf, with a white towel and night-cap hanging from it. A cat, frightened by the angel, bounds across the floor with raised tail and arched back. The angel has waving flaxen hair, and wears a blue robe. He carries the lily in his L. hand, and holds up his R. hand impressively. His bluish-green wings are not like a

THE MADONNA AND CHILD, WITH SAINTS

Löwy photo.] [*Vienna Gallery*

bird's, but like Psyche's. He kneels in front of a 1527-
parapet which borders upon a rose-garden, with a vine- 1528.
trellis, a bower of cut ilex, a stone-pine, and some
cypresses showing clear against the pale blue sky.
Above the garden appears God the Father, in profile,
with arms extended.

Signed, in script: L. Lotus. On canvas, 1·62 m.
h., 1·14 m. w. Well preserved.

Photographed by Anderson and Alinari.

The Madonna would be nearly the same as the
Vienna Madonna if she were seen in profile, and the
angel, also, resembles the one in Vienna, but is here
filled with the awe of his message. The billowy folds
of the Madonna's blue robe are of the same character
as in Vienna. The lights and shadows are treated not
only with great delicacy, but with genuine science.
Carpaccio himself never painted a better interior than
this bedroom of the Virgin. The vehicle is clear, with
subtle qualities of tint. As execution, this is one of
Lotto's best works, and as interpretation—well, nowhere else has a painter of this subject ventured to
portray the woman in the Virgin. This *Annunciation*,
by the way, differs from the rather archaic altar-piece
of 1508 preserved in the Municipio of the same town,
as the Hermes of Praxiteles differs from the Aeginetan
marbles.

To these years belongs a St. Jerome which I found
since the first publication of this book:

HAMBURG. CONSUL WEBER, No. 33. ST. JEROME.

St. Jerome, half wrapped in a blanket-like mantle of
Lotto's characteristic pinkish scarlet, stops reading,
and with a gesture not free from affectation turns
sentimentally to a cross and a skull. His right foot

1527-1528. is stretched out, and his left is doubled up under him. Above him is a shelf of books. Beyond is a room with a lion passing through it. Further still beyond is a colonnade leading to a ruined wall closing in a garden.

On panel, 51 × 40 cm.

Reproduced in Signor Frizzoni's article on Lotto in *Archivio Storico dell' Arte*, 1896, p. 438.

This picture (as is more usual with Lotto's works when not recognized) I found attributed to a non-Venetian painter, in this case to Andrea del Sarto. But the nervous, quick movement is Lotto's; the scarlet is Lotto's; the folds are Lotto's; the lion reminds one of the cat in the Recanati *Annunciation*; the woodwork and the background recall the same picture. The only other St. Jerome which reminds me of this one is a work by Lotto's fellow pupil Marco Basaiti, belonging to Herr R. von Kaufmann of Berlin. (See catalogue of this gentleman's collection.)

BRESCIA, GALLERY TOSIO, No. 34. ADORATION OF THE SHEPHERDS.

On canvas, 1·42 m. h., 1·61 m. w.

Photographed by Alinari, Florence.

The Virgin kneels in a shed, adoring the Child, who lies on the edge of her dress playing with a lamb held over Him by one of the shepherds. The lamb's head casts a cool, clear shadow on the Child's face. The two shepherds have portrait features, and their faces recall the *Andrea Odoni* of Hampton Court. Behind them are two angels, and behind the Virgin, St. Joseph, whose face stands out dark against the pale sky. The lights and shadows, and the billowy draperies, as well as the types, bring this work into line with the two last described, although it seems to be a trifle later than either.

Anderson photo.] [*Recanati, Santa Maria di Sopra*

THE ANNUNCIATION

This is perhaps the picture seen by Ridolfi in the *Padri Reformati* at Treviso. That it came from Treviso is still the tradition at Brescia. 1527–1528.

We have finally to speak in this connexion of a picture which, from whatever point of view we consider it, must be placed among the few most fascinating of Lotto's works. In few others has he combined such beauty and such movement with such poetical suggestions of space and such subtle irony. Lotto was not the man to portray a contrast such as there is in this picture between the unruffled beauty of the Venus and the bad temper of the Chastity without some conscious purpose. And was it as a mere 'academy,' to bring out the greyness of the flesh tints, that he painted the light as just beginning to break in the sky?

ROME, ROSPIGLIOSI GALLERY. THE TRIUMPH OF CHASTITY.

Venus, an exquisitely modelled nude, with streaming hair and a star on her head, floats over a landscape, where dawn is just breaking, holding on her shoulder a casket full of toilet articles, and shielding with her arm the little Cupid from the attack of an infuriated female, who, dressed in green, with an ermine creeping on her breast, has just broken his tiny bow and dashed the still lighted torch out of his hand. The ermine indicates that this figure is meant to represent Chastity.

Signed, in script: Lavrentivs Lotvs. On canvas, 73 cm. h., 1·14 m. w.

Photographed by Anderson, Rome.

This picture must have been painted at the very end of the period we have been studying, as the

1527-1528. Cupid and the outline of the profile of the Chastity would by themselves be taken as belonging to the next period. But the arm of this figure is drawn in the same awkward way as that of the angel in the Recanati *Annunciation*, the flutter of the draperies is the same in both figures, coming close, also, to the angel's draperies in the Vienna *Santa Conversazione*, and the tone, although richer, is the greyish one of the other works of this year. The Venus is modelled in a way that vividly recalls a marble torso visible in Odoni's portrait.

TRIUMPH OF CHASTITY

Anderson photo.] *[Galleria Rospigliosi, Rome*

CHAPTER V

MATURITY

1529–1540

LOTTO was almost fifty years of age at the opening 1529–of the period in his career to which we are now going 1540. to devote our attention. 'Nearly fifty years old,' it may be objected, 'and yet you put the rubric "Maturity" over the chapter treating of his works executed in the next ten years?' Yes, it was only in these years that Lotto at last completely realized himself. Not that many Alvisesque habits did not continue to stick to him, and not that he ceased to feel the magnetism of artists greater than himself, but it was in these years that the man at last attained the full consciousness of his own power as a thinker, poetical interpreter, and creator. In no works of Lotto's previous years do we find, as in the pictures now before us, sacred subjects so profoundly interpreted, and with so distinct a touch of the sublime, or portraits which betray so keen an interest in the human being, an analysis so searching, and a diagnosis so complete, combined with the ideal physician's sympathy, and with the ideal priest's tenderness. Once or twice, it is true, Lotto makes us feel that, like the priest or the physician, he ought to have kept his sitter's secret under the seal of confession, instead of revealing it; but such a feeling disappears as mere

1529-1540. petulance before our gratitude to the artist who opens our eyes to the existence in a time and in a country supposed to be wholly devoted to carnality and carnage, of gentle, sensitive people, who must have had many of our own social and ethical ideas, and been as much revolted by the crimes happening in their midst as we are by the horrors and scandals bursting out frequently among ourselves.

Regarded as composition, structure, and technique, the works of this period, although differing among themselves, hold a high level of excellence. As compositions, there are in art but few dramatic ones so successful as the Monte San Giusto *Crucifixion*, and few which contain such sublime suggestions of space as the Carmine altar-piece at Venice, painted in the beginning, or the Cingoli altar-piece, executed at the end of this period. As structure, the figures in the better works of this decade are built up more solidly, the modelling is more plastic, the draperies more functional. In tone, the grey manner already noticed in the Vienna *Santa Conversazione* prevails, particularly after 1531. But in a few pictures executed in 1529, 1530, and 1531, works ranking among Lotto's best, a manner appears which could not have been merely the natural and inevitable consequence of Lotto's previous evolution, but must have resulted from an attempt to adopt the technique of Titian. Lotto, we remember, had thus far kept faithful to the slow vehicle inherited from Alvise, and his colour-scheme had been blond or grey. We remember, too, that in 1514 he made an attempt to adopt the more fluid vehicle and deeper, richer, more fiery colouring of the Giorgioneschi, as practised by Palma, but that he soon gave up this technique as uncongenial, barely approaching it once again in 1527. In the Carmine altar-piece, however, the first work of the period now before us, the *impasto* and the colour scheme are again, as in the Alzano picture, Giorgionesque, this time, however, not in Palma's but in Titian's manner.

1529-1540.

What was Lotto's relation to Titian at this time? We have not a word in any contemporary writer or document to answer this question, but the Carmine altar-piece reveals clearly enough that Lotto, if not in personal relations with Titian, had at least studied his pictures, and been stung by them to emulation. In 1518, it will be remembered, Titian completed his *Assunta*, which gave him full possession of the place at the head of Venetian painters occupied before him by Giambellino and Giorgione. In 1526, just as Lotto was returning to Venice, Titian was finishing his Pesaro *Madonna*. Two or three years later Titian's supremacy was ratified, as it were, by Imperial decree. No painter at this time could possibly live in Venice taking an interest in his art without hearing of Titian and seeing his works. It is rather surprising, therefore, that Lotto should have been there three years before he began to show signs of an acquaintance with Titian's technique, and this fact may perhaps give ground for the inference that during Palma's lifetime Lotto did not make other acquaintances, and that it was only after Palma's death in 1528 that he came in contact with Titian, or at least had his attention drawn to Titian's works. Whatever the nature of the contact, whether or not personal, as it scarcely could have helped being, its result was the Carmine altar-piece, a work in which the qualities of composition and line, in which the conception and the feeling are to the highest degree characteristic of Lotto himself, but wherein the vehicle and the colour-scheme tend to be Titianesque. The medium must have been (in so far as the present state of the picture permits us to judge) a more fluid one, and the colouring more what is called

1529-
1540.
'Venetian'—that is to say, ruddier, richer, and more fiery—than was usual with Lotto. In the course of two or three years he abandoned this colour-scheme almost as completely as he had abandoned Palma's after 1514, having in the meantime, however, produced several masterpieces. He then returned to his cool grey manner.

Lotto's debt to Titian, then, was restricted to this: that for a year or two he experimented, not unsuccessfully, with Titian's colour-scheme, trying how well he could express *himself* in tones then as fashionable as are purples in landscape pictures nowadays. When he became convinced that his own universe did not look a 'Titian red,' he returned to his blues and greys. But it cannot be said that Lotto shows signs of having taken an idea, a conception of any sort, or even the least *motif*, from Titian[1]. In all such matters he was more than Titian's equal, inferior though he was, as Alvise in the century before had been inferior to Giambellino, in some of the more serious business of painting as a craft. In the next period we shall find indications of another contact between Lotto and Titian, and we shall then have occasion to study further into the relation between these two painters who stood at the opposite poles of Venetian art.

1529.
Lodovico Dolci, a hack writer of some talent, and a parasite of the log-rolling company of which Titian, Sansovino, and Aretino were the chief partners, took occasion in his *Dialogue on Painting* to find fault with Lotto's Carmine altar-piece for its too fiery colouring. No one to-day would be tempted to find fault with it on this score, and it is more than questionable whether such an objection could ever have been made in good

---

[1] The only approach to a *motif* taken from Titian is the angel in the Recanati *Annunciation*, which may have been suggested by Titian's at Treviso.

faith. In all probability Dolci's censure was nothing 1529. but an echo of Titian's fear of being outmatched, or at least equalled, on his own ground. Ruined as this altar-piece now is, we still enjoy in it the glowing reds and whites, and the delicate ruddy flesh tints found in such of Titian's pictures as the Pesaro *Madonna*, the Louvre *Entombment*, or the National Gallery *Bacchus and Ariadne*. Lotto's picture, far from being too fiery, does not quite attain the glow of Titian's masterpieces, but has instead a more than Titianesque subtlety in the juxtaposition and fusion of the colours.

VENICE, CARMINE, SECOND ALTAR, L. ST. NICHOLAS OF BARÌ IN GLORY WITH OTHER SAINTS.

St. Nicholas of Barì, surrounded by three angels bearing his insignia, with St. Lucy and St. John seated on clouds to R. and L. a little below him, floats over a wide stretch of landscape, with a view of the sea from inland, paths winding down to a port, and travellers going toward the coast. In the foreground to R., St. George fights the dragon, while the Princess flees towards a castle.

Of the signature and date there is at present no trace, but Ridolfi says that it was signed and dated 1529, and the style of painting bears out this statement. The picture is mentioned by Vasari also.

On canvas, 3·25 m. h., 1·80 m. w., rounded top.

Photographed by Anderson and Alinari.

The incomprehensible neglect in which this masterpiece is still left is all the more to be regretted because, everything considered, it seems to have been one of Lotto's greatest achievements. In few other works has he created types so strong and beautiful, and seldom has his drawing been so firm, his modelling so plastic, and his colouring so glowing and harmonious.

1529. The landscape must have been one of the most captivating in Italian painting, and, even now, although it is coated with candle-grease, the sweep of its outlines, the harmony of its colours, and the suggestiveness of its lights make an unwonted appeal to the imagination.

1529-1530. The work, which in technique stands closest to the Carmine picture, is an altar-piece at Jesi, for which Lotto received the order as far back as December 11, 1523. He was to be paid 220 ducats for it by the *Società di Santa Lucia*. It was not ready for delivery on June 4, 1527, and on November 20, 1528, his employers threatened to give the commission to another painter unless Lotto made haste. On February 5, 1531, he received his last payment for this work[1]. Judging by the style and technique, Lotto could not have as much as begun it before some time in 1529, and it is probable that he finished it in 1530.

JESI, LIBRARY. ST. LUCY BEFORE HER JUDGES.

On wood, 2.29 m. h., 2.24 m. w. Much darkened and ruined,
Photographed by Alinari.
The treatment of light is almost the same as in the Carmine altar-piece. The Judges resemble the Pharisees in the Louvre *Christ and the Adulteress*, painted somewhat later. The executioners, who are trying to pull the saint away, are in romantic costume. This altar-piece, in its present state at any rate, is much less interesting than the *predelle* which originally belonged to it, but are now preserved in the Municipio.

[1] See Hugo von Tschudi, 'Lorenzo Lotto in den Marken,' *Repertorium für Kunstwissenschaft*, vol. ii.

Anderson photo.] (Venice, Church of the Carmine

THE GLORY OF ST. NICHOLAS

STORY OF ST. LUCY.

Three panels, each 32 cm. h., 69 cm. w. Save for a little rubbing, they are well preserved.
All photographed by Alinari.

1529-1530.

In the first panel—*St. Lucy at the tomb of St. Agatha*—four scenes are represented: (1) Lucy asleep on the steps of the altar; (2) Lucy and her companion hearing mass; (3) Lucy and her companion moving away from the altar; (4) Lucy in a side chapel giving alms. This panel is remarkable for the skilful treatment of lights and shadows within an interior. The architecture is of the peculiar kind found only in the Veneto, in such a church, for instance, as Santa Maria Formosa at Venice. Such small, rather stunted figures as are found here occur frequently in Lotto's less studied compositions, particularly in the Bergamo intarsias.

The second and third panels go together, the second containing *St. Lucy before the Judges*, treated in the same way as in the altar-piece itself, and part of the last scene, concluded in the third, where the attempt is being made to drag her away after the sentence has been pronounced. Eight pairs of bullocks, harnessed to her, extend in a long line, straining every muscle, but fail to move her from the spot.

The tone throughout is rich and glowing, and the treatment of lights and shadows is very elaborate, almost as advanced as in Vermeer van Delft. The dramatic interpretation and the characteristic movement of each individual figure are on a level with the frescoes at Trescorre, and with the Bergamo intarsias. These *predelle* are delightful, not only for their sparkling colour and the grace of the action, but also for the vivid sympathy with which the artist interprets the character of the heroine, who, like the *St. Barbara* at Trescorre, is not a woe-begone martyr, but a sprightly

1529-1530. lass who enjoys witnessing to the faith that is in her, and has the physical energy to remain not only firm but cheerful to the end.

Another picture which Lotto painted, probably in the same year, equally wins our sympathy for its heroine. It is the *Christ and the Adulteress*, a subject very popular in Venice at this time, as may be inferred from the fact that scarcely any painter of note left it untouched. But Lotto treats it with his own peculiar tenderness. The droop of the head and the faltering figure of the lovely woman make it impossible for any but such coarse, vehement creatures as the Pharisees, by whom she is surrounded, to be harsh with her.

LOUVRE, NO. 1351. CHRIST AND THE ADULTERESS.

Christ stands in the midst of the Pharisees, with the woman on the L.
On canvas, 1·24 m. h., 1·56 m. w.
Photographed by Braun.
The Christ is Lotto's usual type. The Adulteress recalls the St. Lucy in the Carmine altar-piece. The Pharisees, although bearing a decided resemblance to the corpulent old men often found in Bonifazio, have here an intentional look of coarseness and vulgarity. This type, by the way, also found in Titian, goes back to engravings of Dürer and Lucas van Leyden, then widely copied in Italy. The crowd stretching away into the darkness is painted with a skill in modelling within deep shadow that surpasses even the altar-piece in San Bartolommeo at Bergamo. There the treatment, though perfect of its kind, is, from a modern point of view, a trifle dry; here the shadow itself is treated atmospherically.
It is curious to note that the painting of armour here

is very different from what we find in the pictures of Bellini's and Giorgione's school, and witnesses once more to Lotto's connexion with Alvise Vivarini. Without the sparkle and iridescence which Titian and Rubens give to metallic surfaces, Lotto's armour, less flashing, but by no means lifeless, resembles that of Rembrandt and the Dutch masters.

1529-1530.

In tone and colour the *Christ and the Adulteress* stands close to the Carmine altar-piece of 1529, but the execution and the treatment of atmosphere indicate a somewhat later date. The crowd most vividly suggests Titian's Vienna *Ecce Homo*, painted, it will be remembered, in 1543.

Lotto is known to have painted this subject a number of times. A replica, originally inferior and totally ruined by recent restoration, still exists.

LORETO, PALAZZO APOSTOLICO, NO. 34. CHRIST AND THE ADULTERESS.

On canvas, 1·05 m. h., 1·32 m. w.
Mentioned by Vasari.
Photographed by Anderson.
Three copies are known, one in the Palazzo Spada at Rome, another at Dresden, and another still at a dealer's in London, the last two by Flemish painters.

Two portraits, which have the characteristics of style and technique of the three last works, and must, therefore, have been executed at about the same time, have also their humane and delicate qualities of interpretation. The one probably first in date is among Lotto's most sympathetic and most expressive. Here, even more than in the Vienna Portrait, the representation of the sitter's physical condition makes us instantly aware of his mental state.

ROME, VILLA BORGHESE, No. 185. PORTRAIT OF
A MAN.

1529-
1530.
On canvas 1·10 m. h., 1 m. w.; three-quarters length.
Photographed by Anderson and Alinari.

He rests one hand upon a tiny flower-wreathed skull, and presses the other to his side, as if in pain. Through the open window is seen a town with hills beyond, and in the foreground St. George and the dragon, treated in the same way as in the Carmine altar-piece.

The other portrait is scarcely so sympathetic. One cannot help feeling, after long study of it, that the artist was not perfectly persuaded of the lady's sincerity, and that he certainly would not have given her such a pose and such accessories unless she had demanded them.

LONDON, COLLECTION OF CAPTAIN HOLFORD. PORTRAIT OF A LADY.

On canvas, 95 cm. h., 1·10 m. w.; three-quarters length.
A copy in the Lichtenstein Gallery at Vienna.

She stands between an empty cradle and a table, holding in her L. hand a drawing of Lucretia, to which she points with the other hand. On the table lies a piece of paper with the inscription: '*Nec ulla impudica Lucretiae exemplo vivet.*' Her expression is discontented and morose. She wears a round turban of white worsted, trimmed with small white ribbons, and

Anderson photo.] [*Borghese Gallery, Rome*

PORTRAIT OF A MAN

Dixon photo. *[Dorchester House, London*

PORTRAIT OF A LADY

a low-cut dress of dull brownish-red striped with green, with puffed sleeves. A gold chain, from which is suspended a jewelled ornament, hangs over the bosom of her dress. The background is a grey wall lighted from the L. The pose of the head suggests the Madonna of 1533 in the Lochis Collection at Bergamo, but the style of painting is more like the works of 1529–1530, while the look recalls the St. Catherine in the Vienna *Santa Conversazione* of about 1528. As colour, this is one of Lotto's most dazzling pictures. *[1529-1530.]*

Although in technique the Holford *Lucretia* (as this picture is sometimes called) is close to the works of 1529 and 1530, we already see in it a departure from the Titianesque fusion and glow of the Carmine altarpiece. Just as we found Lotto, in the portrait of Agostino della Torre, painted in 1515, in reaction against Palma, more than usually Alvisesque in tone and vehicle, so, in the Holford picture, we have a flesh tone almost reverting to Alvise, as if, in the effort to react against Titian, the artist had had to draw back violently and hold on tight for a moment to his oldest, most deeply rooted habits.

In a work executed perhaps immediately after the *Lucretia*, in another altar-piece at Jesi, the reaction is complete, and Lotto has returned to his own grey manner, which has, however, itself undergone a change, emerging firmer and broader, a little turbid, and without the delicacy and freshness of such a work as the Vienna *Santa Conversazione*, which, although executed when the artist was forty-eight years old, does nevertheless produce the impression of having been painted by a young man. But this larger, less transparent technique, goes well with the firmer hold upon life that Lotto betrays in the Jesi altar-piece, and with its greater seriousness. *[1530.]*

JESI, LIBRARY. VISITATION, WITH ANNUNCIATION IN LUNETTE. (Originally in San Francesco in Monte.)

1530. The Madonna, followed by two companions, advances with a graceful, affectionate gesture, bending over and clasping St. Elizabeth's R. hand in both of hers. Zachariah appears in the doorway to L. The ground is strewn with roses. In the lunette the Madonna kneels to R. beside a heavily draped bed, while the beautiful, light-haired angel enters to L.

Inscribed, in script: L. Lotus 1530. On canvas, Visitation, 1.54 m. h., 1.52 m. w.; lunette, 1.03 m. h.

In both pictures the Madonna is dressed entirely in garments of Lotto's characteristic light blue, which fall in billowy folds, such as are found in the pictures of 1528. In the *Annunciation* her expression and pose are eloquent to the highest degree. The tone of the entire work is grey and cool, and the woodwork of the interior is done with a neatness that rivals Catena in his National Gallery picture representing St. Jerome in his study. The brush-work is of a larger, firmer stroke than in any of Lotto's preceding works, and the outlines are done as if with a soft brush which had occasionally stopped and blotted.

1531. In a work of the next year, we note that Lotto still oscillates between his grey manner, as we just found it at Jesi, and the Titianesque colour-scheme of the Carmine altar-piece, as if, after all, he did not find it easy to wholly give up the latter. But the stroke of the brush in the *Crucifixion*, to which we are going to turn, is of masterly firmness and breadth, surpassing not merely all that Lotto himself had ever accomplished before, but even Titian's achievements up to this date. If it were as great in the structure of the single figure

[Jesi Library

THE VISITATION AND ANNUNCIATION

as it is in conception and execution, it would, as a work 1531. of art, rival Titian's greatest masterpieces.

MONTE SAN GIUSTO[1], SANTA MARIA. CRUCIFIXION.

Signature illegible, but date decipherable, '1531.'

On canvas, in original frame (one of the finest now existing). Not repainted, but a little darkened. Figures in the foreground life-size.

Photographed (poorly) by Alinari.

This altar-piece divides itself distinctly into two groups—into Foreground and Middle Distance.

The foreground is almost a complete picture by itself, of splendid dramatic effect. The Virgin, partly supported by one of the Marys, faints into the arms of St. John. To the R., the Magdalen, with streaming flaxen hair, expresses her grief in frantic gestures. In front of her kneels another Mary, in profile, with her eyes turned to the cross, while she holds the arms of the fainting Madonna. John (one of the finest heads ever painted) turns abruptly to look at the donor, Niccolò Bonafede, Bishop of Chiusi and General of the Church, who kneels to the extreme L. Beside the bishop, an angel with arms eloquently outstretched, explains the scene.

In the middle distance rise three tall crosses. The upper part of the picture is veiled in clouds, while the small figures at the foot of the cross stand out clearly against the pale, green sky. Horsemen surround the scene on each side, one on the R. bearing a yellow standard, while the one next to him has his arm around the thief's cross. Two robust lancers stand at the foot of the middle cross, and, beyond them, men are seen hurrying down the hill. At the foot of the cross to

[1] Monte San Giusto is a few miles from the station Morrovalle—Monte San Giusto on the railway from Portocivitanuova to Fabriano.

1531. the left, Nicodemus, on a white horse, starts back, letting fall his lance. Several soldiers surround him, pointing up, and gesticulating. The white draperies of the crucified figures stream out against the clouds.

Nothing can be simpler or more free from entanglement, clearer or grander in action, than is this entire picture. Rarely, if ever, has the Crucifixion been treated so much in the spirit of a Greek tragedy. To an even heightened sense of beauty, Lotto adds here a mastery of construction such as we have never found in him before. The vigour of the execution is so great that we are reminded of Paul Veronese's firm stroke in his Santa Giustina altar-piece at Padua. The colouring, it is true, has darkened a little throughout, but is still glowing. Indeed, all in all, this *Crucifixion* may be regarded as Lotto's most important work, being the largest in scope, the most dramatic in rendering, and of the greatest force [1].

In another work of 1531, we find a technique and scheme of colour recalling, it is true, the Monte San Giusto *Crucifixion*, but greyer and less powerful.

BERLIN, No. 323. ST. SEBASTIAN AND ST. CHRISTOPHER. (Two canvasses framed together.)

R., St. Christopher wading through the sea, bearing the Christ-child on his shoulder.

Inscribed: L. Loto, 1531.

L., St. Sebastian, with his R. hand fastened over his head to the branch of a tree—a soft figure of almost feminine beauty, wearing a waist-cloth of striped India silk, which trails on the ground. Background of sea and rocks.

---

[1] A varied copy of the group of the Marys and St. John, probably by Beccarruzzi, exists in the Strasburg gallery.

Alinari photo. [*Monte San Giusto, Santa Maria in Telusiano*

THE CRUCIFIXION

Signed: L. Loto. Each picture 1·39 m. h., 55 cm. w. 1531.

Photographed by Hanfstängl, Munich.

Lotto seems to have enjoyed the contrast of the Herculean St. Christopher with the feminine St. Sebastian, and he carried out the contrast in the technique. The St. Sebastian has the qualities of the works of 1528, even to the sharp outlines of the shadow sides of the torso and limbs, while the St. Christopher is painted with a larger stroke, and his face has the spotty outlines of the Zachariah in the Jesi *Visitation*. Sebastian's R. thumb, by the way, is exactly like the thumb in the Holford *Lucretia*, the first phalanx much thinner than the second. The big toes have to an exaggerated degree the Alvisesque mannerism of being shorter than the others.

In September, 1531, Lotto in Venice was appointed, along with Titian and Bonifazio, trustee of the fund left by Vincenzo Catena for the dowering of daughters of unprosperous painters (G. Ludwig in *Jahrb. Pr. Kstsm.*, 1901, p. 69).

No dated work of 1532 is known to me, and I know 1532. none that can be assigned with certainty to this particular year. But we have a notice regarding Lotto at this time of greater value to us, at this point, than an ordinary picture. A document in the Treviso archives, dated August 29, 1532, informs us that Lotto was then living at Venice[1]. This notice is of such value, because, aside from a word in the documents concerning the Bergamo intarsias, to the effect that Lotto was in Venice in June, 1530, and the other notice of 1531 just referred to, it is the only positive knowledge we have of his whereabouts during this period. In default, however, of any proof to the con-

[1] See G. Bampo, *Spigolature dell' Archivio Notarile di Treviso*, *Archivio Veneto*, vol. xxxii.

1532. trary—his works of 1530 and 1531 at Monte San Giusto and Jesi being on canvas, and therefore as likely to have been executed in Venice as on the spot—and considering that the only two notices which we do have speak of him as being in Venice, we can take it for granted that he spent most of the decade between 1530 and 1540 in or near Venice, leaving this region, if at all, for only short intervals.

This is the decade, it will be remembered, in which, thanks to the unsettled state of the rest of the peninsula, Italy's intellectual and spiritual activities chose Venice as a centre, making it for a time the gathering-place of all the deeper and more sincere Italian thinkers. And, what was even more foreign to Venice than being an intellectual capital, it became during this decade the religious capital as well. Many of the people who had been touched by Lutheran teachings, and many others who were soon going to be their persecutors, were now at Venice, discussing articles of faith, planning reforms for the Church both from within and from without. That Lotto came in contact with any of these thoughtful, religious people, we have no way of proving by documents, but, considering what Lotto was himself, how personally he took his religion, how he loved to ponder over things, and how profoundly he could interpret Scripture, we can scarcely have a doubt on the subject. Moreover, his Cingoli altar-piece, to which we shall come soon, gives as clear proof of contact between Lotto and the religious reformers as the Carmine altar-piece proved his contact with Titian. (Only where the question is one of technique and colour-scheme, the demonstration is much easier.) What was Lotto's own state of mind regarding life and religion, we already know from the works we have thus far examined. As he grew older, his serious tendencies would under all circumstances have become intensified; but he might have met on 1532. the one hand with opposition, on the other with encouragement, and the effect would have been noticeable in his life and in his art. Now all the pictures that we still have to examine, and all the documents, which, by the way, become more copious, reveal Lotto in his last thirty years to have been not only as religious, as brooding, and as profound as we should have expected, but much more, as if he had in the meantime been in the company of people who had drawn out and fostered in him these very qualities. Such people, we know, he could find then in plenty in Venice, and as we know something about them, we can the easier imagine the atmosphere Lotto was living in at this time.

Turning now once more to his works, we are first 1533. of all greeted by one of great charm, dated 1533, in technical characteristics not far removed from the pictures of 1531:

BERGAMO GALLERY, LOCHIS COLLECTION, No. 185. HOLY FAMILY WITH ST. CATHERINE.

The Child asleep on a parapet within an arbour which opens out on a view of a broad river winding to the sea. Joseph lifts up the coverlet from the sleeping Infant to show Him to Catherine, who kneels to R., and the Madonna, looking up from her book, hushes them with a gesture of her hand.

Inscribed, in script: Lavrentivs Lotvs 1533.

On canvas, 81 cm. h., 1·15 m. w.

Photographed by Alinari.

In 1632 this picture formed part of the famous Collection of Roberto Canonici of Ferrara, where it was valued at 120 ducats. Campori, *Raccolta di Cataloghi*, p. 119.

1533. The Virgin and Catherine as types, might have occurred in Lotto's pictures of an earlier date, but the peculiarly eager look of this saint, the brown outlines, and the general execution, indicate the exact epoch. The landscape is covered with a soft haze, and the effects of light are full of poetical suggestion.

1533 (?). Probably of the same date is a portrait at Berlin, of a youngish man, soft-eyed, soft-voiced, and unassertive, yet not weak nor irresolute, but with a quiet look of intelligence and even of humour in his face:

BERLIN, No. 182. BUST OF A YOUNG MAN.

He seems to be about thirty years old. He has a short black beard, and leans his head a little to the R. He wears a black cap, a black coat, and a double-tipped white collar, and is seen against a green curtain. The outlines are as in the Lochis *Holy Family*. The ear is naturalistic.

On canvas, 47 cm. h., 38 cm. w.
Photographed by Hanfstängl.

An almost effaced portrait in Rome was perhaps also painted in the same year, at any rate no later:

ROME, CAPITOLINE GALLERY, SALA II, No. 74. YOUNG MAN WITH MUSKET.

Attributed to Giorgione, but obviously by Lotto, and already recognized as such by Morelli.

1534. The year 1534 is represented by a dated work in the Uffizi, of unequal quality, painted, perhaps, in a moment of peculiar tension; for it displays a great nervousness of movement, and an exaggerated expressiveness and eagerness in the faces, while at the same

THE MADONNA AND CHILD

[Bergamo, Lochis Gallery
Alinari photo]

time the drawing is very loose—one might add, as 1534.
scrawly as the trembling hand of a man writing under
unusual excitement:

FLORENCE, UFFIZI, No. 575.   MADONNA AND SAINTS.

St. Anne is seated on a cushion with the Virgin
reclining between her knees and holding against her
cheek the naked Child, who draws back as if a little
frightened by the too eager look of St. Joachim, who
stands on a lower level to L. Behind Joachim appears St. Jerome with his cardinal's hat swinging over
his bare shoulder. St. Jerome is of the type of the
Joseph in the Lochis *Madonna* at Bergamo, but a little
older.

Inscribed, in script: Lorenzo Loto 1534. On canvas,
65 cm. h., 82 cm. w.

Photographed by Brogi, Florence.

I would assign to the same date—certainly to no
earlier—a small panel which when I first saw it, after
the publication of the first edition of this book, was
still ascribed to Moretto of Brescia:

WILTON HOUSE.   LORD PEMBROKE.

St. Antony sits on the ground reclining against
a table-like rock. He is within a grotto, and points
to the world without with the thumb of his R. while
his L. hand is eloquently stretched out.

Reproduced in the *Art Journal* for 1899, p. 93, to
illustrate an article by Prof. S. A. Strong.

The large head of the saint is almost certainly
a portrait. The action vividly recalls the Madonna
in the Uffizi picture. The technique and the folds of
the draperies are of this precise period. The landscape—the charming part of this picture—differs but

1534. little from the one in the *Holy Family* in the Lochis Collection at Bergamo, and even less from a work of slightly later date, the Louvre *Recognition of the Holy Child*.

The St. Joachim, the best part of the Uffizi picture, so closely resembles, not only in type but in technique, the St. Roch in the following work, that we cannot hesitate to ascribe it to the same or the following year:

LORETO, PALAZZO APOSTOLICO, No. 30. SS. SEBASTIAN, ROCH, AND CHRISTOPHER.

A slightly varied replica of the Berlin Saints of 1531, with the addition of St. Roch. The giant St. Christopher wades ankle deep in a broad gulf. To the R. stands St. Sebastian, identical with the St. Sebastian in Berlin, except that the waist-cloth here is white. To the L. stands St. Roch, leaning on his staff. Water and landscape background.

Signed: Lavrentii Loti pictoris opus. On canvas, 2·79 m. h., 2·32 m. w.

Photographed by Anderson.

The treatment here is considerably larger than in the Berlin Picture. The St. Roch has a peculiarly sensitive and wistful face.

1535. In 1535 Lotto was called to Jesi to decorate in fresco the chapel of the Palazzo Pubblico, but as nothing came of it[1], we may doubt whether he stayed in the Marches for any length of time; but his presence there for a while helps to account for originals and replicas of works of about this date existing at or near Loreto. Two such we have already noted, and we have to note

[1] See Hugo von Tschudi, 'Lotto in den Marken,' *Repertorium*, vol. ii.

'RECOGNITION OF HOLY CHILD'

still another[1] this time, of a picture now in the Louvre, painted not earlier than 1535, and scarcely later than the next dated work, the Cingoli altar-piece of 1539. Turning first to the original:

1535.

PARIS, LOUVRE, NO. 1351. THE RECOGNITION OF THE HOLY CHILD.

On a flowered meadow in a forest, under the shade of secular trees, the Holy Child lies naked on a white cloth, stretching out His arms to the sturdy little St. John, who points Him out to the Virgin. She sits close by, half reclining, and throws up her hands, looking at the Child as if she had never before realized His nature. To the L., and, as usual, a little out of the composition, St. Joseph rises from his knees to look at the Child. On the R. St. Elizabeth bends eagerly over Him, and behind her St. Joachim, also rising up to look, puts out his hand in wonder. Behind the little St. John, three angels in white with pearly, iridescent wings crossing, crowd forward also to pay homage to the Child.

On canvas, 1.50 m. h., 2.17 m. w.

Photographed by Braun.

1537 (?).

As may be inferred, even from the bald description just given, this is a picture remarkable for its *motif*, and for its dramatic unity. The meaning of the artist is unmistakable. It was to represent the recognition of the divine character of the Christ-child by the human beings in the midst of whom He was born. I need scarcely say that this *motif*, although it was at times vaguely approached by Italian painters, particularly by Leonardo in the *Virgin of the Rocks*, was

[1] This, however, Lotto brought with him when he finally settled at Loreto. On leaving Venice in 1549 he left it with Sansovino, who soon sent it after him. Lotto valued it at forty-five ducats. Cf. *Nuova Rivista Misena*, March-April, 1894, P. Gianuizzi, 'Lotto nelle Marche.'

1537 (?). never treated with such obvious intention, and with so much feeling, such solemnity, and such pathos as here. In a work like this Lotto comes, perhaps, as close as an Italian could come to the lowliness, pathos, and solemnity of Rembrandt's pictures of scenes from the Gospels.

Considered as technique, also, there is something almost Rembrandtesque in the brush-work of this picture and in the treatment of the light and shade, with the highest light in the centre almost veiling the angels. But the tone, as a whole, is a bluish grey, such as we shall presently find in the Cingoli picture, and in type the Madonna stands close to the one in that same altar-piece. The St. Joseph recalls the St. Jerome in the Uffizi picture of 1534, and the St. Joseph in the Lochis *Madonna* of 1533 at Bergamo. The St. Anne has the eager look of the St. Joachim in the Uffizi picture. The St. Joachim in the picture before us is not altogether Lottesque in type. He reminds us of Savoldo's *St. Jerome* in the collection of Lady Layard, and of Savoldo's charcoal drawing in the Louvre (Braun, 435), for the head of that saint. No matter precisely how we account for this likeness, we have in it, be it noted, a proof that the two artists, precise contemporaries, and, in all probability, fellow pupils under Alvise Vivarini, were at this time in contact with each other. We shall have occasion to return to this point in a subsequent chapter.

The Loreto replica of the *Recognition of the Holy Child* is slightly varied and of inferior workmanship, indeed, not entirely from Lotto's own hand:

LORETO, PALAZZO APOSTOLICO, NO. 42. RECOGNITION OF THE HOLY CHILD.

On canvas, 1.72 m. h., 2.46 m. w.
Mentioned by Vasari.

'RECOGNITION OF HOLY CHILD' 203

At Osimo there is a work to which my attention was drawn after the publication of this book, by Signor Frizzoni's articles in the *Archivio Storico dell' Arte* for 1896. It is certainly of the same date.

1537 (?).

OSIMO, MUNICIPIO. THE HOLY CHILD ON HIS MOTHER'S KNEE PRONOUNCES A DISCOURSE TO WHICH SHE AND THREE ANGELS ARE LISTENING.

The Holy Child is on His Mother's right knee, His left hand pressing down upon it, His right blessing. The Madonna has stretched out her hands in astonishment, and the angels make gestures of amazement and worship.

Figures half the size of life.
Photographed by Alinari.

The angels recall at once the Brescia *Nativity*, and the Louvre *Recognition of the Holy Child*. The colouring and the folds suggest the last works at Jesi. The motive is as unusual and fresh as that of the Louvre picture just mentioned; and the spirit of both is identical. Very effective here are the greens and yellows.

The Rembrandtesque technique that we have just noted in the Louvre picture occurs again in one of the most pathetic portraits ever painted :

1535, circa.

ROME, DORIA PALACE. PORTRAIT OF A MAN OF THIRTY-SEVEN.

A look of great pain draws up his brows, as he points at himself with his R. hand, holding his L. to his breast. He is evidently in distress over his physical condition, which the painter seems to have considered no less desperate than did the sitter himself. He has a short beard, and wears a dark cap and

1535, a plain long coat. He stands against a wall over
circa. which ivy is straggling. To the R. is a stone with
the inscription: ANN. ÆTATIS SVE XXXVII. To
the L. is a little winged genius looking up as he
balances himself on a pair of scales which he holds
in his clasped hands. This same figure, by the way,
occurs in the Bergamo intarsias.

On canvas, life-size, three-quarters length.
Photographed by Braun, and Anderson.

1535-1539. In contrast to the Doria sick man stands the
portrait of an architect painted at about this time, as
if to assure us that Lotto did not insist on seeing
sensitiveness and physical and mental delicacy except
where they actually existed:

BERLIN, No. 153. PORTRAIT OF AN ARCHITECT.

Black beard, dark biretta, and dark blue mantle.
In his L. hand a scroll, in his R. a pair of compasses.
Brownish background.

Signed: LL. On canvas, 1·05 m. h., ·82 m. w.
Three-quarters length.

Photographed by Hanfstängl, Munich.

This portrait is even more interesting for its interpretation than for its great technical merit. In most of Lotto's other portraits the faces are sensitive almost to morbidness. Here, on the contrary, we have the bluff, rather loud-spoken face of a practical house-builder, who is, however, by no means devoid of feeling.

Even closer in style and technique to the Doria portrait, but scarcely less contrasted in conception is a work at Vienna which, seen by me some years before the publication of this book, did not impress

[Anderson photo.] [Doria Palace, Rome

PORTRAIT OF A MAN

me as a Lotto, but amply convinced me of being his when I saw it again :

1535-1539.

VIENNA, IMPERIAL MUSEUM, 220. THREE VIEWS OF A MAN.

The same man, aged somewhat over thirty, is represented full face, turned to R. and again to L. He has luxuriant curly hair, and wears a dark coat with the white shirt showing.

On canvas, 53 cm. h., 79 cm. w.

Photographed by Löwy, and Hanfstängl.

The interpretation of a commonplace, prosperous person is here no less complete than of refined, ailing people in the Doria and Borghese portraits. Perhaps the breadth of Lotto's range is nowhere better revealed.

Between 1535 and 1539 we have neither mention of Lotto nor dated works from his hand. He remained in Venice, most of the time, probably, painting the works we have just examined. In Venice also, and not necessarily or even likely at Cingoli, he may have painted the important canvas for that little town in the Marches. But before we turn to that, we must give a glance to a little picture which betrays, in contrast to the modern feeling that we shall find in the Cingoli altar-piece, an almost mediaeval view of Christianity, as if to remind us, this time, that in Lotto, as in so many of his contemporaries, the old and the new could lie peacefully in separate strata of a man's nature, unconscious as yet of their reciprocal antagonism [1] :

[1] The following significant inscription on the back of the panel had escaped my attention when I first published this book :—' *Questo quadro è fatto di mano di Messer Lorenzo Lotto, omo molto divoto, et per sua divotione* [i. e. as a spiritual exercise] *il fece la septimana santa et fu*

MILAN, BORROMEO COLLECTION. CRUCIFIXION.

1535-1539. Painted on a convex wooden panel for a portable shrine. Considerably under a foot square.

Photographed by Marcozzi, Milan.

Christ is hanging on the Cross, with the various scenes of the Passion indicated in a kind of pictorial shorthand, as in a number of Giottesque pictures, of which the well-known *Lorenzo Monaco* of the Uffizi is an example. The modelling and the effects of light bring this little panel close to the Ancona altarpiece to be described hereafter, but I place it considerably earlier because it usually happens that the signs of an advanced style appear sooner in pictures with small figures than in important works of larger size, and also because in type and action the Christ is scarcely changed from the one at Monte S. Giusto. Indeed, in some respects, this panel stands closer to the St. Lucy *predelle* of about 1530 than to any other works.

We come now to the last important work of this period:

CINGOLI (PROVINCE OF MACERATA), SAN DOMENICO. MADONNA IN A ROSE-GARDEN WITH SIX SAINTS AND THREE PUTTI.

Inscribed: L. LOTVS. MDXXXIX. On canvas, 3·84 m. h., 2·64 m. w., and fair condition, except for a recent scratch, and two tinsel crowns nailed on to the Virgin and Child.

Photographed by Alinari.

1539. The Madonna, dressed in Lotto's characteristic blue,

finito il Venerdì Santo all'ora della Passione di N.S. Gesù Cristo. Io Zanetto del Co. o scritto acciò si sappia e sia tenuta in quella veneratione che merita essa figura.' Frizzoni, *op. cit., p.* 428.

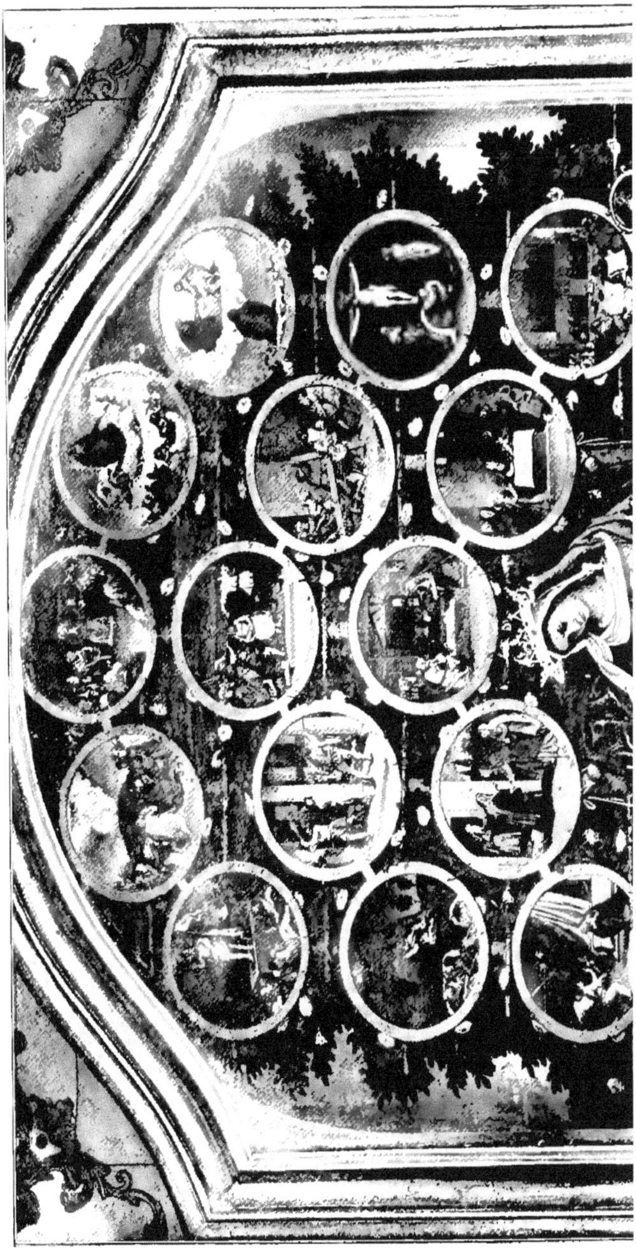

Alinari photo.] [*Cortona, San Domenico.*

THE MADONNA AND SAINTS

sits on a stone platform, her chair draped with crimson 1539. brocade. She bends forward to present a pearl rosary to St. Dominic, who kneels to the L., looking up at her with arms outstretched. Behind him stands St. Thomas, pointing up with an eloquent gesture, and to the extreme L. stands the Magdalen. She has a bewitchingly beautiful face, and golden hair braided with pearls. She seems like the St. Barbara of the Bergamo altar-piece, grown to full womanhood, and at the same time she recalls the Venus in the Rospigliosi picture. The fingers of her hand holding the vase still recall Alvise and Bonsignori. The Child in His mother's lap, stretches out His arms toward the model of the town held up to Him by the patron saint, Esuperanzio, who kneels opposite to Dominic, forming with him, the *putti*, and the Madonna, a well-arranged pyramidal composition. St. Esuperanzio wears a mitre, a purplish-pink mantle and maniples, and a hood of cloth of gold, upon which is embroidered the Coronation of the Virgin. Behind him stands a nun, St. Sperandia, with lilies and a crucifix in her hands, and beside her, to the extreme R., St. Peter Martyr, who has a peculiarly sensitive and refined face. It is to be noted, by the way, that here, as in one or two of Lotto's earlier pictures, and as frequently in Cima, the Madonna turns to one group of saints and the Child to another.

Under the lichen-covered stone platform, at the Madonna's feet, a playful *putto* gathers up handfuls of rose-petals from a wicker basket and scatters them like a meteor-shower over St. Dominic. Another *putto* presents a rose to St. Sperandia, and the infant John points up to the Christ Child[1].

A stone wall stretches behind the group of saints,

---

[1] It still is the custom, in Central Italy at least, to strew rose-petals on Corpus Domini.

dividing the picture almost in half. Over it grows a tall, spreading rose-hedge, sharply outlined against a greyish-blue sky. From its branches hang, like Japanese lanterns, fifteen *tondi*, each one containing a picture. These, although wonderful in themselves, must be looked at apart from the rest of the work, for, taken together, the effect is not satisfactory.

The lower part of the picture, containing the Madonna and saints, is painted in a style evolved from the splendid grey manner of the Jesi *Visitation*, and is even more forcible. It is unrivalled among Lotto's works for its cool shadows, for its general tone, and especially for a treatment of values, which, in the three *putti* around the rose-basket, actually calls to mind Velasquez' *Weavers*. Again and again in Lotto's works we have come upon scattered rose-leaves and rose-buds; here they fairly invade the picture, playing at least as important a part as any of the saints themselves.

Each one of the fifteen *tondi* is an interesting design by itself. They are all characterized by the extreme depth with which space is indicated, the largeness of the workmanship, and the presence of atmosphere, going with a perfection of cool, low tone. Many of them are of great importance, because they show how Lotto treated certain subjects otherwise unrepresented in his existing works. The originality of his mind manifests itself particularly in the *Christ among the Doctors*, a scene taking place in a hall of vast dimensions, and in the *Coronation of the Virgin*, the one really adequate treatment of this subject in art; in the *Ascension*, in which we see only the feet of Christ in a cloud, and the *Agony in the Garden*, which is rendered with great probability and impressiveness. In these small scenes, we already see Lotto as we shall find him in his latest pictures, not only in his skilful treatment of space, but in his frequent use of 1539. the purplish-pink peculiar to his last works at Loreto.

The *tondi* contain the following scenes, arranged in curving rows of five across the hedge: *The Annunciation, The Visitation, The Nativity, The Circumcision, Christ among the Doctors, The Agony in the Garden, Christ at the Column, The Crowning with Thorns, Christ Falling under the Cross, The Crucifixion, The Resurrection, The Ascension, The Descent of the Holy Spirit, The Assumption,* and *The Coronation.* The last scene, the *Coronation of the Virgin*, deserves special mention. The Madonna prostrates herself in space, separated by what seems an endless stretch of ether from Christ and God the Father who are crowning her. Lotto attains here a sublimity which is rare elsewhere in painting, and which I can compare to Milton only. The gulf between the human and the Divine has never been indicated with more spiritual suggestiveness. This *tondo* makes one regret even more than did the Bergamo intarsias, that Lotto was not also an engraver. But to fully appreciate the value of these little pictures, one should compare them with Titian's later ecclesiastical pictures. One need only look at these Cingoli *tondi*, and then at Titian's *Religion Succoured by Spain*, or even at his *Trinity*, to see that genuine religious feeling inspires the one painter, and mere compliance the other.

In exact agreement of colour and tone with the figure of the Magdalen in the Cingoli altar-piece, and therefore to be assigned to about the same time, are two full-length figures of saints on separate canvasses:

LORETO, PALAZZO APOSTOLICO, NOS. 25 AND 27.
SS. LUCY AND THECLA.

The *St. Thecla* has as illustration some of the

qualities of the Louvre *St. Margaret* attributed to Raphael [1].

On canvas, each 1·69 m. h., 60 cm. w.

With these two pictures, executed in Lotto's grey manner, but with touches which anticipate his very last works, closes the period of Lotto's 'Maturity.' The next works that we shall study will surprise us by their Titianesque qualities.

---

[1] Signor Frizzoni, in his articles on Lotto in the *Archivio Storico dell' Arte* for 1896, protests vehemently against the attribution to our painter of these two saints. I have not seen them since, and Signor Frizzoni may be right.

CHAPTER VI

OLD AGE

1540-1550

JUST as we are beginning to feel that, after following Lotto for forty years, we can understand him sufficiently to study the rest of his career without the aid of documents, documents become unusually plentiful; yet, although they would have spared us much labour had they come earlier, they do not come too late to be of great service.

Old age is a period in an artist's life which repays study almost as well as early youth. If a man's beginnings are of peculiar interest because they reveal, so to say, his genus and species, because they indicate the traditions in the midst of which he was reared and the habits to which he was trained, his last years, although lacking that charm which youth must ever have simply because it is youth, are scarcely less interesting to the student. It is in these years, when the physical system is already on the decline and the will no longer has the energy to reinforce this or that element which needs especial support, when old habits are no longer to be changed or new ones acquired, that the man most clearly manifests his native temperament, the almost *chemical* change it underwent in youth, and what it made of itself in middle age. The less tenacious, the more recently acquired habits drop away, ambition flickers low, and the man himself appears with a distinctness never perceived before. As he now stands before us, thus he essentially was

1540-1550. through life, but so disguised by physical vigour and joy in living and by the absorption in the struggle for self-assertion, that we found it difficult to recognize him. But with this image of the man, as we see him in old age, clear in our minds, we can go back to the problems regarding him that we have hitherto had to deal with, and we shall find that they lose the vagueness they had when we first encountered them, and that they resolve themselves into distinct factors leading quickly to results that we reached before only after great labour. If, moreover, any solution hitherto attained prove incompatible with the knowledge we now have of the artist's temperament, we can rest assured that in that solution there lurks some fallacy. We cannot therefore be too eager to acquire any bit of information that will reveal to us Lotto's state of mind, temper, and habits of life, during his last years.

The amplest revelation of the man we find in his will of 1546, all the interesting points of which will be given either in this chapter or in the final one. A letter written in 1548, by no other, oddly enough, than Aretino, touches especially on Lotto's religious feelings and piety. But we have a still further source of information, unfortunately not so illuminating as it is copious. This is nothing less than a codex in Lotto's own hand, discovered two or three years ago in the Archives of Loreto. In the spring of 1893 it was in the hands of Signor Guido Levi of Rome, who was intending to publish it[1]. He was good enough to let me look through it and extract the items that seemed to me of the greatest importance. This I did, taking care to confine myself strictly to our subject; for, interesting as this codex will be to the general student of Italian art and civilization, it is com-

---

[1] Since the first edition of this book it has been published, admirably edited, in the first volume of *Gallerie Nazionali Italiane*.

paratively meagre in personal items, in spite of being, 1540-
as I have said, in Lotto's own hand. 1550.

This codex of foolscap size is, in fact, nothing but an account-book kept by Lotto from about 1539 to his death. The debits are entered on one page and the credits on the opposite page, as might have been done by any other business-like Venetian. It is, however, difficult to consult, because the items are entered under the Christian names of the debtors, and even when the debtor was a community, Lotto did not enter the transaction under the name of the community, but under the Christian names of the delegates. All the items of special interest that a rapid glance through the codex discovered, will be found duly entered in this chapter; but they contain little, if anything, that adds to the knowledge of Lotto's personality which cannot be derived from documents already published and from his works. Certain inferences that we can draw from these are, however, confirmed by the codex. That he was exceedingly nervous, for instance, and at the same time pietistic, is put beyond further doubt by such items as the one clearing his account with an apprentice named Ercole whom he had kept for a year and more. At last, Lotto writes, he became 'a cross too burdensome,' and his master dismissed him, but 'in all friendliness,' and in 1552 he says that he will never again take an apprentice, 'because they are so ungrateful.'

The codex is more interesting for the light it throws on the business relations between the Italian artist and his employers than for its illumination of Lotto's own character. Yet on one point it is of importance in helping us to estimate Lotto, proving, as it does, that he must have been an artist of unusual industry. The works mentioned by him as executed in these declining years are more than double the number of the pictures

1540-1550. of his entire career which are left to us. The codex establishes also the ingenuousness of Lotto's nature. Again and again he speaks of having done excellent work for people who remunerated him with pence where, if a contract had been made, they would have had to pay him in pounds. One case was too much for even Lotto's patience, and he turned the portrait of a miserly prelate into the figure of a saint, selling it, in this disguise, to a church.

This account-book kept in his last years could not have been the only one he kept. The 'Sunto di li quadri .. a miser Zanin Casoto' of which I spoke in the fourth chapter must have been the fragment of a similar earlier one. Another indication of Lotto's business-like habits of mind may be seen in the fact that a large number of his works are signed and dated.

Lotto spent most of the decade we are now going to study in or near Venice, and toward the end of it we are at last informed of his relations to Titian. In a letter addressed to Lotto in 1548, Pietro Aretino writes that Titian wishes to be remembered, and that he values Lotto's judgement and taste as that of no other. Titian was at this time at Augsburg, honoured by Charles V as perhaps no painter had yet been honoured in modern times, and if he could think of Lotto under such circumstances and wish that he were present to aid him with his taste and judgement, as Aretino writes, we may safely infer that they had been acquainted for some time.

Titian himself was one of those people who are for ever determined by the first strong influence they fall under, remaining henceforth insensible to other influences. He developed continuously on a line which, in so far as mere craft is concerned, was as necessitated by the Bellini and Giorgione and his own temperament as if they formed a mathematical

equation of which he, as an artist, was the result. 1540–
There can therefore be no question of his art betraying 1550.
signs of his contact with Lotto. But it was not so
with his friend. We have already seen Lotto in 1529
and 1530 experimenting with the technique of Titian,
and we shall find him making a similar experiment
once more in the years from 1542 to 1545. In the
St. Antonino at Venice, in the Ancona altar-piece, and
in the Brera portraits, the *impasto* is, for Lotto, thick,
the vehicle comparatively fluid, and the tones fused
into a rich scale as hard to describe as it is easy to
name 'Titianesque.' Even in structure these works
suggest Titian, being more solid and better put together than Lotto's figures usually are. But here,
again, I must insist on the fact that this experimenting
with another man's technique did not in the least
entail the pilfering of the other man's ideas. No one
well acquainted with Titian would find reminders of
him in the conception or interpretation of the Brera
portraits, for instance, Titianesque although they are
in technique. But even as workmanship, and as a
colour-scheme, though Lotto never would have painted
them as they are had he not been under Titian's
influence, they differ widely from Titian, the stroke
being larger—at any rate than the Titian of this time
—and the fusion more subtle. There is a certain
modernity of technique in these Brera portraits which
reminds one of some of the great masters of our own
times, of Degas, for instance.

It is curious that one of the earliest entries in Oct. 17,
Lotto's account-book should concern Martin Luther in 1450.
a phase most abhorrent to Catholicism. Luther, it is
well to remind people nowadays, was not only an arch-
heretic, but a priest who had married, thereby com-
mitting one of the most horrible and at the same time
most disgusting crimes that the Catholic mind can

1540. conceive of. Well!—on October 17, 1540, Lotto completed the portraits of Martin Luther and his wife, not for himself, it is true, but without the least disapproval, excepting, I believe, that he does in one of the two entries speak of the wife as 'druda'[1]. These portraits were executed by Lotto at the commission of his nephew, Mario, with whom he was then living at Venice, Mario himself intending them as a gift for a friend named Tristan. It is just possible, of course, that they were painted for somebody who had in Luther and his wife only the curiosity of scandal, a curiosity that would to-day be satisfied by the illustrated newspaper or the photograph. But this is not likely—for one reason, because the illustrated newspaper was already in existence in one of its first stages, the fly-sheet engraving. In 1540 such engravings of Luther and his wife were already numerous, and indeed Lotto must have made use of them in painting the portraits, for it is practically out of the question that he himself had ever seen Luther. The Tristan for whom the portraits were intended was in all probability not a mere scandalmonger but a sincere admirer of Luther, whom Lotto's nephew, Mario, wished to please, and Lotto himself speaks of this Tristan as if he knew him well. We have thus a chain of argument, not altogether made of sand, in support of the inference we made in the last chapter, that Lotto must have come in close contact with the religiously minded people of Protestant tendencies, who were unusually numerous in Venice at this time [2].

---

[1] Queen Elizabeth's treatment of Bishop Parker's wife shows how difficult it was for certain people, otherwise strongly inclined to the Reformation, to stomach the clergyman's wife.

[2] What it signified to have anything to do with portraits of Luther we may infer from the way the broad-minded and indifferent Bembo writes in September, 1541, about Vergerio's having portraits of Lutherans in his house. M'Crie's *Reformation in Italy* (Edinburgh, 1827), p. 136.

Although Lotto's account-book furnishes copious items for every year, we shall consider only such as concern works still existing, and no work of 1541 is known to me.

1541.

The year 1542 was more eventful. Toward the end of it Lotto went to live with friends at Treviso, as is proved by his will of 1546. After a trial of three years he gave up this arrangement and returned to Venice, partly because of the irksomeness of the situation, and partly because he could not earn enough at Treviso. To this episode in his life we shall return in the last chapter, but meanwhile we still have a large number of works to consider, and, in the first place, two executed in 1542.

1542.

The more important of the two is a famous picture in Venice which used to be assigned to a date following close upon Lotto's return from Bergamo, thus proving, as it was supposed, that Lotto at that time had been suddenly drawn out of his own orbit by the overwhelming attraction of Titian. What makes any such theory improbable on the face of it, is the fact that Titian himself in 1530 was not 'Titianesque' in the way that he became after 1540. Now, happily, we are at last certain from Lotto's account-book that he finished this picture on March 28, 1542. The price was to be one hundred and twenty-five ducats; but in his will of 1546 he mentions that he reduced the price to ninety ducats on the condition that on his death he should be buried without charge by the monks of San Giovanni e Paolo, in the habit of their order.

VENICE, SAN GIOVANNI E PAOLO, R. TRANSEPT.
 ST. ANTONINO OF FLORENCE AND THE POOR.

Signed: Laurentio Loto. On canvas, 3·32 m. h., 2·35 m. w.

1542. Mentioned by Vasari.
Photographed by Anderson, Rome.

Two *putti* poised in air draw aside a red curtain revealing the saint seated on high, in front of a rose-hedge, looking into a scroll which he holds with both hands, while two angels float beside him, whispering into his ears, interceding with eloquent gestures for the poor below. Under the saint, behind a parapet hung with a Turkey carpet, are two deacons, in face and gesture so individualized and yet so typical that in similar circumstances you still see their like anywhere in Italy. One of them receives petitions and tries to control the crowd, while the other, with a look of compassion, is taking money out of a bag to give to the poor, who hustle up, a dozen heads producing the impression, of a multitude. The deacon receiving the petitions is one of Lotto's best figures, considered both as painting and as psychology. The crowd would be scarcely inferior to him, if it were not for the unwarranted disproportion between the different heads. The colouring throughout is deep and rich, but a little turbid in the shadows. The draperies have life and movement. The hands have the characteristic thumb, be it noted, and the hand in the extreme R. has, moreover, the fore- and middle-fingers stretched out and the other two curled in, as in the St. Thomas in the Recanati altar-piece of 1508. It is interesting to note this Vivarinesque habit, reappearing so late in Lotto's life.

The other extant work of this year is of less importance, and is painted hastily in the grey manner. Lotto notes in his account-book that he began this picture on December 28, 1541, and finished it August 5, 1542. It was painted at Treviso for Ser Antonio Chugier de' Gatti, Ser Piero di Bernardo, and

Ser Salvino di Zambon, all from Sedrina, wine- 1542. merchants on the Riva di Ferro at Venice. Lotto was to be paid fifty gold *scudi* and all expenses:

SEDRINA, NEAR BERGAMO. MADONNA AND SAINTS.

The Madonna in a glory of cherubs floats above SS. Joseph, Jerome, Francis, and John the Baptist. In the middle distance, a view of the Val Brembana.
Signed: Laurentio Loto. On canvas, 2·93 m. h., 1·96 m. w. The lower part is somewhat ruined. There is also an inscription, as follows: 'Hoc opus fecit fieri fraternitas Sante Marie de Sedrina MDXXXXII[1].'

Photographed by Taramelli of Bergamo.

On the 19th of April, 1543, Lotto himself writes 1543- that he began the half-length portraits of 'Messer 1544. Febo of Brescia, and Madonna Laura da Pola, his wife,' finishing them on May 19, 1544. It is highly probable that these are the portraits of a man and woman, obviously *pendants* (being of the same size and identical in workmanship), now hanging close to each other in the Brera. The technique is the subtle Titianesque one of just this time, the lights and shadows, and even the draperies, would compel us to

---

[1] On June 16, 1542, Lotto, as appears from his account-book, undertook to paint a triptych for Giovenazzo in Apulia. It was to contain St. Felix between St. Antony of Padua and St. Nicolas of Tolentino, was to cost thirty ducats, and to be finished by the end of the year.

Happening to be in Apulia during the spring of 1897, I stopped at Giovenazzo to see what had become of Lotto's work. After a number of more than ordinary adventures I found the one figure of St. Felix, much the worse for wear, in a dust-heap at the back of the high altar in the church of St. Domenic. Of the rest of the triptych I could discover no trace; nor indeed did the one figure I found still pass under Lotto's name. There was a tradition, however, that it had come from a church of St. Felix.

1543-1544. assign them to about this date, and the portrait of the woman has a strong likeness, not only in technique but in type and conception, to the head furthest back under the R. hand of the deacon receiving petitions in the S. Giovanni e Paolo altar-piece. The only apparent difficulty in accepting these Brera portraits as those mentioned by Lotto is his speaking of them as *mezza figura*, when we should speak of them as 'three-quarters length.' But we know that all such phrases even now are vague, and that they were very much more vague in the sixteenth century:

MILAN, BRERA, NO. 255 AND NO. 253. PORTRAITS OF (?) MESSER FEBO OF BRESCIA, AND MADONNA LAURA DA POLA.

The man is of middle age, with long dark beard and short cropped hair, leaning against a parapet with his R. hand resting upon it. He wears a fur-trimmed mantle, and holds a pair of gloves in his L. hand. He is a simple, straightforward man, painted as simply and straightforwardly as Veronese's portrait of Barbaro in the Pitti. His L. hand, it should be noted, has between two of the fingers a curve like a 'lancet window,' such as we also have in the S. Giovanni e Paolo altar-piece, in the R. hand of the deacon who receives petitions. Even the signature is the half-Latin, half-Italian one of the works of 1542.

Signed, in script: Laurent. Loto p.

Madonna Laura is a woman of about thirty, richly dressed, sitting on a draped chair beside a curtain and a *prie-dieu*, on which rests her L. arm. She holds an ostrich-plume fan in her R. hand, and a missal in her L. Her head is inclined a little to the

[Brogi photo.]   [Brera Gallery, Milan

PORTRAIT OF A GENTLEMAN

L., and she looks pensively out of the canvas. (See frontispiece.) 1543-1544.

Signed, in script: Laurent. Loto p.

Both portraits are on canvas, each 91 cm. h., 76 cm. w.

Both photographed by Alinari, Anderson, and Brogi.

Both these portraits are executed with a breadth and mastery, with a subtlety of light and shade, and with a delicate fusion of tones, which put them, technically considered, in a niche apart among Lotto's works. Their only rival, and, as it happens, their superior, is a portrait hanging between them in the Brera, which is, morphologically and technically, so like them that their all belonging to the same time can be safely taken for granted:

MILAN, BRERA, No. 254.   PORTRAIT OF AN OLD MAN.

He has a long yellow beard, and is dressed in black, with grey gloves and white handkerchief.

On canvas, 89 cm. h., 73 cm. w. Life-size, three-quarters length.

Photographed by Alinari, Anderson, and Brogi.

This is the most subtle of all Lotto's portraits in characterization, and, considered merely as technique, it is his most masterly achievement. It would be hard to find elsewhere flesh so delicately modelled as this, showing every vein, and yet treated so largely. The skin has the texture suitable to the man's age.

To the same epoch must belong another portrait in the Brera in which I recognized Lotto's hand only after the publication of the first edition of this book:

MILAN, BRERA, GALLERIA OGGIONO, No. 67. PORTRAIT OF A MAN.

1543-1544. He is seen down to the knees, is dressed in black, and has a blond, longish beard. With one hand he points insistently, and the other is on the hilt of his sword.
On canvas. Under life-size.

This portrait is described as 'Venetian school,' but despite its ruined condition, the form, and the movement, and the dramatic conception clearly reveal Lotto as its author.

We remember that when Lotto was only five and twenty years old, he was already spoken of at Treviso as 'pictor celeberrimus,' and that soon after this he quitted that town so penniless that he had to leave his furniture and clothing behind him to pay for the
Oct.1544. rent of his lodgings. A similar contrast between the esteem in which he was held at Treviso and his inability to find sufficient employment greets us now, forty years later in his career. In October, 1544, the vestrymen of Santa Maria at Valdobbiadena (near Treviso) chose Lotto to estimate an altar-piece painted for them by Francesco Beccarruzzi, and on that occasion they spoke of Lotto in the following terms, which I quote in their own quaint Latin: 'Habita fides,' they say, 'tam in Civitate Venetiarum quam Tarvisii ... de prudentia, integritate et peritia Domini Laurentii Lotti Pictoris et de presenti Tarvisii Commorantis, ipsum Dominum Laurentium unanimes et concordes elegerunt ad estimandam picturam et Palam artis pictorie concernentem, &c., &c.[1]'

But although he was receiving such praise, he found it hard to get commissions of his own, or to

[1] Federici, *Memorie Trevigiane* (Venice, 1803), vol. ii, p. 33.

sell the pictures he painted on speculation. Thus, he speaks of a number of works, among them a subject treated by him, as we happen to know, with the greatest impressiveness—the *Sacrifice of Melchizedec*—which he sent from Treviso to Venice to be offered for sale, but which remained unsold until he returned to claim them. He had to leave Treviso finally, because, as we have already noted, he could not earn enough for his support. 1544.

In 1545, by his own account, Lotto executed for San Polo, at Treviso, a picture painted in his greyish manner, and possessing considerable technical merit, although our enjoyment of it is spoiled by the fact that it reminds us in sentiment both of the overwrought grief of the *Pietà* as they were painted in the middle of the fifteenth century, by such artists as Crivelli and Niccolò da Foligno, and of the swooning, fainting saints of the later Bolognese painters: 1545.

MILAN, BRERA, NO. 244. THE DEAD CHRIST.

Christ is supported on the lap of His fainting mother, who in turn is supported by John. Two *putti* pityingly hold the limbs of Christ. 1545, circa.

Signed: Laurentius Loto. On canvas, 1·80 m. h., 1·52 m. w.

Of about the same date[1] must be the smallish picture painted rapidly and thinly, but with a masterliness recalling the *Madonna* painted by Titian thirty years later, which was once in the Dudley gallery, and now belongs to Mr. Mond, of London.

---

[1] I note subsequently to the publication of the first edition of this book that I am but little, if at all, out in the dating of this picture. Two or even three versions of this precise subject are mentioned in Lotto's account-book between the end of 1545 and the end of 1546.

224 OLD AGE

MILAN, POLDI-PEZZOLI MUSEUM, No. 86. MADONNA AND SAINTS.

1545, circa.

The Madonna, wearing a pointed hood (as in Lotto's earliest works), bends over and puts her R. hand on the shoulder of the infant John, whom Zachariah is presenting to her, while the Christ-child, seated on His mother's knee, blesses. The two children are painted exactly as the *putti* in the Brera *Pietà*.

On canvas, 50 cm. h., 64 cm. w.

Photographed by Marcozzi, Milan.

To the same date also can be safely ascribed two pictures representing St. Jerome in prayer, a subject which, as we know from Lotto's account-book, he painted a number of times in his later years. One of these is now in Rome, and the other in Madrid [1].

ROME, DORIA GALLERY, No. 159. ST. JEROME IN PRAYER.

The saint kneels in front of the cross with a stone in his hand, his body bent forward, his head hanging down, and both arms outstretched in an attitude of passionate prayer. To R. and L., wooded hillocks, and at the back a stretch of landscape.

Photographed by Anderson.

On canvas, 51 cm. h., 43 cm. w.

Nothing could be more interesting than to contrast

---

[1] Still another, which I have not seen, is said to be at Hermannstadt in Siebenbürgen, but judging from the description and the signature, 'LAVRE LOTUS,' this must be a work of considerably earlier date. See T. von Frimmel, *Kleine Galerienstudien*, Neue Folge (Vienna, Gerold & Cie., 1894), p. 82 et seq. It should be noted that violent as is the action it recalls but one picture in the world, and that one is a St. Jerome (in the National Gallery) by Lotto's elder fellow-pupil, Cima. The Hermannstadt picture has been photographed by Ludwig Michaelis of that town.

this intensely passionate picture with Lotto's treatment of the same subject in 1500, when he was twenty years old.

1545, circa.

MADRID, No. 478. LARGER REPLICA OF THE DORIA ST. JEROME, WITH THE ADDITION OF AN ANGEL IN THE AIR.

On wood, 99 cm. h., 90 cm. w. (Attributed to Titian.)

In November, 1545, Lotto returned to Venice, and on March 25, 1546, while lodging in the '*Volta della Corona in Rialto presso San Matio*,' he made the will to which I have already had occasion to refer a number of times, leaving all his belongings to be disposed of by the Hospital of San Giovanni e Paolo, and directing, by special bequest, that his cartoons for the Bergamo intarsias should be given to two able-bodied female wards of the Hospital, 'quiet in disposition,' on their marriage to painters' apprentices. He dwells in this will upon certain antique cameos and rings which he valued for their symbolical import[1].

March 25, 1546.

In the earlier months of 1546, Lotto probably painted the splendid altar-piece seen by Vasari in San Agostino at Ancona, which is now in the communal gallery of that town. It is an interesting work, betraying in the *impasto*, in the saturated colouring, and in the vehicle, a renewed contact with Titian, and at the same time a return to old habits, and the cropping up of early memories.

1546 (?).

---

[1] Among his possessions at this time is a Marcus Aurelius, bought in 1543.

ANCONA, PINACOTECA, No. 37. MADONNA ENTHRONED BETWEEN SAINTS.

1546 (?).

Signed in large, rather fanciful lettering: Lorenzo Lotto. On canvas, figures about life-size.

Photographed by Anderson, Rome.

The devout-looking Madonna, seated on a draped throne, holds her hands in prayer, while the somewhat burly Christ-child leans back, as if struggling to free Himself from the pressure of her arm, at the same time throwing a blessing at St. John the Evangelist. The latter is a well-constructed, well-draped figure, who trips up, a little too eagerly perhaps, pen in hand, ready to write. St. Matthias, balancing the Evangelist on the R., looks out of the picture, and beside him stands St. Lawrence, with his hand on an enormous gridiron. Beside the Evangelist stands St. Stephen, also looking out of the picture, pensively. Above the Madonna, holding a crown, flutter two angels, whose white robes reflect the greenish-grey light coming from behind, over the parapet of an open *loggia*.

Of the technical qualities of this work, I have already spoken. As feeling, it is uneven. The Madonna and the angels are graceful and tender, but the St. John is a little theatrical, and the other figures have small connexion with the principal one. The greatest merit of this altar-piece is its treatment of light and shade, which is subtler here than in any other work by Lotto, showing a preoccupation with *chiaroscuro* that suggests the great Dutch masters. This preoccupation itself reminds us of Alvise Vivarini and his contrasted lights and shadows, and of him, or his school, we are reminded by still other features in this picture. The Madonna, for instance, is enthroned between two lights, as in Alvise's Venice Academy 1546 (?). *Madonna* of 1480. Her hand recalls Bonsignori's *Madonna* in San Paolo at Verona, and her big toe is shorter than the other, as always in the Alviseschi. Other details recall Lotto's own earlier works, as, for example, the footstool, which occurs in a number of his Bergamask pictures, and the Child, whose movement recalls the Child in Signor Piccinelli's *Madonna*. But the colouring, as I have said, is Titianesque, closely resembling the Brera portraits and the St. Antonino altar-piece. As to the latter work, the points of special resemblance with it are the likenesses in type as well as in execution between the deacon receiving petitions there and the St. Lawrence here, between the *putti* drawing the curtain in the one and the Christ-child in the other, and between the angels in both.

Of this Ancona altar-piece, a hasty and slightly varied replica, which was begun, as Lotto tells us, on August 26, and finished on November 15, 1546, for the price of twenty ducats, still remains on the altar for which it was intended:

VENICE, SAN GIACOMO DELL' ORIO. REPLICA OF ANCONA ALTAR-PIECE.

The Madonna is enthroned between SS. Jacob, Andrew, Cosmas, and Damian.

Inscribed: 'In tempo de Maistro Defendi de Federigo e compagni 1546. Lor. Lot.' On canvas.

To my knowledge no works by Lotto of 1547 or 1549 now exist.

On Nov. 16, 1547, he was commissioned to paint for Mogliano near Macerata an altar-piece for 130 gold ducats. In February of 1548 the work was so far advanced that he ordered the frame for it, and in July

1546 (?). it was already up[1]. I knew when preparing the first edition of this book that such a picture had been painted, but the knowledge that it still exists we owe to Mr. Charles Loeser[2].

MOGLIANO, MADONNA AND SAINTS.

The Madonna with hands eloquently outspread soars upward with a look of pious ecstasy. Devout angels accompany her. Below, following her flight with upturned faces, stand Francis and the Magdalen flanked by Domenic and the Baptist. Behind them the temples of a town.

Signed, as at Ancona, LORENZO LOTTO.
Life-size figures.
Photographed by Houghton, Florence.

The Madonna is like the one in the Brera Pietà, Domenic and the Baptist are replicas of two figures at Sedrina.

That he spent these years in Venice, we know from his own account, and it is precisely at this time that his intimacy with Titian and his 'set' seems to have been the greatest. Aretino's letter, from which we draw our information, is such a curious mixture of good criticism, stabs in the back, and the usual log-rolling in Titian's favour, that we must know the whole of it, which I therefore translate, printing in italics passages which otherwise would require special comment: 'O Lotto, as goodness good, and as talent talented, Titian from Augsburg, in the midst of the high favour everybody is eager to show him, greets and embraces you by the token of the letter which I received from him two days ago. He says that it would double the pleasure that he takes in the Emperor's satisfaction with the pictures he is now

April, 1548.

---

[1] *Gallerie Nazionali Italiane*, i. 165, 166, 139, 144.
[2] *Repertorium*, xxii. 319.

painting, if he had your eye and your judgement to approve him. And, indeed, the painter is not mistaken, for your judgement has been formed by age, by nature, and by art with the prompting of that straightforward kindliness which pronounces upon the works of others exactly as if they were your own; so that the painter may say that in placing before you his pictures and portraits, he is showing them to himself, and asking himself his own opinion. Envy is not in your breast. Rather do you delight to see in other artists *certain qualities which you do not find in your own brush*, although it performs those miracles which do not come easy to many who yet feel very happy over their technical skill. *But holding the second place in the art of painting* is nothing compared to holding the first place in the duties of religion, *for heaven will recompense you with a glory that passes the praise of this world. Venice, April*, 1548[1].'

To make us quite sure of Lotto's intimacy at this time with the entire Titian 'set,' Lotto himself informs us that on quitting Venice in 1549, he left a number of pictures with the third chief partner of the Titian-Aretino Mutual Benefit Society, Jacopo Sansovino, in the hope that the latter would find buyers for them. But Sansovino hastened to send them after Lotto, wishing doubtless to be rid of them. Cellini gives us a good instance of how Sansovino treated people from whom he had nothing further to gain.

Early in June, 1549, Lotto quitted Venice for Ancona, having undertaken to paint, at the expense of a certain Lorenzo Todini, for the price of four hundred *scudi*, an *Assumption*, intended for the church of Santa Maria della Scala at Ancona. He arrived there in July, but the altar-piece was not ready till November of the

---

[1] The original is most accessible in Bottari e Ticozzi, *Lettere Pittoriche*, vol. v, p. 183.

1549. following year. Meanwhile, early in that year, in
1550. 1550, that is, he must have already made up his mind to remain for the rest of his life in the Marches, for otherwise the pictures left with Sansovino would have awaited his return to Venice, instead of being sent after him, reaching him on May 12. He himself seems to have brought along with him a large number of pictures of different sizes to Ancona, and in August of this year we find him [1] putting up forty-six of them in a raffle, provided he could gather a subscription of four hundred *scudi*. But buyers here seem to have been as scarce as in the North, the subscription failing to mount to even forty *scudi*. For this sum he disposed of seven of his smaller works, and to the titles of three of them, as given by himself, I desire to call the attention of those who may be tempted to think that I have seen in Lotto more religious and symbolical purpose than he really had. I give the titles in his own words: '*El quadro de lanima rationale*' —the picture of the rational soul; '*el quadro de lo abatimento de la forteza con fortuna*'—the picture of the combat between strength and fortune; '*el quadro del putin che porta la croce*'—the picture of the Child carrying the cross. The two tendencies of Lotto's mind come out in these titles alone, one thoughtful and profound as in the 'rational soul,' betraying a spirit of allegory which anticipates John Bunyan, and the other, in the contrast of the Child and the cross, the sentimental, over-tender spirit such as crops up later in the Bolognese painters, and in the Catholic Reaction in general [2].

[1] See Pietro Gianuizzi, *Lorenzo Lotto e le sue Opere nelle Marche* in the *Nuova Rivista Misena*, March–April, 1894. Also Lotto's account-book.

[2] Two other titles are worth adding:—Apollo asleep on Parnassus, with the Muses going each her way, and Fame taking flight. The Infant Christ in mid-air surrounded with the symbols of the Passion.

We must now return to the work which was the 1550 immediate occasion of Lotto's leaving Venice for the Marches, the last large work of his remaining, and the last of the period we have been studying:

ANCONA, PINACOTECA, No. 13. ASSUMPTION OF THE VIRGIN.

Inscribed, in large, fantastic letters: LORENZO LOTTO 1550.

On canvas, figures more than life-size.

The Apostles in the lower part of the picture are most brutally repainted. The upper part, although very solidly modelled, is hardly worthy of Lotto; yet the five angels who support the Virgin still retain something of his character. But in its present state the picture as a whole is hardly to be counted as being by him.

CHAPTER VII

LAST YEARS

1550-1556

Aug. 30, 1552.   UNTIL August 30, 1552, when Lotto settled down at Loreto under the protection of the Governor, he remained at Ancona, executing works of various kinds, chiefly portraits and altar-pieces for various towns
Sept. 8, 1554.   in the neighbourhood. On September 8, 1554, he made over himself and all his belongings to the Holy House, 'being tired of wandering, and wishing to end his days in that holy place.' Among the conditions of the deed of transfer[1] were that he was to have rooms, a servant, and clothing, that he was to enjoy the consideration of a canon, to be prayed for as a benefactor, and to have one florin a month 'to do what he pleased with.' At Loreto, then, as a slave of the Blessed Virgin, he spent the last four years of his life, uneventful[2] except for an occasional quarrel with his servants, growing feebler and feebler, it would seem, 'having entirely lost his voice'[3] as early as

---

[1] Published in the *Nuova Rivista Misena*, May-June, 1894. P. Gianuizzi, *Lotto nelle Marche*.

[2] See G. Annibaldi in the *Nuova Rivista Misena*, July, 1892, for notice of an important altar-piece in many parts begun for Jesi in 1552, which was never quite finished, and of which there is now no trace. From his account-book it would seem that Lotto had finished it. Cf. p. 188 of *Gal. Naz. Ital. anno* I.

[3] See Lermolief, *Galerien zu Dresden und München*, p. 61.

1550. He continued painting to the end, and as the fruit of these last years must be regarded a series of pictures at Loreto—nearly all that now is left for us to examine. Pictures with the same subjects are mentioned, it is true, in his account-book under earlier dates, but as he seems to have repeated himself a good deal toward the end of his life, and as the style of these paintings is far more advanced than any works prior to 1550, we need not hesitate to regard them as later than that date. In all probability they were executed in the last two years of his life[1].

Sept. 8, 1554.

But before turning to these pictures at Loreto, we must devote our attention for a moment to a portrait at Nancy, the style of which indicates it as a work executed by Lotto toward the very end of his life. It is doubtless one of the number mentioned by him in his account-book under the years 1550-1552:

1550-1552.

NANCY, PUBLIC GALLERY. BUST OF A MAN.

On canvas, 57 cm. h., 48 cm. w. (Ascribed to Pordenone.)

He seems to be between forty and fifty years old, has a slightly forked auburn beard and moustache, and deep-set brown eyes. He wears a dark cap, and his brown coat is buttoned close over his chest, while a cloak is draped over his R. shoulder. To the L. a cloudy grey sky and the shoulder of a hill. To the R. a greyish-brown wall.

In type, this portrait recalls the *Old Man* of the Brera, but is less carefully painted. The lights and shadows, and the sensitive nostrils are characteristic, but most indicative of Lotto is the heavy line of shadow

---

[1] This I infer from the fact that there is no mention of them in his account-book, which in 1554 he ceased keeping with precision.

1550–1552. between the folds of the cap, and similar lines in the drapery across the shoulder. The whole manner of execution leaves no doubt as to the authorship, and at the same time determines the date.

1554–1556. The pictures at Loreto are of unequal merit, but deserve far more attention than they have ever received. Their chief characteristic is an almost monochrome effect of tone, and a seeming looseness of drawing such as is found in Titian's last works, which is more than made up for, in Lotto as well as in Titian, by a modelling from within of the most plastic kind. Those acquainted with modern French art will seize my meaning when I refer them to M. Henner's and to M. Carrière's way of modelling. In his last works, Lotto's colour also acquired new notes. His white became as chalky as the old Titian's with an even bluer tinge, and he made great use of a peculiar purplish pink:

LORETO, PALAZZO APOSTOLICO, NO. 50. SACRIFICE OF MELCHIZEDEK.

On canvas, 1·72 m. h., 2·48 m. w. Somewhat ruined.
Mentioned by Vasari as *Sacrifice of David*.
Photographed by Alinari and Anderson.
Abraham, accompanied by his warriors, comes up to the altar, on the other side of which stands Melchisedek, who lifts his hands up to heaven, while the attendants are bringing in the sacrifice. The scene takes place in a wood at dawn. The rendering is as dramatic as ever, the feeling well interpreted, the tone low, but rich. The group of warriors still has the Giorgionesque glamour, but the armour to the last recalls Alvise. The composition is almost identical with the one of the same subject in the Bergamo intarsias.

No. 24 AND No. 28. TWO PROPHETS.

On canvas, each 2·08 m. h., 63 cm. w. 1554–1556.

They stand on granite pedestals. The drapery and modelling of the limbs underneath are done exactly as in such of Titian's last works as the two in San Salvatore, the *St. Nicholas* in San Sebastiano, and the *Pietà* in the Academy, all in Venice.

The four following pictures form a series, and are all mentioned by Vasari.

No. 31. ST. MICHAEL DRIVING LUCIFER FROM HEAVEN.

On canvas, 1·70 m. h., 1·37 m. w.

Vasari speaks of this picture as a composition containing many figures. It is, however, very much ruined.

Photographed by Anderson.

The interpretation here is noteworthy, for Lotto represents Lucifer as an angel of great beauty.

No. 32. THE PRESENTATION IN THE TEMPLE.

On canvas, 1·70 m. h., 1·57 m. w. Not quite finished.

Photographed by Anderson and Alinari.

The figures stand around a white-covered table in what looks like the choir of a church. On the L. St. Simeon lifts up his hands in exultation as the kneeling Virgin presents the Infant. A number of women crowd about her, and to the R. stand two acolytes, St. Anne, and a group of men. St. Anne and St. Simeon have that look of extreme old age

1554-1556. which, one thinks, only a man who himself felt old could have painted.

The tension of feeling over an event which all the bystanders recognize as more than human, expresses itself on every face, and on each in a different way. As interpretation, in fact, Lotto never before did anything quite so wonderful, and almost as much may be said of the workmanship.

The paint is put on in a way even more modern than in Titian. Indeed, to find the like of it, we have to turn to the works of contemporary 'Impressionists'—to Manet, in particular. The youth behind St. Anne, for instance, with two dabs of red on the sallow cheeks, reflecting the lights of the red cloak and harmonizing with it in tone, is, singularly enough, almost identical with a figure in Manet's *Spanish Dance*, belonging to M. Durand-Ruel at Paris. As general tone and as drawing, this *Presentation* suggests the work of M. Degas. It is, in short, one of Lotto's greatest achievements, and is perhaps the most 'modern' picture ever painted by an old Italian master.

No. 21. THE BAPTISM.

On canvas, 1·72 m. h., 1·37 m. w. Much darkened and ruined.

The modelling is solid, and the landscape still has fine effects.

No. 20. ADORATION OF THE MAGI.

On canvas, 1·78 m. h., 1·36 m. w.

A work not at all to be compared to the rest of the series. It was probably executed by Baghazotti of Camerino, Lotto's assistant at this period.

[Aninari photo.] [Loreto, Santa Casa

THE PRESENTATION

The last entry in Lotto's account-book dates from 1556. late in the year 1556. His death could not have occurred until toward the end of the year 1556.

It is a singular coincidence that Lotto ended his career nearly on the spot where he began it. The works of his adolescence were once at Recanati; the works of his extreme old age are still at the neighbouring town of Loreto. He did not merely begin and end his career in the March of Ancona, but all through his life he kept in communication with this part of the Adriatic coast, visiting it himself from time to time, or sending it his pictures. This fact also connects him with his Muranese predecessors, who supplied the Marches with works of art, as their fellow citizens supplied it with merchandise. Works by the Vivarini were once numerous in this region, and Crivelli entirely deserted Venice to settle down at Ascoli, whence he supplied the neighbourhood with those resplendent altar-pieces which now form oases in the wastes of archæology and 'masterpieces' that our great collections have become. Lotto, then, in this particular also, continued the Muranese tradition, exploiting the market created for him by his predecessors.

With one of these, Carlo Crivelli, probably the fellow pupil of his master Alvise, we have had, at different times, occasion to note Lotto's special likeness. The one in certain aspects seems but the reincarnation, in an advanced age, of the other. In both we find feeling that tends to be too intense; in both great daintiness, love of elegance and of finery, in both a supreme sense of decoration. And now we have to note a likeness even in their careers—they both haunted the Marches and ended there.

Furthermore, it is not without interest that two artists of such high rank as Crivelli and Lotto, both

1556. among the few Venetian masters of note who were actually natives of Venice, should have been the ones to spend a great deal of their lives away from home. Another native Venetian who lived and died even farther away from Venice was Jacopo di Barbari, between whom also, and Lotto, as we recall, we found strong resemblances. Now, what was it that drove these artists away from home? If the cause lay in the lack of appreciation for them at home, that itself would be a most interesting comment—that Crivelli, and Barbari, and Lotto should have found no employment in Venice, when Lazzaro Sebastiani, Mansueti, Benedetto Diana, and Girolamo Santa Croce found plenty! Yet some such reason there may have been. Crivelli, Barbari, Lotto, and still another, Sebastiano del Piombo, all left Venice urged probably by necessity or the hope of greater gain. But in all these cases the point to bear in mind is that they yielded to a pressure that might not have been able to move others; and they yielded so readily because they all were sons of a race accustomed to trafficking abroad, to colonizing, to taking flight in their numerous galleys at the least provocation. They had the blood of rovers in their veins, and the wandering that to their ancestors had been a necessity, became in them an impulse.

With the taste for wandering, all the artists I have mentioned, except Sebastiano del Piombo, who was more of the mere trafficker, combined certain fanciful qualities of mind and bizarre traits of character—at least if we may, as we must, trust their works to be the revelations of themselves. They seemed possessed with a taste for the extraordinary, for what was subtle and refined, and there was in all of them just a touch of what we now should call the 'decadent.' There would be nothing of general interest in this if it were not that of the only five or six artists of nearly the first order born in Venice between 1412 and 1512, three had the qualities I have noted. And in this fact we have a comment on the Venetian temperament that supplements, to say the least, the current notion of the Venetian character—a notion based chiefly, on the one hand, upon the study of merely political history, and on the other, upon the art-product of the Bellini, who were perhaps not even brought up in Venice, and upon the art-product of Giorgione, Titian, and Veronese, none of whom was by birth or blood a real Venetian.

1556.

APPENDIX TO CHAPTER VII

COPIES OF LOST ORIGINALS. DRAWINGS

In the study of a given master we cannot afford to neglect such valuable sources of information as are the copies of his lost works, and his drawings. The former often help to complete the image we have constructed of the master in our study of his original paintings. The latter may reveal nooks and corners of the artist's personality to which his pictures have failed to draw our attention. Unfortunately, in the case of Lotto, the few copies of works not extant, with the exception of one in the Borghese Gallery already discussed, and the few drawings I have been able to find, do not add to our knowledge of Lotto: the copies because they are not of works diverging in character from the originals we have been studying; the drawings either because they are portrait heads in which no peculiar qualities of draughtsmanship come to the surface, or too few to give anything like an adequate idea of the master's talent as a draughtsman. But such as these copies and drawings [1] are, here is a list of them.

COPIES

MILAN, ARCHBISHOP'S PALACE. MADONNA WITH ST. CATHERINE AND ST. JEROME.

The original must have been a work of 1522, the Madonna being the same as in the pictures of that date at Costa di Mezzate, and at Mrs. Martin Colnaghi's in London. St. Catherine is almost identical with the same saint in the former, the Jerome with the same person in the latter work. Copy, old, Italian.

ROME, COLONNA GALLERY. PORTRAIT OF POMPEO COLONNA.

The original may have been a Bergamask work. Copy, almost contemporary, Italian.
Photographed by Alinari, Florence.

FLORENCE, GALLERIA FERONI (NOW AMALGAMATED WITH THE CENACOLO DI FOLIGNO). NATIVITY.

Photographed by Brogi.
A night scene. The original could have been neither the picture mentioned by Vasari as belonging to Tommaso da Empoli, nor the one mentioned by Ridolfi as belonging to Van Reynst of Amsterdam,

---

[1] We shall not forget that in its place we already have spoken of the original drawing for the Borghese copy of a lost Santa Conversazione.

because this copy does not answer exactly to the description of either. Lotto's original must have been a work of about 1530. The copy is obviously Flemish.

Another copy of the principal part only of the picture exists in the Uffizi under the name of Michelangelo Anselmi, No. 1210.

VENICE, SIGNOR GUGGENHEIM.

Portrait of a man of about forty, and his wife, seated at a table. Her R. hand rests on his shoulder, and in her L. she holds a little white dog. The original must have been an interesting work of about 1535. Copy, old, Italian.

DRAWINGS

LONDON, MR. G. T. CLOUGH.

A design in india ink and wash for a Peter and Paul upholding a monstrance which is being incensed by two angels. The subject recalls a picture that Lotto tells us he painted for Breda in 1543. The saints suggest those at Sedrina, the angels those in the Ancona altar-piece of about 1545. We shall thus not stray far in placing this interesting but scarcely brilliant drawing between the three works just mentioned.

LONDON, MR. HENRY WAGNER.

Cartoon in black chalk, heightened with white, and with a touch of pink on the lips, for the life-size portrait of a young man. The toss of the head, the vivacity, and all the morphological peculiarities are characteristic of Lotto. The date can be no other than that of the Della Torre Portraits at the National Gallery. This is the one and only drawing by Lotto that merits consideration as draughtsmanship. 33½ cm. h., 27 cm. w.

FLORENCE UFFIZI. Frame 333, No. 1860 F. Black chalk on brown paper, 25 cm. h., 18½ cm. w.

Head of a man of about thirty, full face, with beard and moustache, wearing a round cap. My attention was first drawn to this splendid drawing by Signor Enrico Costa.

Photographed by Alinari, Florence.

UFFIZI. Frame 333, No. 1741 F. Black chalk on brownish paper, 21 cm. h., 16½ cm. w. Considerably rubbed.

Head of a young man, almost full face, with short beard and moustache, wearing a cap, and having long hair falling on each side of his face. This head seems to have all the characteristics of Lotto's earlier works— the eyes, the Alvisesque mouth, the sensitive nostrils, and the somewhat dry modelling. It stands particularly near to such a work as the Recanati altar-piece of 1508.

Photographed by Alinari, Florence.

VIENNA ALBERTINA.

Cartoon in black chalk, for the bust of a man of about thirty, wearing a short beard, hair down to the shoulders, and a hat. 42½ cm. h., 27½ cm. w.

It would be idle to discuss why I have attributed this head to Lotto. I would date it about 1530.

Reproduced as Plate 280 of Schönbrunner's Albertina Publication.

[H. Wagner, Esq., London

CARTOON FOR THE PORTRAIT OF A MAN

CHAPTER VIII

LOTTO'S FOLLOWING AND INFLUENCE

To fully understand an artist we must know more than how he came by his style, and what was its character. We must also know not only how he was received by his contemporaries—that we partly infer from the number of his works and the prices they fetched—but we must further know what power of kindling others he possessed, and whether his style was one that could easily be imitated, and one that the merely venal painter found it worth while to imitate.

Of Lotto's power of kindling his contemporaries I shall speak later. As to his imitators it is significant that they were few. His style apparently was never so popular as to make it worth while to retail it largely as an article of commerce; and he invented no formula which, as, for instance, in the case of Botticelli, a pupil could imitate with success. Even his types, in so far as they differ from those of his precursors, were so much the expression of his own personality, so charged with emotion, that imitation of them could lead only to caricature. Like Raphael, like Michelangelo, like Correggio, Lotto completely exhausted a certain vein, leaving nothing for followers; and it must be added that Lotto himself approached too close to the brink of decadence for imitators not to plunge into the gulf.

Such caricaturists, then, as his imitators were bound to be, Lotto did not altogether lack; in Bergamo,

Caversegno. Caversegno, and, in the Marches, Antonio da Faenza, Caldarola, Durante da Force, and others. Caversegno may have been Lotto's direct pupil or assistant during Lotto's Bergamask years. He finished the polyptych left uncompleted by Previtali in Santo Spirito at Bergamo, and other pictures by him may be seen in the sacristy of the same church, and elsewhere in the town. A more than usually Lottesque work, recounting the story of St. Julian, belongs to Mr. Ludwig Mond, of Rome. He approaches nearest to Lotto in a *Madonna with St. Roch*, No. 493 in the Ferdinandeum at Innsbruck. Another Bergamask who seems to have come

Fra Damiano da Bergamo. under Lotto's influence is Fra Damiano da Bergamo, who executed the intarsias on the choir-stalls in San Domenico at Bologna (1528–30). A scarcely definable trace of Lotto is visible throughout these compositions, particularly in the allegorical and decorative bits. In the *Maryrdom of St. Catherine* the movement of the executioner is distinctly Lottesque. In the *Stoning of Stephen* a figure to the R. is taken from Lotto's *predella* for the San Bartolommeo altar-piece (1516).

Antonio da Faenza. Antonio da Faenza[1] was active in or near Loreto during the earlier decades of the sixteenth century. An elaborate altar-piece of his at Montelupone containing the Madonna enthroned on a high pedestal under a magnificent coffered vaulting with seven male saints to the sides, betrays intimate acquaintance with Lotto's S. Bartolommeo altar-piece at Bergamo. The architecture differs only in the absence of the apse; the Sebastian is almost a copy from the figure in that

Simone da Caldarola. work. Caldarola painted in the last half of the sixteenth century. His works are found in the Franciscan church at Matelica, in the Pinacoteca of Fabriano, and elsewhere in the Marches. A *Crucifixion* at

---

[1] P. Gianuizzi, Antonio da Faenza, in *Arte e Storia*, xiii, Nov. 19, 1894.

Matelica, dated 1568, is nothing but a free rendering of Lotto's Monte San Giusto altar-piece (1531). But the *predelle*, although they can scarcely be direct copies, seeing that the Monte San Giusto *Crucifixion* never had *predelle*, are quite as Lottesque as the picture itself, and point to Caldarola's having been a real imitator, and not a mere copyist. At Cingoli also, in San Domenico, there is a picture by him, representing a saint raising a sick woman, which is equally Lottesque, even to the treatment of lights and shadows. Durante of Force may be seen in a picture in San Francesco at Massa Fermese—the *Madonna in Glory, and Twelve Saints*. It is dated 1549, but the character of the painting shows that the author must have come under Lotto's influence at least fifteen years earlier. It is known from the account-books of the Santa Casa that in 1555 a certain Baghazotti of Camerino was paid twenty-four *scudi* a year to assist Lotto. Possibly two prophets in the storeroom of the Palazzo Apostolico, very Lottesque, but not worthy of Lotto himself, are by this Baghazotti. In Santa Maria in Monte Morelli at Recanati there is a Madonna with SS. Flavian and Vito by an unknown imitator of Lotto's middle manner. He comes nearer to his master than any of the known followers. Another unknown imitator of Lotto's style of about 1533 is the author of the *St. Sebastian* at Dresden[1]. The landscape in this picture recalls the one in the Berlin *St. Sebastian*, the draperies and the general grey tone are distinctly Lottesque; but the quality throughout is too feeble for Lotto, and betrays the imitator. An imitator of about 1540 appears in a small Madonna with two angels holding a crown over her head, in the Museo Correr at Venice (Phot. Anderson, 12,483). A Flemish imitator reveals himself

{Durante of Force.}
{Baghazotti.}
{Unknown imitators.}
{Flemish imitator.}

---

[1] Photographed by Tamme, Dresden.

in a landscape in the National Gallery (No. 1298), now ascribed to Patinir.

Lotto's influence. Palma.
His direct following, then, was slight and unimportant, but the influence he exerted upon his contemporaries was by no means so slight. His own indebtedness to Palma was touched upon sufficiently in previous chapters of this work. We cannot enter so fully into the study of Palma's debt to Lotto. Suffice it to say that, although Palma never becomes so obviously Lottesque as Lotto in his Alzano altar-piece is Palmesque, he nevertheless felt the return influence much more lastingly, and was much more permeated by it. In the case of Lotto the inclination was towards Palma's technique only; but Palma was taken captive by Lotto's point of view also. This is fully attested by such of Palma's works as the Louvre *Adoration of the Shepherds* and the Naples *Santa Conversazione*, by certain of the female portraits at Vienna, by the male portrait at Berlin (No. 174), and most of all by the male portrait in the Querini-Stampalia Collection at Venice.

Savoldo.
In analysing Lotto's *Recognition of the Holy Child*, a picture of about 1538, now in the Louvre, we discovered a great likeness between the head of the St. Joachim in that work, and the head of a St. Jerome in a picture belonging to Lady Layard, painted by Savoldo. As this type of head is more characteristic of the latter than it is of Lotto, we may assume that in this case Lotto took a suggestion from Savoldo; but this is the only case of the kind, while Savoldo on his side seems to have owed much to Lotto's inspiration. Exact contemporaries, and pupils, as I believe, of the same master, they probably were friends from their youth up. Savoldo's career is still a mystery, and the story of his life is known to us in fragments only. In one, however, of his few dated

works, *The Nativity*, at Hampton Court (No. 139), executed in 1527, Savoldo has introduced a portrait of pronouncedly Lottesque character. His masterpiece, the Brera altar-piece (No. 234), is not dated, but the kindred work in Santa Maria in Organo at Verona is dated 1533. The composition and landscape in both pictures recall Lotto's Carmine altar-piece of 1529. A similar landscape occurs in Savoldo's *Rest in the Flight*, now in the Casa Albani at Urbino, but this landscape is full of little figures that recall Lotto's intarsias, the cartoons of which Savoldo may have known. The instances cited make it more than probable, therefore, that at least from 1527 to 1533 Savoldo was largely under Lotto's spell.

Lotto's Bergamask contemporaries took, as was natural, a great deal from him. In the case of Previtali, Lotto's influence is most evident in an altar-piece in the Bergamo Cathedral, and, above all, in its *predelle*, now in the sacristy, which Messrs. Crowe and Cavalcaselle actually attribute to Lotto himself. Cariani's most Lottesque works are a *St. Sebastian*, at Vienna (No. 162), attributed to Correggio, and a *Madonna with a Donor*, dated 1520, left by the late Signor Baglioni to the gallery of Bergamo—works in which Cariani succeeds in catching much of Lotto's intimate charm. Cariani's *Lot and his Daughters*, in the Museo Civico of Milan (No. 106), and the portrait of a man seizing a sword while pointing to an apparition of the Virgin, in the Tadini Gallery at Lovere (No. 378), deserve mention in this connexion. That Lotto was not forgotten at Bergamo in the seventeenth century is proved by Salmeggia and Cavagna, who imitated him as closely as Padovanino and Liberi imitated Titian and Paul Veronese.

In the Trevisan also one frequently stumbles upon paintings betraying the influence of Lotto. This is

Previtali.

Cariani.

Seventeenth-century Bergamask painters.

Becca- particularly true of the works of Francesco Beccaruzzi,
ruzzi. an estimate of an altar-piece by whom Lotto was, in 1544, requested to make. An adaptation by Beccaruzzi of the lower part of Lotto's M. San Giusto *Crucifixion* I have already mentioned as being at Strasburg. In the Giovanelli Collection at Venice there is a *St. Roch in Ecstasy*, attributed by most authorities to Lotto himself, which I believe to be by no other than Beccaruzzi.

CHAPTER IX

RESULTING IMPRESSION

Up to this point, we have been occupied in reconstructing, bit by bit, the personality and career of Lorenzo Lotto. The detailed analysis of his earliest works, with which we began, yielded the conclusion that Lotto could not have been the pupil of Giovanni Bellini, as he has been considered hitherto, but that he must have been the follower of Alvise Vivarini, and we had then to set to work to gather as much knowledge as we could about Alvise and his school, because it has been a comparatively neglected chapter of art history. With this light on our path, much in Lotto that would otherwise have remained unexplained assumed a natural appearance, and his way through life became easier to follow. Every further work by him that we examined was like a new image added to the images of his personality we had already acquired. At last, we had a composite picture, made up of the impressions left upon our minds by the painter's various artistic achievements, and this composite picture was only strengthened, framed in, as it were, by an acquaintance with his last works and with his own scattered utterances.

But as there were many points to prove by the way, and much mere cataloguing to be done, we are only now free to ask ourselves what is our final impression of the artist. This final impression is, of course, nothing else than the composite image of the man that our detailed study has yielded—an image which makes no claims to scientific accuracy. Art deals with the emotions, and do what we will to pump ourselves dry of prejudices and accidental feelings, do what we will to be cautious and judicious, our final impression of works of art remains an equation between them and our own temperament. Every appreciation is, therefore, a confession, and its value depends entirely upon its sincerity. But such a confession may end by having something of the interest of the work of art itself. The perfect masterpiece, among the many requirements it must fulfil, must give us the attitude of a typical human being towards the universe. The perfect criticism should give us the measure of the acceptability at a given time of the work of art in question.

I happen to have a temperament which inclines me to forgive much to an artist like Lotto. In thinking of him, I find it difficult to dwell upon his faults: my composite visual image tends to be an image of his qualities only. This, however, may be not an unmixed evil. Faults are so obvious as compared with qualities, and pointing out the qualities may lead a few people to enjoy and profit by an artist to whom they otherwise might remain indifferent. A person with another temperament, it is true, might have, as the result of studies similar to those I have made, a different and much less agreeable impression of Lotto. But a sympathy kept under the control of reason has a penetrating power of its own, and leads to discoveries that no coldly scientific analysis will disclose. I mean, however, not to exaggerate Lotto's qualities, and to avoid, above all things, making any statement not warranted by the conclusions at which we have arrived in previous chapters.

To bring out clearly the composite image of Lotto's qualities, it is necessary to do something more than merely describe them. We must relieve them against the epoch in which he was living, and contrast them with the qualities of his parallel, Correggio, and of his great rival, Titian; we must see why he was so much less appreciated than they in his own times, and why he is beginning to find a tardy appreciation at this day.

In 1480, when Lotto was born, Giorgione, Titian, and Palma were already alive. These three pupils of Giovanni Bellini form a group who carried painting beyond the methods and ideals of their master, even before his death; and Lotto, although not their fellow pupil, but attached to the kindred school of Alvise Vivarini, kept abreast of the advance they made. Bellini retains to the last a vigour and freshness in which there is not the least suggestion of his great age. But if we recall that he was seventy at a time when the younger painters were between twenty and twenty-five, we can easily understand that there should be in them a quality which is more than vigour and freshness, a quality which is youth—quicker senses for the passing moment, greater joy in looking forward to the morrow. But this youthfulness is not necessarily personal, and it may be questioned whether Bellini's own pupils, Giorgione, Palma, and Titian, were by temperament any more personal than their master himself. Giorgione died young; Palma's talents were not of the highest order; Titian, therefore, remained without a rival among the younger generation of Bellini's followers, taking that place in the Venice of the sixteenth century which was Bellini's in the fifteenth. This position he took and continued to hold, not by mere chance, but by right, for his genius was of the kind which enabled him to embody the dominant tendencies of his age, as Bellini had embodied those of an earlier generation. Titian alone, of all the Italian painters of the sixteenth century, expressed the master feelings, the passions, and the struggles then prevailing; the impotence no less than the energy; the cowardice as well as the noble-mindedness; the pretence as well as the boundless zeal. The expression Titian gave to the ideals of his own age has that grandeur of form, that monumental style of composition, that arresting force of colour, which make the world recognize a work of art at once, and for ever acclaim it a classic; but with all these qualities, Titian's painting is as impersonal, as untinged by individuality, as Bellini's. Indeed, to express the master passions of a majority implies a power of impersonal feeling and vision, and implies, too, a certain happy insensibility—the very leaven of genius, perhaps.

This insensibility, this impersonal grasp of the world about him, Lotto lacked. A constant wanderer over the face of Italy, he could not shut his eyes to its ruin, nor make a rush for a share in the spoils. The real Renaissance, with all its blithe promise, seemed over and gone. Lotto, like many of his noblest countrymen, turned to religion for consolation, but not to the official Christianity of the past, nor to the stereotyped Romanism of the near future. His yearning was for immediate communion with God, although, true to his artistic temperament, he did not reject forms made venerable by long use and sweet association. He is thus one of the very few artists who embodies in his works a state of feeling in Italy which contained the promise of a finer and higher civilization, of a more personally responsible moral life, and a more earnest religion. As these promises were never realized, Lotto at times seems more like a precursor of the Counter-Reformation[1], but at all events, he is there to witness to an attitude of mind in Italy which, although not the dominant, could have been by no means rare. For the dominant tendencies of an epoch are never so predominant as to give a complete idea of it. To know the sixteenth century well, it is almost more important to study Lotto than Titian. Titian only embodies in art-forms what we already know about the ripe Renaissance, but Lotto supplements and even modifies our idea of this period.

Art so faithfully registers the struggles and aspirations of humanity that, to understand in what way it expresses a certain epoch, it may be needful to venture beyond its narrow limits into the region of general history. Christianity, it will be remembered, owed its rapid growth and final triumph, in large measure, to the personal relation it attempted universally to establish between man and God. Pushed into the background while the Church was devoting itself to the task of civilizing barbarian hordes, this ideal of a close relation between God and man revived with the revival of culture, and became in the sixteenth century the aim of all religious striving. A brave Italian band trusted that they would be able to make religion personal once more without becoming Protestants. We all know of the sad failure of Contarini and Sadolet. Lotto had the same temper of mind, and he remained as unappreciated as they, for Titian and Tintoretto swept him into oblivion, as Caraffa and Loyola effaced the protestantizing cardinals.

Italy was tired of turmoil, and was ready to pay any price for fixed conditions and settled institutions. It

[1] Among the premonitory symptoms of the new Catholicism may be noted the importance which Lotto begins to give to St. Joseph. In the Jesi *Madonna with Joseph and Jerome*, for instance, we already find him as in Seicento art, fully installed as *the* foster father of the Holy Child.

soon appeared that the price demanded was abject submission to the decrees of the Council of Trent, and Italy paid it with scarcely a murmur. If the Council of Trent meant anything, it meant the eradication of every personal element from Christianity. Bearing this in mind, we can see how inevitable was the failure of such men as Contarini, Sadolet, and Lotto—men to whom their own souls were more than Christianity itself, for in Christianity they sought only the satisfaction of their aspirations and longings. They wanted more personality rather than less, and Italy was not ready to see that personality was a very different affair from the individualism of which she was heartily weary.

The chief note of Lotto's work is not religiousness, then—at any rate not the religiousness of Fra Angelico or the young Bellini—but personality, a consciousness of self, a being aware at every moment of what is going on within one's heart and mind, a straining of the whole tangible universe through the web of one's temperament. This implies exquisite sensitiveness, a quality which could not be appreciated by a people who were preparing to submit to the double tyranny of Spain and the Papacy. Nor was a man who strained the whole universe through a sensitive personality likely to interpret Scripture and the legends of the Saints in a way that would be pleasing to the new Catholicism.

Lotto's temper of mind was thus a hindrance to his success, but a sensitive personality has a more vital drawback still, in those inevitable fluctuations of mood which make it so much more difficult for a man like Lotto than for one like Titian to keep the level he has once attained. But Lotto's very sensitiveness gave him an appreciation of shades of feeling that would utterly have escaped Titian's notice. Titian never painted a single figure that does not have the look and bearing rank and circumstances require. His people are well-bred, dignified, represented at their best—that is to say, conforming perfectly to current standards. We cannot find fault with Titian for having painted nothing but prosperity, beauty, and health—man on parade, as it were—but the interest he himself arouses in the world he painted, makes us eager to know more of these people than he tells us, to know them more intimately, in their own homes, if possible, subject to the wear and tear of ordinary existence. We long to know how they take life, what they think, and, above all, what they feel. Titian tells us none of these things, and if we are to satisfy our curiosity, we must turn to Lotto, who is as personal as Titian is typical. If artists were at all as conscious of their aims in the sixteenth century as they are supposed to be now, we might imagine Titian asking of every person he was going to paint, Who are you? What is your position in society?—while Lotto would put the question, What sort of a person are you? How do you take life?

Lotto was, in fact, the first Italian painter who was sensitive to the varying states of the human soul. He seems always to have been able to define his feelings, emotions, and ideals, instead of being a mere highway for them; always to recognize at the moment the value of an impression, and to enjoy it to the full before it gave place to another. This makes him pre-eminently a psychologist, and distinguishes him from such even of his contemporaries as are most like him: from Dürer, who is near him in depth; and from Correggio, who comes close to him in sensitiveness. The most constant attitude of Dürer's mind is moral earnestness; of Correggio's, rapturous emotion; of Lotto's, psychological interest—that is to say, interest in the effect things have on the human consciousness.

The critic who attempts to write about a painter must beware of many dangers, but he must be especially careful to avoid being vague and fanciful. The surest way of keeping clear of these dangers is to treat the painter chronologically, touching upon the various influences he came under, and considering the various phases of his art in connexion with corresponding epochs in his life. I shall, therefore, so far as practicable, follow this plan in endeavouring to reconstruct Lotto's artistic personality. In the almost total lack of important documents to throw light upon the greater part of his career, we turn with gratitude to the fact that he seldom forgot to date his pictures— a significant trait, it may be, of his consciousness of self, and one, at any rate, which helps us to follow him in his wanderings, and to trace the evolution of his personality through his successive works.

Like other painters of the Italian Renaissance, Lotto, precocious as he seems to have been, did not attain full expression of his genius at a single bound. Although the entire series of his early works, from Prof. Conway's *Danaë* (London), painted before 1500, to the Recanati altar-piece of 1508, have qualities of drawing, of chiaroscuro, and of colour, which clearly distinguish them from the work of any other artist of the time, nevertheless the dominant note of his spirit is as yet scarcely apparent. Nor is this surprising, when we stop to reflect that even the born psychologist must have the material of experience to work upon. In these early essays, therefore, we find Lotto even more dependent in spirit than in technique upon the school he comes from. The religious severity and asceticism which characterize the school of the Vivarini, even at a time when the Bellini had become paganized, stamp all Lotto's youthful works. They have none of the pagan quality that marks the Madonnas Giorgione and Titian were painting at the same time, and nothing could be more utterly opposed to them in feeling than the decorous little garden parties—the '*Sante Conversazioni*'—infallibly called to mind when the name of Palma is mentioned. Although the first of Lotto's known pictures is a mythological subject, a Danaë, it is treated far more ascetically than was the penitent Magdalen by Italian painters of a generation or two later. She illustrates, indeed, a tendency in the Renaissance exactly opposed to the one that is usually pointed out : instead of paganizing Christianity, Lotto, perhaps following the example of one of his predecessors, Jacopo di Barbari, here Christianizes paganism. Nothing could be less premeditated than this little picture, in which the childlike Danaë sits fully clothed in a wooded landscape. Sincerity and *naïveté* are its distinguishing qualities, as indeed of all of Lotto's early pictures. Yet that we note such qualities as sincerity and *naïveté* at all, proves that the painter has already passed beyond the stage in which impersonal feelings and beliefs find unconscious expression. Unpsychological as Lotto is in these first works, he is groping toward something far more conscious and personal than any of his Venetian predecessors had attained; and it is this initial note of personality, added to the asceticism of the school in which he was trained, that gives his own early pictures a moral earnestness, and a depth of feeling which place them beside Dürer's.

The first indication of Lotto's psychological bent appears in a *Portrait of a Young Man*, at Hampton Court, dating from about 1509. Here, Lotto obviously sought to catch the pose and expression that were most characteristic. Instead of gazing straight out of the canvas, and looking grave and stately as people always do in Giorgione's and Titian's early portraits, this young man throws back his head with a toss, as if about to assert an opinion of his own. With the exception of the portraits painted by Lotto's master, Alvise, there is no existing Venetian head of about this date half so unconventional. Venetian portraiture, as a whole, was still held in bondage by the ecclesiastical and ceremonial painting to which it had hitherto been a mere adjunct. Giorgione and the young Titian posed people as if they were assisting at some solemn religious festival or state ceremony. But in this portrait Lotto has already shaken himself free from such restraint, and anticipates that intensely individual kind of characterization which Moroni attains in his happiest works, as for example in the portrait of Pantera in the Uffizi.

It is a temptation to speak of the portraits at greater length than their relative number warrants, because they gave freest scope to psychological treatment. But Lotto was not like Moroni, a mere portrait painter. Religious subjects occupied most of his energies, and we shall see presently to what extent his psychological spirit permeates these works as well. Devoting our attention for the moment, however, to his portraits, we find that not one of the score still existing leaves us indifferent. They all have the interest of personal confessions. Never before or since has any one brought out on the face more of the inner life. We should be tempted to think that Lotto had purposely chosen somewhat morbid subjects, people peculiarly sensitive and self-conscious by nature, or, at any rate, made sensitive by disease or sorrow, if we had not several instances to the contrary, such as the *Young Man*, at Hampton Court; the three portraits in the Brera, and the *Architect*, at Berlin. One of his most sympathetic interpretations is a portrait in the Borghese Gallery of a man who rests his hand on a tiny flower-wreathed skull. He looks as if the world were just dawning upon him again after a sorrow that had overwhelmed him like a terrible illness. In a portrait by Lotto in the Doria Gallery, a man presses his hand to his heart as if to allay a pain, seeming only too well aware of a disease, perhaps mortal, that may at any moment snatch him away from all he holds dear.

Lotto's psychological interest is never of a purely scientific kind. It is, above all, humane, and makes him gentle and full of charity for his sitters, as if he understood all their weaknesses without despising them, so that he nearly always succeeds in winning our sympathy for them. This is true even where they were evidently antipathetic to himself, as in the portrait of Andrea Odoni, at Hampton Court, where the painter seems as much as to say: 'What can you expect from a man of this temperament?' Yet, in one of his latest portraits, that in the Brera, of an old man whom life seems to have turned to flint, Lotto shows himself at need a keen and merciless judge. Even where he has sitters to whom no other painter of the time would have managed to give a shred of personality, Lotto succeeds in bringing out all that is most personal in them, all that could possibly have differentiated them from other people of their age and station. Perhaps the best example is the portrait at Bergamo of a middle-aged woman who certainly could have had little to distinguish her from a hundred other Bergamask gentlewomen, but on whose face Lotto portrays all the kindliness, motherliness, and neighbourliness of which such a woman is capable. Again, in the portraits of Niccolò della Torre and his brother in the National Gallery, and in the Brera *Portrait of a Lady*, his sitters were in no way remarkable. Nevertheless he gives them a look of refinement and innate sweetness of nature, which brings us very close to them. Taken all together, Lotto's portraits are full of meaning and interest for us, for he paints people who seem to feel as we do about many things, who have already much of our spontaneous kindness, much of our feeling for humanity, and much of our conscious need of human ties and sympathy. The charity of Lotto's spirit gives us a very different idea of the sixteenth century from that which our fancy conjures up when we concentrate our attention upon the murder of Lorenzino de' Medici, or the tragic end of the Duchess of Palliano. Indeed, the study of Lotto would repay if it did no more than help us to a truer and saner view of the sixteenth century in Italy than has been given by popular writers from Stendhal downwards, writers who too exclusively have devoted themselves to its lurid side. That side, it is true, is the prominent one, yet we feel a generous suspicion that another side must have existed, and Lotto helps to restore that human balance without which the Italy of the sixteenth century would be a veritable pandemonium.

Among the works of this category, two form a class apart, because they unexpectedly anticipate the spirit of the modern psychological novel. The *Family Group* of the National Gallery, far from being painted as such groups usually were in Italy—a mere collection of faces looking one like the other, but with no bond of sympathy or interest uniting them—is in itself a family story, as modern almost as Tolstoi's *Katia*. Lotto makes it evident that the sensitiveness of the man's nature has brought him to understand and condone his wife's limitations, and that she, in her turn, has been refined and softened into sympathy with him; so that the impression the picture leaves is one of great kindliness, covering a multitude of small disappointments and incompatibilities.

The Madrid *Couple*, painted in 1523, may be

compared to an American novel, but the story is obviously only at its beginning. One cannot look at the broad, smiling face of the young bridegroom, or at the firm mouth and clever eyes of the young bride, without sharing the amusement of the roguish little Cupid who maliciously holds a yoke suspended over their necks. Lotto had studied the psychology of this Bergamask couple too well not to interpret the situation somewhat humorously; and, in fact, a psychological humour of this kind is by no means rare in his works. It is so delicate, however, that in a well-known picture it has escaped attention. The Lotto in the Rospigliosi Gallery at Rome has long been miscalled *The Triumph of Chastity* [1]. It is true that Venus and the scared little Cupid are fleeing before the fury of a female who evidently personifies Mrs. Grundy, but their innocent looks betray their belief that she has been seized by a sudden and unaccountable madness, for which they are in no way responsible. In the intarsias in one of the Bergamo churches, for which Lotto supplied the designs, and in a chapel at Trescorre, near Bergamo, which he covered with frescoes, the humour is not quite so subtle, but gay and playful. Among the designs of the intarsias are some which recount the story of David, and Lotto treats it with that half-conscious touch of modernization (turning, for instance, the messenger into a country postman), which plays so great a part in the humour of Ariosto. In Trescorre, a little boy, bored by the religious ceremony to which his father has brought him, and absorbed, as children are, in his play, takes advantage of a peculiarly solemn moment to snatch at the Bishop's glittering robe.

I have said that Lotto, as distinguished from other

[1] In French guide-books, however, it is entitled, *La Force qui frappe l'Innocence*. See illustration.

artists of his time, is psychological. He is intensely personal as well. But these qualities are only different aspects of the same thing, psychological signifying an interest in the personality of others, and personal, an interest in one's own psychology. In his portraits, Lotto is more distinctly psychological; in his religious subjects—the only other class of paintings which, with few exceptions, he ever undertook—he is not only psychological, but personal as well. Psychology and personality mingle to a wonderful degree in his renderings of sacred themes. He interprets profoundly, and in his interpretation expresses his entire personality, showing at a glance his attitude towards the whole of life.

. . . .

In 1513 Lotto was called to Bergamo, where he remained at work for twelve years. When he went there he was thirty-three years old, and complete master of his craft. He was in the full vigour of manhood and entering upon the happiest period of his career. His pictures of this time, particularly those still preserved at Bergamo, have an exuberance, a buoyancy, and a rush of life which find utterance in quick movements, in an impatience of architectonic restraint, in bold foreshortenings, and in brilliant, joyous colouring. There is but one other Italian artist whose paintings could be described in the same words, and that is Correggio. Between Lotto's Bergamask pictures and Correggio's mature works, the likeness is indeed startling. As it is next to impossible to establish any actual connexion between them, this likeness may be taken as one of the best instances to prove the inevitability of expression. Painters of the same temperament, living at the same time and in the same country, are bound to express themselves in nearly the same way—not only to create the same ideals, but to have the same preferences for certain attitudes, for certain colours, and for certain effects of light. Yet Lotto, even in these Bergamask works, differs from Correggio by the whole of his psychological bent. Correggio is never psychological; he is too ecstatic, too rapturous. A sensation or a feeling comes over him with the rush of a tidal wave, sweeping away every trace of conscious personality. He is as tremulously sensitive as Lotto, but his sensitiveness is naïvely sensuous, while Lotto, as has been said, reserves his most exquisite sensitiveness for states of the human soul. In these years Lotto felt that immense joy in life, that exultation of man realizing the beauty of the world and the extent of his own capacities, which found perfect expression in Titian's *Assunta* and Correggio's Parma *Assumption*. Lotto's expression is less complete than either Correggio's or Titian's, for in him there is ever the element of self-consciousness, of reflection, reduced for a brief while within the narrowest limits, yet never entirely absent. The altar-pieces at San Bartolommeo, at Santo Spirito, at San Bernardino, the larger intarsias at Santa Maria Maggiore in Bergamo, and the frescoes of the chapel at Trescorre, are all full of this Renaissance intoxication, sobered down before it grows Dionysiac by a correcting touch of self-consciousness. They have beauty, they have romance, they have quickness of life, and a joy in light, as if sunshine were the highest good; but the beauty is an extremely personal ideal, too strange, too expressive to be unconscious; the romance is too delicate, the quickness of life too subtle, and the joy in light too dainty, not to betray an artist vividly conscious of it all as he lives and creates.

This consciousness is at the very opposite pole from ordinary self-consciousness. It is in no way connected with social ambitions or unattainable ideals. Its whole result, so far as beauty is concerned, is to make the artist linger more over his work, with a more intimate delight. Lotto has too keen a joy in his art to treat any detail, even the smallest, as a matter of indifference or convention. His landscapes never sink to mere backgrounds, but harmonize with the themes of his pictures, like musical accompaniments, showing that he was well aware of the effect scenery and light produce upon the emotions. In one of his earliest works, the Louvre *St. Jerome*, dated 1500, the landscape has a hush and retirement as if it had sprung up in answer to the studious hermit's longing for solitude. The marvellous panorama of land and sea in the Carmine altar-piece of 1529 at Venice, ruined as it is, stirs the soul with cosmic emotion. Far from treating the hand as a mere appendage, he makes it as expressive, as eloquent, as the face itself, and in some of his pictures, in such an one, for example, as the *Assumption*, at Celana, the hands form a more vital element in the composition than even in Leonardo's *Last Supper*. Even in decoration Lotto entirely casts loose from architectural convention, letting himself be swayed by his personal feeling only for what is tasteful. He displays a sense, almost Japanese, for effects to be obtained from a few sprays of leaves and flowers, arranged, as it were, accidentally, or joined loosely with a ribbon so as to form a frame—for scattered rose-petals, or trees blown by the wind on a cliff. So little is his decoration merely in the nature of a trimming that at times, as in the Bergamo intarsias, it is hard to tell where decoration ends and allegory begins. Wherever he is left free to deal with it in his own spirit, his allegory has the allurement of a realm of beauty or thought which reveals itself for a bare instant, as if by the accidental lifting of a curtain.

It is in this period of his career, while he was at Bergamo, that Lotto, as we have seen, is most in touch with the general spirit of his time. This explains why his Bergamask pictures appeal far more than his earlier or later works to all lovers of classic Italian painting—that is to say, to all people who feel the spell of the Italian Renaissance. Yet even here, his way of painting separated him widely from his more successful Venetian contemporaries. They were without exception followers of Giorgione. It is true that in delicacy of touch and refinement of feeling no one came so near to that great master as Lotto, but these qualities counted for little with a public indifferent to what was individual in Giorgione's spirit, but so enamoured of the glitter and flash, the depth and warmth of his colouring, that they would welcome no picture which did not give them a distinctly Giorgionesque effect. Lotto's colouring is never distinctly Giorgionesque. In the works of his earlier and of his Bergamo years it is subtle, it is spontaneous, but it is a world removed from Titian's—and Titian's friends, such as Lodovico Dolce, seem to have taken great care that the difference was not reckoned to Lotto's credit. His type of beauty also, although during these Bergamask years it comes nearest to being a definite type, differs from Titian's and Correggio's in the same way in which his spirit differs from theirs, being more refined, more subtle, more expressive, and, as compared with Titian's at any rate, less like a mask. Lotto cannot always reproduce the same face. He colours it too much with his own mood; it is too highly charged with expression to conform to any fixed ideal of outline or feature.

The Madonnas of Botticelli, if we may trust Mr. Pater, are so wholly out of sympathy with the Christ-child they bear in their arms, that they feel Him like an 'intolerable honour' thrust upon them. The exact contrary is the truth about Lotto's Madonnas. They seem to realize to the full what new life the Child brings, and they do not humbly treasure the secret in their hearts, but long rather to enlighten all the world, and to fill it, in like measure with themselves, with the new hope and the new joy. In the San Bernardino altar-piece, for example, the Madonna, with inspired look and eloquent gesture, seems to expound the Child's message to the listening saints, to argue, to persuade, and convince them of the miracle.

A strictly Christian or religious strain, is, despite these Madonnas, less common in Lotto's Bergamask years than earlier or later in his life. Religion being with him rather a need for support and consolation than the object of artistic striving, it plays a less important part when the tide of life is highest in him. But the psychological interest—the essential element of his genius—is never absent, never wholly pushed out of sight by the most joyous of feelings. In these Bergamask pictures, and indeed in all his sacred subjects, his psychology finds employment in interpretation. He seems never to have painted without asking himself what effect a given situation must have on a given character. Thus it is rare to find in any one of his canvases, two faces which wear the same expression, which view an event in precisely the same way, which receive a message with the same degree of attention.

Let us compare to illustrate the point, such a well-known work as Titian's *Presentation of the Virgin*, in Venice, or the *Ecce Homo* at Vienna, with one of Lotto's more important compositions, such as the scene in the Piazza in the Trescorre frescoes, or the *Crucifixion* of 1531, at Monte San Giusto. We find in both of Titian's pictures differences of type, class, and station, but we find, at the same time, that the event produces nearly the same mental and emotional effect on all the bystanders. Lotto, on the contrary, makes each class and condition view the occurrence with varying degrees of sympathy, antipathy, interest, or indifference. But he goes still further: each person in the different groups is a distinct individual, with individual feelings, largely dependent upon his state and condition, but not entirely limited by them.

Both Titian and Lotto are dramatic. Titian attains his dramatic effect by a total subordination of individuality to the strict purposes of a severe architectonic whole. The bystanders are mere reflectors of the emotion which it is the purpose of the artist their presence should heighten; their personality is of no consequence. Lotto, on the other hand, attains his dramatic effect in the very opposite way. He makes us realize the full import of the event by the different feelings it inspires in people of all kinds. He does this, of course, because his real interest is psychological, while Titian's method follows with equal consequence from the epic nature of his genius. The psychological talent as inevitably adopts a treatment allowing great diversity of character and incident, as the epic spirit tends to eradicate every trace of what is not typical and strictly to the purpose. The study of character being the real aim of the psychological artist, and not the ethical situation or problem, he reverses the procedure of the epic artist, and makes the situation or problem an excuse for the study of character. Individuality, which the epic treatment subordinates almost to extinction, receives an importance which makes it seem nearly independent of the general plan. But what makes both Titian and Lotto in their different methods equally dramatic, is that they have an equal power of vivid representation. In the one case, the subject is the event itself, in the other, the emotion roused by the event—not the emotion of a chorus, which is perhaps as strongly brought out in the epic treatment, but the emotion as felt by distinct individuals.

. . . .

Lotto left Bergamo in 1525, when he was forty-five years old. In the next ten years he painted some of his greatest works—works retaining much of the health and blitheness of spirit of his Bergamask time, but of larger scope and deeper feeling. The two pictures of this period already mentioned—the Carmine altar-piece at Venice, and the Monte San Giusto *Crucifixion*—both have a breadth and sweep, a suggestiveness of large emotions, which remind us, though we are in Italy, that Luther was already preaching, and that the great chorals of the Reformation were beginning to be heard. Lotto's humanity grows deeper and even more refined, as we see in the *Annunciation* and *Visitation* of 1530 at Jesi. To give any idea of these at all, they must be contrasted with other treatments of the same subject. Mediaeval Christianity, remembering only the 'Ecce Ancilla Dei,' always represented the Madonna in the Annunciation as the handmaiden so meek and characterless, that it is impossible to imagine her bursting forth in the 'Magnificat,' that song of rejoicing as exultant as Miriam's. The fifteenth century continued this tradition, in spite of the innovations of the great sculptor, Donatello. In the early years of the sixteenth century, during the brief period of triumphant paganism, the Annunciation also was paganized, and thus we find it in both of Titian's earlier versions, one in Treviso, and one in the Scuola di San Rocco. We have nothing to indicate how Lotto may have treated the subject in his youth, but in the Jesi pictures his treatment shows that he had dwelt long and lovingly upon Luke's Gospel, and had lived himself into its strong, joyous spirit, which he interprets with all the sympathetic insight of his

LOTTO AND THE REFORMATION 269

nature. The *Visitation* shows even more clearly than the *Annunciation* Lotto's evangelical familiarity with the Bible, and personal rendering. The same may be said of his treatment of another subject which seems to have been, perhaps because of its deep humanity, a favourite one just at this time, the *Christ and the Adulteress* (Louvre, painted about 1529), which is as full of charity as the Gospel itself. Indeed one of the points distinguishing Lotto from early painters, and even from his contemporaries, is that he drew his inspiration as directly from the Scriptures as if he were a militant Lutheran, whereas other painters were content with the semi-mythological form given to Biblical episodes by centuries of popular tradition.

It is unfortunate that the records of Lotto's life up to his sixtieth year are so scant. That he was living in Venice between 1527 and 1544 is fairly certain, but it would be of greater interest to know to what extent he came in contact with the many Reformers who then frequented Venice[1]. It will be remembered that not only those Italians who hoped to reconcile Protestantism with the Church by returning to a more evangelical form of Christianity were to a great extent Venetian subjects, or living and working in Venice, but also that the Theatines, the Somascan Order, and the Jesuits themselves, either had their roots or took their final shape there. The accounts of the early Theatine movement, the letters of Contarini or Pole, convey exactly the same impression of charity, of large humanity, and evangelical feeling, that is conveyed by the pictures Lotto was painting at the same time.

The likeness between Lotto and the Italian Reformers is nowhere else so striking as in a work painted at the moment when hope was strongest

[1] It is significant that in 1540 Lotto was commissioned by a nephew to paint for a common friend the portrait of Luther and his wife.

among all who longed for a purified and humanized Church—a work executed in 1539, two years before the fatal Conference at Ratisbon. This altar-piece, made for Cingoli, a little mountain village lost in the March of Ancona, contains beside the large Madonna and saints, fifteen small pictures which render the most important episodes from the lives of Christ and the Virgin. Lotto treats each one of these episodes with a depth of conviction, with a sublimity of conception, with an earnestness of piety, with an eloquence of appeal, which have a kindling power, such as the early Protestant preachers are reported to have had over those who heard them. We have here the expression of a noble and inspired soul endeavouring to reconcile itself with eternity by the only means within its reach, the symbols and allegories of Christianity. The gulf between the human and divine has never been indicated with more spiritual suggestiveness than in the last scene, the *Coronation of the Virgin*. Lotto here attains a sublimity which can be compared with Milton's. Contrasting such a picture with Titian's *Religion Succoured by Spain*, or even with his *Trinity* (both in Madrid), it is at once evident that genuine religious feeling inspired the one artist, and ostentatious conformity the other. One cannot help regretting that these small pictures at Cingoli were not at the very time of their painting engraved and scattered over the world, like Dürer's engravings. That they would have found intense appreciation in the North there can be no doubt, but in Italy the fatal reaction set in almost at once, and put an end to any chance Lotto might have had of helping to 'kindle a new birth.'

This great expansion of soul, let it be understood, by no means dulled Lotto's sense of beauty. The Magdalen in the Cingoli altar-piece is one of the most bewitchingly beautiful women ever painted, and a *motif*

WILL OF 1546

so poetical, so gay, so care-free, as the *putti* scattering showers of rose-petals over the kneeling saints exists perhaps nowhere else in the Italian painting.

. . . .

Apart from his pictures, the only glimpses we get into Lotto's personality are in an account-book he kept from 1540 to 1556, and in a will he made out at Venice, in 1546, and these but confirm the idea of his character, which we deduce from his paintings. At the time he made this will he was sixty-six years old, and had just returned from an absence of three years in Treviso, where he made the unfortunate experiment of living with friends. He had hoped to find among them that attention and sympathy for which he felt a great longing, 'seeing' as he himself relates, 'that I was advanced in years, without loving care of any sort, and of a troubled mind.' He was induced by a friend, a Trevisan goldsmith, to become the guest of a common acquaintance, Zuane del Saon. Zuane's son, Lotto hoped, 'would be benefited by me in the art and science of painting, for my friend greatly delighted in me, and it was very dear to him to have me in his house, not only to him, but to his entire family, by whom I was respected and honoured. Nor would he have me spend anything or pay a farthing, but remain always with him. And thus I was persuaded to enter into such fellowship united in Jesus Christ, with the firm intention, however, of repaying so much courtesy and Christian kindness. So I went there. Then they besought me to be pleased to assure them that in case of my death he' [their son, who was to be Lotto's heir] 'should not be molested or annoyed in any way by my relatives. Thereupon I most willingly set my signature to a declaration that in case of my death, no relative of mine was empowered to ask for an account of any goods left over by me.'

This declaration in writing was read to 'Gossip Saon' and the common friend, Carpan, in the presence of the confessor, 'dear to them all,' and was authenticated by the witness of a notary in whose hands it was left. 'Gossip Saon,' on his side, made a declaration in writing that it was 'for the greatest delight of himself and his family that Lotto stayed in his house, and that no payment should ever be asked of him.' But no sooner was this compact known in Treviso than 'respectable people,' Lotto says, turned a cold shoulder to me, saying that I had become a child's nurse, eating away under the roof of another without earning my salt.' Lotto could not endure this, and so he drew up another agreement in which Saon had to fix a sum to be paid him annually for board and lodging —this also meeting with the confessor's approval. But after three years, 'for divers reasons,' Lotto writes, 'I found it necessary to get up and go away from Treviso, chiefly because I did not earn enough by my art for my own support.'

The will from which this quaint and pathetic bit of autobiography is taken, makes it clear that Lotto had no close family ties, although his account-book proves that in 1540 he was living with a nephew. His life must always have been that of a lonely wanderer, of a person more or less improvident, very industrious, as the number of his works indicates, but laying up no store whatever. A Trevisan document of 1505, for instance, speaks of him as '*pictor celeberrimus*,' but we learn from a statement of the very next year that he left Treviso with a bare shirt to his back. While in Venice, he seems to have been intimate with the monks of San Giovanni e Paolo, to the hospital of which he, on two separate occasions, bequeathed all his goods, both times on the condition that he should be buried in the habit of the Order.

The second of these wills, from which I have been quoting, contains a few further indications of his temper and ideas. Among his scanty possessions were a number of antique gems of which he speaks lovingly, because they were engraved with mystic symbols for the spirit to brood upon. The cartoons for the Bergamo intarsias were still in his hands, and he left them as a dower for two girls, 'of quiet nature, healthy in mind and body, and likely to make thrifty housekeepers,' on their marriage to 'two well-recommended young men starting out in the art of painting, likely to appreciate the cartoons, and to turn them to good account.' One of the items in his account-book is a large picture he finished for the young widow of a fellow artist, on the condition that she 'should marry again quickly, so as to avoid being talked about.'

These indications would be but trifling if we could not read them in the light his pictures throw upon his personality. Some notion of his place among the artists of Venice is given by a letter written in April, 1548, by Pietro Aretino, wherein Lotto is addressed as 'Good as Goodness.' Aretino forwards the remembrances of Titian, who was then at Augsburg enjoying the favour of Charles V, 'but not so carried away that he would not greatly appreciate the opinion and criticism of his friend Lotto, whose judgement he valued as he scarcely valued that of any other man.'

But this company was not perfectly congenial to Lotto, or else his *inquiete mente* made him restless in Venice, for soon afterwards he is found at Loreto, and in 1554 he made over himself and all his goods to the Holy House. There can be no doubt that he knew Loreto from earlier years, for works by him of various dates are found there, and it is perhaps not surprising that a man of his temperament should have sought the

T

solitude and the inspiring beauty of this serene retreat in preference to the society of such men as Titian, Aretino, and Sansovino. Of the sympathetic, fervently religious people who crowded Venice fifteen years earlier few probably were left, considering with what a rush the Catholic reaction set in and continued after 1541.

. . . .

Long familiarity with the work of an artist often ends by creating a visual image which rises invariably before the mind at the mention of his name. This image is the result of a slow process of selection and combination; certain qualities of expression, certain types of face, certain attitudes, a given scheme of colour, a prejudice for certain effects of light, recur at the thought of the artist with ever greater persistency. At last, by the elimination of all accidental elements, the connexion between the artist and a perfectly individualized face and expression becomes fixed. This face is, at bottom, nothing else than a sort of composite mental photograph of all the impressions received from the artist's works. It happens sometimes that among these works one figure or face occurs which answers exactly to this composite mental photograph, and the natural looseness of the mind leads it to regard the image, in some vague way, as the portrait of the painter himself. It is curious that the figure among Lotto's works which answers to such a description should be at Loreto, and it is a stranger coincidence still that it should represent St. Roch, the restless and compassionate wanderer, whom Lotto, it is hardly fantastic to imagine, may have looked upon as his special patron. The St. Roch, although he has a certain resemblance to the print given by Ridolfi as Lotto's portrait, can scarcely be an actual likeness of the painter by himself, for it represents a man of about forty, and Lotto must have been over fifty when he painted it; yet it contains all that refinement, all that unworldliness, and all that wistful unrest which were at the very foundation of his nature [1].

. . . .

Age crept upon him very fast in these last quiet years. His voice almost entirely failed him, and it is not hard to imagine that most of his time was taken up with his devotions. He did not wholly give up painting, but among the few works produced in the last years of his life, only two deserve comment here. These, however, are of surpassing interest. They show that their painter was to the last a psychologist, and indicate even more than any earlier works great familiarity with the Scriptures, and an intensely personal way of taking religion. As technique also they sum up all the tendencies of his career, particularly in its later phases. In these pictures he produces with few strokes, and with one or two colours, effects of tone approaching greyish monochromes that vividly call to mind Velasquez and the greatest living French painters. This style of painting is scarcely popular even now, and it is easy to understand that it found no recognition then. Titian himself painted in this fashion during the last twenty years of his life, but even Titian with all his fame could not make it acceptable. In this connexion one need only refer to the story of 'Fecit, Fecit.' A public to whom the splendid *Annunciation* of San Salvadore at Venice seemed such a daub that they refused to believe Titian had painted it until he signed it twice over, may be excused for neglecting the works of Lotto's last years. In them they would have found only lack of finish and

[1] A type very close to this occurs in the Uffizi picture of 1534 in the figure of St. Joachim, whose age would correspond with Lotto's own at this date.

the signs of dotage. Until the other day, in fact, a work of this kind, not by Lotto, but by Titian himself, a work to be reckoned a masterpiece among Titian's masterpieces, remained buried away in a lumber-room, and now that it is exhibited, it is catalogued in the Imperial Gallery of Vienna as an 'unfinished sketch.'

But the Pantheon of the arts has been wonderfully enlarged and changed of late. Franz Hals, Rembrandt, and Velasquez have been added, and since their admission these new reputations have tended to play with the old ones the part of the Ark of the Lord in the Temple of Dagon. Consistency compels us to admit elsewhere the qualities we admire in them, and the result is that we are beginning to understand the greatness of some of our living painters, instead of waiting until death calls attention to their genius, and to find in certain Italian masters beauties of workmanship unappreciated by their contemporaries. We are beginning to see that the achievements of Titian's old age are at least as important as those of his youth, and one might hazard the prophecy that before long Loreto will again become for intelligent people a place of pilgrimage, but this time to Lotto's later works.

Among his last pictures, two, as I have said, are especially important. The first, *The Sacrifice of Melchizedek*, is a deeply poetical scene, such as the subject would naturally suggest to an imaginative mind. It is early dawn, and the cool grey light falls upon the armour of the warriors assembled in the quiet forest-clearing, and upon the white-stoled priests and acolytes. Melchizedek is an old man who throws up his hands to heaven with a rapt look of piety and devotion rising from the very springs of life. Lotto here betrays an insight into the psychology of old age, which becomes even more penetrating and subtle in what was probably the last picture to which he ever set his hand. In the *Presentation in the Temple*—perhaps the most modern picture as regards technique ever painted in Italy—Simeon and Anna have that crumbled look of the whole osseous frame, that toothless, almost effaced, physiognomy of those upon whom the years have pressed heavily; yet in their eyes, and in every line of their figures, there is an expression of satisfied yearning taking the most exultant form it can in such aged bodies. Religious awe and profound interpretation rise to a higher pitch in this last work than ever before. The tension of feeling over an event which all the bystanders recognize as more than human, expresses itself on every face, and on each in a different fashion. To the end Lotto remains a psychologist, using psychology not for its own sake, but as an instrument with which to give a finer interpretation of character than was given by any of his contemporaries; as a means of drawing closer to people, and of looking deeper down into their natures; as a guiding power for the recreation in painting of the most symbolic events of sacred story. These, as we have seen, he interprets with earnest piety and profound sincerity at a time when Titian was painting Jesuitical pictures which met with the exact approval of his Spanish patrons, and when even Tintoretto was mingling with all his sublime inspiration a strong dose of apologetic sophistry. Where Tintoretto sought to explain, and Titian to comply, Lotto sought only to interpret the beliefs which had permeated and coloured his whole personality.

Lorenzo Lotto was, then, a psychological painter in an age which ended by esteeming little but force and display, a personal painter at a time when personality was fast getting to be of less account than conformity, evangelical at heart in a country upon which a rigid and soulless Catholicism was daily strengthening its hold. Even the circumstances of his life, no less than his character, were against his acquiring a reputation. Restless and a wanderer, he left but few pictures in Venice, his native town, so that the sixteenth-century amateurs, from whom we have derived our current notions about the art of that time, did not find there enough of Lotto's work to carry away enthusiastic accounts of it. But even if circumstances had been more favourable, it is probable that Lotto's reputation would have paled before that of his great rival, who gained and kept, through a long lifetime, the attention of the public. Achievements so brilliant and so well advertised as Titian's could leave but scant room for the European fame of a painter, the appreciation of whose peculiar merits required a better trained eye and a more delicate sense of personality than were common in the camp of Charles V or court of Philip II.

But for us Lotto's value is of a different sort. Even if modern art were not educating us, as it is, to appreciate the technical merit of work such as his, nevertheless, in any age personality moulding a work of art into a veritable semblance of itself is so rare a phenomenon that we cannot afford to neglect it. Least of all should we pass it by when that personality happens to be, as Lotto's was, of a type towards which Europe has moved, during the last three centuries, with such rapidity that nowadays there probably are a hundred people like Lotto for one who resembled him in his own lifetime. His spirit is more like our own than is, perhaps, that of any other Italian painter, and it has all the appeal and fascination of a kindred soul in another age.

INDEX

TO PHOTOGRAPHS OF PICTURES AND DRAWINGS NOT BY LOTTO MENTIONED IN THE COURSE OF THIS MONOGRAPH.

NOTE.

Al. = Alinari Bros., of Florence.
An. = D. Anderson, of Rome.
Br. = Braun, Clément & Cie., of Paris.
Hnf. = Hanfstängl, of Munich.

ANTONELLO DA MESSINA.

ANTWERP.	Crucifixion. Br.
BERLIN.	18. Youth. Hnf.
DRESDEN.	St. Sebastian. Br. Tamme, Dresden.
LONDON.	Portrait ; Crucifixion. Br.
PARIS.	Condottiere. Br.

ANDREA DA MURANO.

VIENNA.	13. Crucifixion. Löwy, Vienna.

BARBARI.

BERGAMO. LOCHIS. Portraits. Al. R. Lotze, Verona.
BERLIN. Madonna and Saints. Hnf.
CASSEL. HABICH. Black chalk drawing, well reproduced in Morelli, *Galleries of Munich and Dresden.* Red chalk drawing, in *Handzeichnungen Alter Meister aus der Sammlung Habich*, edited by Dr. O. Eisenmann. (Lübeck, Nöhring, 1890.)
DRESDEN. All. Tamme, Dresden.
FLORENCE. PITTI. St. Sebastian. Al., An.; under name Pollajuolo.
UFFIZI. Red chalk drawing. Al., Br.; under name Garofalo.
TREVISO. S. NICCOLÒ. Frescoes. Al.

BASAITI.

BERLIN.　　　40. Madonna. Reproduced in Morelli, *op. cit.* Hnf.

BELLINI, GIOV.

BERGAMO.　　Madonna. Lotze, Verona.
TURIN.　　　Madonna. Brogi, Florence.
VENICE.　　　All. Al., An.

BONSIGNORI.

BERGAMO.　　LOCHIS. Portrait of a Gonzaga. Al.
CHANTILLY.　Portrait. Br., B. Arts, 179.
FLORENCE.　 UFFIZI. Portrait. Al.
LONDON.　　 Portrait. Morelli, London.
MANTUA.　　 Accademia Virgiliana. All. An.
MILAN.　　　BRERA. All. Al.
ROME.　　　 SCIARRA (formerly). Portrait. Br.; under name Mantegna.
VENICE.　　　S. GIOV. E PAOLO. Polyptych. An.; under names of Vivarini and Carpaccio.
VIENNA.　　 Portrait. ALBERTINA. Gerlach and Schenk's Albertina Publication.
VERONA.　　All. Al.

CARIANI.

BERGAMO.　　BAGLIONI. Madonna. Lotze, Verona.
MILAN.　　　MUSEO CIVICO. Lot and his Daughters. Brogi, Florence; under name Lotto.
VIENNA.　　St. Sebastian. Löwy, No. 162.

CATENA.

LONDON.　　Oriental Warrior adoring the Infant Christ. Hnf.

CIMA.

BERLIN.　　　Madonna and Donor. Hnf.
BOLOGNA.　　Madonna. An.
MILAN.　　　BRERA. All. Al. Brogi, Florence.
　　　　　　POLDI. Head of Female Saint. Marcozzi, Milan.
MODENA.　　GALLERY. Deposition. An.
MUNICH.　　Madonna and Saints. Hnf.
PARMA.　　　All. An.
VENICE.　　　All. Al., An.
VICENZA.　　Madonna and Saints. Al.

CORREGGIO.

DRESDEN. Madonna with St. Francis. Br. Tamme, Dresden.

CRIVELLI.

MASSA FERMANA. Polyptych. Houghton.

GIORGIONE.

CASTELFRANCO. Madonna and Saints. Al., An.
ST. PETERSBURG. Judith (copy). Br.; under name Moretto.
VICENZA. CASA LOSCHI. Christ bearing Cross. Al., An.

MANTEGNA.

BERLIN. Scarampo. Hnf.
MILAN. BRERA. Polyptych. Brogi, Florence.

MONTAGNA.

BERGAMO. LOCHIS. Madonna and Saints. Al.
BERLIN. Madonna and Saints. Berl. Phot. Gesell.
CASSEL. HABICH. Drawing, in Dr. Eisenmann's publication.
CERTOSA. (Near MILAN.) Madonna and Saints. Brogi, Florence.
MILAN. BRERA. Madonna and Saints. Al.
VENICE. ACADEMY. Madonna. An.
VICENZA. All mentioned. Al.

PALMA.

BERLIN. Male Portrait. Hnf.
NAPLES. Santa Conversazione. Brogi.
PARIS. Louvre. Nativity. Br.
VENICE. QUERINI-STAMPALIA. Portrait. An.
VIENNA. Female Heads. Löwy.

PORDENONE.

VENICE. S. Giovanni Elemosinario. Altar-piece. An.

SAVOLDO.

MILAN. BRERA. Madonna and Saints. Marcozzi, Milan. Al.
PARIS. Head in black chalk. Br., No. 435.
VENICE. LADY LAVARD. St. Jerome. Al.
VERONA. S. MARIA IN ORGANO. Madonna and Saints. Lotze, Verona.

TITIAN.

MADRID.	The Trinity. Religion Succoured by Spain. Br.
VENICE.	Nearly all. Al., An.
VIENNA.	All. Löwy.

ALVISE VIVARINI.

BERLIN.	Madonna and Saints. Hnf.
LONDON.	MR. SALTING. Head of Youth. Br.; Palais Bourbon, 3.
NAPLES.	Madonna and Saints. Brogi, Florence.
OXFORD.	CHRIST CHURCH. Head. Grosvenor Gallery Publication, Oxford, 3.
PADUA.	Bust of Man. An. 10364.
PARIS.	Head of Man. Br.; under name Savoldo.
STUTTGART.	Bust of Man. Fr. Hoefle, Augsburg.
VENICE.	ACADEMY. All. Al., An.
	FRARI. Altar-piece. Al., An.
	S. GIOVANNI IN BRAGORA. Madonna. An. No. 14001.
	REDENTORE. Madonna. Al., An.
	LADY LAYARD. Head of Man. Al.; under name Antonello.
	MUSEO CORRER. St. Antony of Padua. An.

ANTONIO VIVARINI.

ROME.	LATERAN. Polyptych. Al.

ANTONIO AND BART. VIVARINI.

BOLOGNA.	Polyptych. An.

BARTOLOMMEO VIVARINI.

VENICE.	ACADEMY. All. An.
VIENNA.	Polyptych. Löwy, Vienna.

INDEX TO NAMES MENTIONED INCIDENTALLY

Lotto, Alvise, Jacopo di Barbari, Bonsignori, Cima, and Montagna will not be found in this index; the chapter and page headings, and the index of place where each separate work is entered, making it easy to find any item concerning them.

ANTONELLO DA MESSINA, and the Venetians, 28; his forms and mannerisms, 85.
ANTONIO DA FAENZA, 244.
ARETINO, PIETRO, letter to Lotto, 214, 228, 229.
ARIOSTO, his humour compared with Lotto's, 261.

BAGHAZOTTI OF CAMERINO, 236, 245.
BASAITI, his touch, 82; share in Frari altar-piece, 83.
BECCARUZZI, picture estimated by Lotto, 222; his debt to Lotto, 248.
BELLINI, GIOVANNI, his impersonality, 252.
BOCCACCINO, BOCCACCIO, and Alvise, 95 note.
BOTTICELLI, his Madonnas, 265.
BRAMANTE, 125.
BUONCONSIGLIO, 52, note 2.

CALDAROLA, 244.

CARAFFA, CARDINAL, 253.
CARIANI, 173; his debt to Lotto, 247.
CARPACCIO, not Montagna's master, 49; his earliest works, 49; his drawings, 50.
CATENA, 76.
CAVAGNA, 247.
CAVERSEGNO, 243, 244.
CONTARINI, CARDINAL, 253, 269.
CORREGGIO, compared with Lotto, 131-6, 255, 262, 263; his antecedents, 133 note.
COSTA, and Alvise, 136 note.
CRIVELLI, CARLO, and the Vivarini, 32; and Lotto, 147, 237, 238.

DAMIANO, FRA DA BERGAMO, 244.
DONATELLO, 98, 268.
DURANTE DA FORCE, 245.
DÜRER, letter from Venice, 34; and Barbari, 36; and Lotto, 37, 255; and the Vivarini, 38 note.

FOGOLINO, in London, 52 note.

INDEX TO NAMES

GIORGIONE, and Alvise, 78 note; forms and antecedents, 78, 81; grade, 98; impersonality, 251; portraits, 258.

LEONARDO, and Verrocchio, 62.
LOMBARDI, and Barbari, 31.
LOYOLA, IGNATIUS, 253.
LUCAS VAN LEYDEN, engravings copied in Italy, 188.
LUTHER, Lotto's portrait of, 261.

MANET, 236.
MANTEGNA, classicism, 42; quality, 42.
MICHELANGELO, grade, 98; and Lotto, 105.
MORONI, 258.
MURANO, ANDREA DA, and Bonsignori, 40.
MURANO, ANTONIO AND BARTOLOMMEO DA, and Alvise, 67, 68.
MURANO, GIOVANNI AND ANTONIO DA, and the Squarcioneschi, 67 note.

PADUA, SCHOOL OF, its influence on North Italian Art, 134.
PALMA, and Lotto, 112-6, 170; debt to Lotto, 246; *Sante Conversazioni*, 257.
PATINIR, 246.
PERUGINO, 102.
POLE, CARDINAL, 269.
PORDENONE, 75.
PREVITALI, earliest work, 23; debt to Lotto, 247.

RAPHAEL, and Timoteo Viti, 62; grade, 98; *Stanza della Segnatura*, 102; and Lotto, 103-5; source of his forms, 134.
REMBRANDT, and Lotto, 202.

SADOLET, 253.
SALMEGGIA, 247.
SANSOVINO, JACOPO, and Lotto, 229.
SAVOLDO, descent, 88 note, 202; debt to Lotto, 246, 247.
SEBASTIANI, LAZZARO, at Vienna, 27; career and quality, 34.
SEBASTIANO DEL PIOMBO, pupil of Cima, 23; compared with Lotto, 105; cause of leaving Venice, 238.
SODOMA, and Lotto, 105.
SOLARIO, and Alvise, 95 note.
STENDHAL, 260.

TINTORETTO, 253, 277.
TITIAN, and Giorgione, 62; and Alvise, 77; development contrasted with Lotto's, 152; influence on Lotto, 183-5; feeling towards Lotto, 214; development, 215; impersonality, 252; takes Bellini's place, 252; and his times, 252; effaces Lotto, 253; type of man, 255; early portraits, 255, 258; colour and ideal compared with Lotto's, 265; dramatic sense contrasted with Lotto's, 267; Annunciations, 268; his orthodoxy, 270.

VALENZA, JACOPO DA, 31.

INDEX TO PLACES

ALZANO:
    Lotto, Peter Martyr, 102 note, 111-4, 116.

ANCONA—*Pinacoteca*:
    Lotto, Altar-piece, 225-7; Assumption, 229, 231.

ANTWERP—*Gallery*:
    Antonello da Messina, Crucifixion, 28.

ASCOLI:
    Crivelli, 237.

ASOLO—*Duomo*:
    Lotto, Assumption, 8.

BARLETTA—*S. Andrea*:
    Alvise, 71.

BERGAMO—*Cathedral*:
    Previtali, 247.

  S. Alessandro in Colonna:
    Lotto, Deposition, 129.

  S. Alessandro in Croce:
    Lotto, Trinity, 128.

  Signor Baglioni (now Public Gallery) *Cariani*, 247.

  S. Bartolommeo:
    Lotto, Altar-piece, 83, 109; Sketch for, 110; in general, 119-28, 263.

BERGAMO (*continued*):
  S. Bernardino:
    Lotto, Altar-piece, 143, 144, 166 note, 263, 266.

  Signor Antonio Frizzoni:
    Lotto, Fragments of fresco, 162.

  Gallery Carrara:
    Lotto, *Predelle* to S. Bartolommeo altar-piece, 127, 128; Portrait, 148, 149, 259; Marriage of St. Catherine, 152-4.

  Gallery Lochis:
    Barbari, 28.
    Bonsignori, Portrait of a Gonzaga, 43, 45, 46.
    Lotto, Sketches for *predelle* to S. Bartolommeo altar-piece, 127; Holy Family, 197.
    Montagna, 49, 52 note.
    Pensabene, Madonna, 3 note.

  Signor Gritti (formerly):
    Lotto, Allegory, 5.

  S. Maria Maggiore:
    Lotto, Intarsias, 157, 162-5, 261, 263, 264.

  S. Michele:
    Lotto, Frescoes, 161.

  Signor Piccinelli:
    Lotto, Madonna, 147, 148.

INDEX TO PLACES

BERGAMO (*continued*):
  S. Spirito:
    Caversegno, 244.
    Lotto, Altar-piece, 144-6, 263.
    Previtali, Polyptych, 244.

BERLIN—*Gallery:*
  Alvise, Early altar-piece, 72 et seq.; Second altar-piece, 75.
  Antonello, Portrait of Youth, 28, 29.
  Barbari, Madonna and Saints, 30.
  Basaiti, Madonna (labelled School of Alvise), 52 note.
  Carpaccio, 49.
  Cima, Madonna and Donor, 56.
  Lotto, Christ taking Leave of His Mother, 146, 147; Portrait of Young Man, 169; SS. Sebastian and Christopher, 194; Portrait (no. 282), 198; Architect, 204, 258.
  Mantegna, Scarampo, 42.
  Montagna, 52 note.
  Palma, Male Portrait, 246.
  Previtali, Madonna, 3 note.

Prof. R. von Kaufmann:
  Basaiti, St. Jerome, 178.
  Lotto, Portrait, 118.

BOLOGNA—*Gallery:*
  Cima, 56.

S. Domenico:
  Fra Damiano da Bergamo, Intarsias, 244.

BRESCIA—*Tosio Gallery:*
  Lotto, Nativity, 178.

BUDA-PESTH—*Museum:*
  Lotto, Angel, 126.

CASSEL—*Habich Collection* (formerly):
  Barbari, Drawings, 32.
  Montagna, Drawing, 50.

CASTELLO DI COSTA DI MEZZATE:
  Lotto, Madonna, 149.

CELANA:
  Lotto, Assumption, 171, 172, 264.

CESENA—*Duomo:*
  Lombardi, 31.

CHANTILLY—*Musée Condé:*
  Bonsignori, Drawing, 32.

CHATSWORTH—*The Duke of Devonshire:*
  Lotto, Cartoon for Portrait of Piero Soderini, 109.

CINGOLI:
  Caldarola, 244.
  Lotto, Altar-piece, 206-9, 270.

CRACOW—*Count Sigismund Puslowski:*
  Lotto, Madonna and Saints, 15.

CREDARO:
  Lotto, Frescoes, 104, 160, 161.

DRESDEN—*Gallery*
  Antonello, St. Sebastian, 29, 30, note 2.
  Barbari, The Saviour, and two other panels, 31; Galatea, 32.
  Correggio, Madonna with St. Francis, 131-3.
  Giorgione, Venus, 79.
  Lotto, Copy of Bridgewater Madonna, 5; Madonna, 140, 142; Copy of Christ and the Adulteress, 189.
  Palma, Holy Family with St. Catherine, 114.
  Unknown Imitator of Lotto, St. Sebastian, 245.

INDEX TO PLACES

FABRIANO—*Gallery:*
  Caldarola, 244.

FLORENCE—*Cenacolo di Foligno:*
  Copy after lost Lotto, 240.
  Pitti:
    Barbari, St. Sebastian, 32.
    Lotto, 'Three Ages,' ascribed to, *preface*.
    Raphael, Granduca Madonna, 79.
  Uffizi:
    Barbari, Drawing, 33.
    Bonsignori, Drawing, 32.
    Carpaccio, Drawings, 50.
    Dürer, Adoration of Magi, 38.
    Lotto, Holy Family, 199, 275 note; Drawings, 242.
    Moroni, Portrait of Pantera, 258.
  Mr. B. Berenson:
    Costa, Madonna, 136 note.

GIOVENAZZO:
  Lotto, St. Felix, 219 note.

GOSFORD HOUSE, N.B.—*Lord Wemyss:*
  Alvise, Portrait, 90.

HAMBURG—*Consul Weber:*
  Lotto, St. Jerome, 177.

HAMPTON COURT:
  Lotto, Bust of Young Man, 15, 257; Andrea Odoni, 174, 259; 'Concert,' ascribed to, *preface*.
  Savoldo, Nativity, 287.

HERMANNSTADT:
  Lotto, St. Jerome, 224 note.

INNSBRUCK—*Ferdinandeum:*
  Caversegno, 244.

JESI—*Library:*
  Lotto, Entombment, 103, 105; Annunciation, 167; Madonna and Saints, 167; St. Lucy altar-piece, 186; St. Lucy *predelle*, 187; Visitation and Annunciation, 192, 195, 268.

LONDON—*National Gallery:*
  Alvise, Portrait, 75.
  Bonsignori, Portrait, 43, 46.
  Catena, 76.
  Cima, St. Jerome, 224 note.
  Lotto, Agostino and Niccolò della Torre, 110, 111, 117, 259; The Prothonotary, 151; Family group, 155, 156, 260.
  Patinir, Landscape, 246.
  Solario, Portraits, 95 note.

Mr. Robert Benson:
  Fogolino, 52 note.

Bridgewater House:
  Lotto, Madonna and Saints, 4.

Mr. G. T. Clough:
  Lotto, Drawing, 241.

The Misses Cohen:
  Alvise, Portrait, 89.

Mrs. Martin Colnaghi:
  Lotto, Madonna, 150.

Sir William Martin Conway:
  Lotto, Danaë, 1, 256, 257.

Late Mr. Henry Doetsch:
  Lotto, Bust of Piero Soderini, 108; Bust of Man, 118; Altar-piece, 130.

Dorchester House:
  Lotto, 'Holford Lucretia,' 190, 191.

LONDON (*continued*):
  Grosvenor Gallery:
    Lotto, Copy of Bridgewater Madonna, 5.
  Miss Hertz:
    Montagna, 50, 52 note.
  Dr. J. P. Richter:
    Solario, Madonna, 95 note.
  Mr. George Salting:
    Alvise, Portraits, 84, 86.
  Mr. Henry Wagner:
    Lotto, Drawing, 241.

LORETO—*Palazzo Apostolico:*
  Baghazotti, 245.
  Lotto, Christ and the Adulteress, 189; SS. Sebastian, Roch, and Christopher, 200, 274; Recognition of Holy Child, 202; SS. Lucy and Thecla, 209; Sacrifice of Melchizedek, 234, 276; Two Prophets, 235; Michael and Lucifer, 235; Presentation in Temple, 235, 236, 276; Baptism, 236; Adoration of Magi, 236.

LOVERE—*Tadini Gallery:*
  Cariani, Portrait, 247.

MADRID—*Gallery:*
  Lotto, Bridal Couple, 154, 155, 260; St. Jerome, 225.
  Titian, Religion succoured by Spain, the Trinity, 209, 270.

MANTUA—*Accademia Virgiliana:*
  Bonsignori, 44, note 2; 45.
  Camera degli Sposi:
    Mantegna, 42.

MASSA FERMANA—*S. Francesco:*
  Durante da Force, 245.

MATELICA—*S. Francesco:*
  Caldarola, Crucifixion, 245.

MILAN—*Archbishop's Palace:*
  Lotto, Copy after, 240.
  Bagati-Valsecchi Collection:
    Alvise, S. Giustina, 78 et seq.
  Bonomi-Cereda Collection (formerly):
    Alvise, Portrait, 84.
  Borrommeo Collection:
    Lotto, Crucifixion, 206.
  Brera:
    Bonsignori, 44 note.
    Cima, St. Peter enthroned, 57.
    Lotto, Assumption, 107; Laura di Pola and Febo of Brescia, 219–21, 258, 259; Old Man, 221, 258; Dead Christ, 223; Portrait, 222.
    Montagna, 51, 52 note.
    Savoldo, 287.
    Solario, 95 note.
  Signor B. Crespi:
    Lotto, Portrait of Niccola Leonicinio, 118.
  Signor Gustavo Frizzoni:
    Lotto, St. Catherine, 162.
  Museo Civico:
    Cariani, Lot and his Daughters, *preface*, 247.
    Lotto, Portrait of a Youth, 169.
  Poldi-Pezzoli Museum:
    Cima, 30, note 2; 57.
    Lotto, Holy Family, 224.

MODENA—*Museo Civico:*
  Alvise, Portrait, 90.
  Solario, 95 note.

MOGLIANO:
  Lotto, Madonna and Saints, 228.

INDEX TO PLACES

MONTEFIORENTINO:
   Alvise, Polyptych, 66 et seq.

MONTELUPONE:
   Antonio da Faenza, 244.

MONTE S. GIUSTO:
   Lotto, Crucifixion, 193.

MUNICH—*Gallery*:
   Cima, Madonna and Saints, 56.
   Lotto, Marriage of St. Catherine, 9.

NANCY—*Gallery*:
   Lotto, Portrait, 233.

NAPLES—*Gallery*:
   Alvise, Madonna, 71.
   Barbari, Portrait, 90.
   Lotto, Madonna and Saints, 3; Bust of Man, 116.
   Palma, 'Santa Conversazione,' 114, 246.
   Vivarini, Bartolommeo, Altarpiece, 70.

NEWPORT, U.S.A.—*Mr. Theodore M. Davis*:
   Giovanni Bellini, Madonna, 67 note.

OSIMO—*Municipio*:
   Lotto, Madonna and Angels, 203.

OXFORD—*Christ Church Library*:
   Alvise, Drawing, 92.

PADUA—*Gallery*:
   Alvise, Portrait, 84.
   Previtali, Madonna, 23.

Eremitani Church:
   Mantegna, 42.

S. Giustina:
   Paul Veronese, 194.

PARIS—*Beaux Arts, Exhibition of* 1879:
   Alvise, Drawing for Portrait, 91.

Comtesse de Béarn:
   Alvise, Portrait, 89.

M. Durand-Ruel:
   Manet, Spanish Dance, 236.

Louvre:
   Alvise, Portrait, 87.
   Antonello, 'Condottiere,' 29 note.
   Lotto, St. Jerome, 2, 264; Christ and the Adulteress, 188, 269; Recognition of Holy Child, 201, 202.
   Mantegna, 'Madonna of Victory,' 133.
   Palma, Nativity, 114, 246.

M. P. Mathey:
   Alvise, Drawing, 93.

Mündler Collection (formerly):
   Lotto, St. Jerome, 110.

PARMA—*Duomo*:
   Correggio, Assumption, 263.

Gallery:
   Cima, Endymion, 2; Apollo and Marsyas, 2; Madonna with six Saints, 57, 121.

PAVIA—*Certosa*:
   Montagna, 52 note.

PEGHERA:
   Palma, 116 note.

PIOVE DEL SACCO:
   School of Alvise, Madonna, 151.

PONTERANICA:
   Cariani, 173.
   Lotto, Polyptych, 172, 173.

RECANATI—*Municipio:*
   Lotto, Altar-piece, 11 et seq.;
   Transfiguration, 103, 106.
S. Domenico:
   Lotto, St. Vincent, 104, 106.
Oratorio di S. Giacomo:
   Lotto, St. James, 107.
S. Maria sopra Mercanti:
   Lotto, Annunciation, 176.
S. Maria in Monte Morelli:
   Imitator of Lotto, Altar-piece, 245.

ROME—*Barberini Gallery:*
   Dürer, 37.
Villa Borghese:
   Lotto, Madonna and Saints, 10; Portrait, 190, 258; Copy after lost original, 114, 115.
Capitoline Gallery:
   Lotto, Portrait, 198.
Colonna Gallery:
   Lotto, Copy after, 240.
Doria Gallery:
   Lotto, St. Jerome, 224.
Doria Palace:
   Lotto, Portrait, 203, 259.
Lateran Gallery:
   Vivarini, Antonio, 80.
Mr. Ludwig Mond:
   Caversegno, 244.
Quirinal:
   Lotto, Marriage of St. Catherine, 157.
Rospigliosi Gallery:
   Lotto, Triumph of Chastity, 179, 261.
Sciarra Palace (formerly):
   Bonsignori, Portrait, 41 et seq.

ROME (*continued*):
Spada Palace:
   Lotto, Copy after, 189.
Sterbini Collection:
   Alvise, Portrait, 90.
Vatican:
   Raphael, School of Athens, 125.

SEDRINA:
   Lotto, Altar-piece, 219.
SERINA:
   Palma, 116 note.
ST. PETERSBURG—*Leuchtenberg Gallery:*
   Lotto, St. Catherine, 81, 150.
STRASBURG—*Gallery:*
   Beccaruzzi, Copy after part of Monte S. Giusto Crucifixion, 194 note.
STUTTGART—*Gallery:*
   Alvise, Portrait, 90.
   Basaiti, Madonna, 4 note.

TRESCORRE:
   Lotto, Frescoes, 158-60, 261, 263, 266.
TREVISO—*Duomo:*
   Titian, Annunciation, 268.
   S. Cristina (near Treviso):
   Lotto, Altar-piece, 6.
S. Niccolò:
   Barbari, Frescoes, 27.
Gallery:
   Lotto, Portrait, 168.

URBINO—*Casa Albani:*
   Savoldo, 247.

VALDOBBIADENA:
   Beccaruzzi, 222.

INDEX TO PLACES

VENICE—*Academy:*
  Alvise, 'Madonna of 1480,' 68; Single Figures, early, 70 note; later, 75, 76.
  Basaiti, Agony in Garden, 6; Calling of Zebedee's Children, 83.
  Boccaccino, *Santa Conversazione*, 95 note.
  Cima, *Pietà*, 55; Madonna with Paul and Baptist, 57; Tobias and Angel, 57; Madonna with six Saints, 129.
  Montagna, 52 note, 123 note.
  Titian, Assumption, 183, 263; Presentation of Virgin, 266.

Museo Correr:
  Montagna (?), Portrait, 50 note.
  Imitator of Lotto, 245.

Querini-Stampalia Gallery:
  Palma, Male Portrait, 170, 246.

Frari:
  Alvise, Altar-piece, 82 et seq.

S. Francesco della Vigna:
  Lombardi, 31.

S. Giacomo dell' Orio:
  Lotto, Altar-piece, 227.

S. Giovanni in Bragora:
  Alvise, Resurrection, 60, 71, 77; Madonna, 71; Saviour, 71.
  Cima, 59 et seq.

S. Giovanni Crisostomo:
  Lombardi, 31.

S. Giovanni Elemosinario:
  Pordenone, Altar-piece, 75.

S. Giovanni e Paolo:
  Alvise, Christ bearing Cross, 78 note.
  Bonsignori, Polyptych, 43 et seq.

VENICE (*continued*):
  Lotto, S. Antonino Altar-piece, 217, 218.

Giovanelli Palace:
  Beccaruzzi, St. Roch in Ecstasy, 248.

Signor Guggenheim:
  Lotto, Copy after, 241.

Lady Layard:
  Alvise, Portrait, 85 et seq.
  Savoldo, St. Jerome, 202, 246.
  S. del Piombo, *Pietà*, 23.

S. Maria del Carmine:
  Lotto, Altar-piece, 185, 264, 268.

S. Maria dell' Orto:
  Cima, 55.

Redentore:
  Alvise, Madonna, 76.

S. Rocco, Scuola di:
  Titian, Annunciation, 275.

S. Salvatore:
  Titian, Annunciation, 275.

Seminario, Stanza del Patriarca:
  Alvise, Portrait, 89 note.

VERONA—*S. Bernardino:*
  Bonsignori, 41, 46.

Gallery:
  Bonsignori, Madonna and sleeping Child, 40; Altar-piece, 40.
  Valenza, Jacopo da, 31.

S. Maria in Organo:
  Savoldo, 247.

S. Paolo:
  Bonsignori, 39.

VICENZA—*Santa Corona:*
  Montagna, 51.

VICENZA (*continued*):
  Gallery:
    Cima, 54.
    Montagna, Altar-piece, 48; Nativity, 50; Madonna, John, and Onofrio, 50; Presentation in Temple, 52 note.
  Monte Berico:
    Montagna, 51.

VIENNA—*Academy:*
  Alvise, St. Clare, 75; other female Saint, 79 note.
  Albertina:
    Bonsignori, Drawing, 32.
    Lotto, Drawing, 242.
  Gallery:
    Alvise, Madonna, 71.

VIENNA—*Gallery* (*continued*):
  Cariani, St. Sebastian, 247.
  Lotto, Portrait, 173; 'Santa Conversazione,' 175; Three Views of a Man, 205.
  Murano, Andrea da, 40 note.
  Sebastiani, Lazzaro, 27.
  Titian, 'Ecce Homo,' 189, 266; Shepherd and Nymph, 276.

WILTON HOUSE—*Lord Pembroke:*
  Lotto, Sketch for Borghese 'Santa Conversazione,' 115, note 2; St. Antony, 199.

WINDSOR:
  Alvise, Portrait, 88; Drawing, 93.

ImTheStory.com

Personalized Classic Books in many genre's

Unique gift for kids, partners, friends, colleagues

Customize:

- Character Names
- Upload your own front/back cover images (optional)
- Inscribe a personal message/dedication on the inside page (optional)

Customize many titles Including
- Alice in Wonderland
- Romeo and Juliet
- The Wizard of Oz
- A Christmas Carol
- Dracula
- Dr. Jekyll & Mr. Hyde
- And more...

Emily's Adventures in Wonderland

Ryan & Julia

CPSIA information can be obtained
at www.ICGtesting.com
Printed in the USA
LVHW081234100519
617379LV00033B/329/P